The Office of Management and Budget
and the Presidency, 1921–1979

Planning a Tragedy

You are now getting some unjust criticism, but remember that the most criticized men in American history were those whose names shone brightest in history—such as Lincoln, Wilson and Roosevelt. Also, remember they crucified Jesus within three years after He began His ministry. It is what God thinks about our actions—and what history will say a hundred years from now—that really counts. Therefore, it is my prayer now that you will continue to face the somber realities of this hour with faith and courage. The Communists are moving fast toward their goal of world revolution. *Perhaps God brought you to the Kingdom for such an hour as this—to stop them. In doing so, you could be the man that helped save Christian civilization.*

—Personal letter from the Rev. Billy Graham to President Johnson, July 11, 1965 (emphasis added)

Planning
a Tragedy

The Americanization
of the War in Vietnam

LARRY BERMAN

W • W • NORTON & COMPANY • NEW YORK • LONDON

First Edition

Copyright © 1982 by Larry Berman
All rights reserved.
Published simultaneously in Canada by George J. McLeod Limited, Toronto.
Printed in the United States of America.

Library of Congress Cataloging in Publication Data

Berman, Larry.
  Planning a tragedy.

  Bibliography: p.
  Includes index.
    1. Vietnamese Conflict, 1961–1975—United States.
  2. United States—Politics and government—1963–1969.
  3. Political science—Decision making. I. Title.
  DS558.B47 1982   950.704′3   81–22570
  ISBN 0–393–01602–1   AACR2

W. W. Norton & Company, Inc. 500 Fifth Avenue, New York, N.Y. 10110
W. W. Norton & Company, Ltd. 37 Great Russell Street, London WC1B 3NU

For my mother and the memory of my father

Contents

CONTENTS

Preface

President Johnson preferred to describe the period as "the most productive and most historic legislative week in Washington during this century,"[1] but it will be remembered as the week Lyndon Johnson led America into war on the Asian mainland. The lead stories of late July 1965 in the *New York Times* and *Washington Post* focused neither on the final stages of Medicare nor on the historic Voting Rights Bill, but rather on the Vietnam policy review then underway within the White House. A war climate permeated the nation's capital, fueled by such foreboding headlines as "Johnson Probes Vietnam Crisis with Top Aides—Parley Viewed as Prelude to Troop Buildup" and "U.S. Moves Closer to Policy Decision on Vietnam—President Holds Talks With Joint Chiefs of Staff and Foreign Relations Aides—Reserves Are Studied—Committing of Up to 200,000 Men Weighed in a Mood of Secrecy and Urgency."[2]

By July 1965 the political and military conditions within South Vietnam were in a state of such turmoil that the policy options confronting President Johnson were infinitely more complex than those which had faced his predecessors. No longer would increments in financial aid, verbal support, or military personnel be sufficient to constitute U.S. policy. No, the fundamental fact of international politics in July 1965 was South Vietnam's impending fall to Communist control, *unless* the United States provided enough ground support to deny Hanoi its goal of unifying Vietnam under Communist leadership. Lyndon Johnson's time of reckoning had arrived—would he bite the bullet and, in his favorite phrase, "turn in his stack" to meet the needs of a fledgling and free South Vietnam or would he lead a systematic reappraisal of U.S. interests and objectives which concluded that no matter how much the ante was raised, the United States could not achieve its goal of containing communism in the jungles of Vietnam? Moreover, could Lyndon Johnson have then led the country away from war in the summer of 1965?

On July 28 President Johnson announced that U.S. fighting strength in Vietnam would immediately be increased from 75,000 to 125,000 and that additional U.S. forces would be sent as they were requested by field commander Gen. William Westmoreland.[3] This military obligation, taken in response to the rapidly deteriorating political and military situation in South Vietnam, would be achieved through substantial increases in monthly draft calls but, contrary to all previous indications from the White House, no Reserve or National Guard units would be called into service.

The president's decision resulted from extensive deliberations among foreign policy advisors and between these advisors and the president. In his backgrounding of the press, Secretary of Defense Robert McNamara emphasized that "not since the Cuban missile crisis had such care been taken in making a decision. On the average of four hours per day has been spent with the President in discussing the problem. In addition, the President sought the advice of every responsible government official in coming to a decision."[4] These White House deliberations reflected what is generally assumed to be one of the few times that the principal Vietnam advisors focused intensively on fundamental questions of policy and not solely on the technicalities of military strategy. For approximately one month the president and his chief foreign policy advisors faced crucial questions concerning America's global objectives, vital interests, policy options, and their probable effects. All of those involved understood that to proceed as indicated above would mean a lengthy American military commitment to a land war in Vietnam.

The case selection was based on the significance of a decision which fully committed the United States to a land war in Vietnam as well as the availability of recently declassified primary source documents from the Lyndon Baines Johnson Library. These materials provide a detailed, dramatic, and often compelling perspective of how advisors worked in what can only be described as a "decision-making microcosm." The documents graphically depict the human element, perhaps a human tragedy, of president and advisors searching for a way out of sending American troops to fight and die on the Asian mainland, yet each unwilling to accept the consequences of such logic. Readers of earlier drafts urged me to "tell the story by letting the documents speak." This historical record illustrates how events can often shape the parameters of decision choice; how situations can deny flexibility in response; how individual world view influences the definition of a situation; how official institutional rank can place advisors in quite unequal advocacy positions; how advisor role definitions can influence advocacy strategy; and most important, how no one decision can be studied in isolation from what preceded it.

A descriptive narrative of the decision process constitutes the core of the text. I have no grand theory for explaining the failure of Vietnam decision-making, nor do I believe that one is necessary. One of the lost arts in the discipline of political science is analyzing the impact of political institutions, processes, and personalities during critical turning points in history. The Vietnam War was, at once, a human and a national tragedy. Yet the complete record of that episode is just now being made available through declassification of White House records. The background chronology in Chapter Two relies on previously published and secondary sources. In Chapters Three and Four I have tried to capture the dynamics of decision choice by utilizing the hitherto unavailable materials. From the complete written record I then draw conclusions for how and why such a tragic decision was made.

Retrospective evaluation of the Vietnam War should be approached with great care. The foreign policy failed, driving a president and the architects of that policy from office. I have tried always to recall McGeorge Bundy's personal advice that "the trick to bringing documents into history is not to neglect the rest of history." But the reader should know that *this history* is viewed primarily as a projection of how decision-makers *themselves* viewed the world and American politics in 1965. Wherever possible I have supplemented the written record with personal interviews and oral history transcripts. Manuscript drafts were circulated to each of the principal decision-makers identified in the text. I have also benefited from the recent declassification of the BDM Corporation study "The Strategic Lessons Learned in Vietnam."[5]

A final caveat. On July 22, 1965, President Johnson met with his Joint Chiefs of Staff to consider a range of military options for Vietnam. It was a depressing meeting. The military advisors made it clear that without extreme and punishing military measures against North Vietnam, this would be a long, costly, and possibly inconclusive war. In the middle of an important debate on military strategy the president drew back and, totally out of the context of the discussion, but so totally within the context of his personality, admonished his military advisors, "but remember, they are going to write stories about this like they did in the Bay of Pigs. Stories about me and my advisors."[6] What follows is such a story, narrated by the president and his foreign policy advisors. It is not the type of script they hoped would be written.

Acknowledgments

"I can't get out. I can't finish it with what I have got. So what the hell do I do?"[7] So Lyndon Johnson once bemoaned to Lady Bird with respect to his Vietnam options. How often I muttered those very words to colleagues, friends, and family as what started as a brief case study developed into a major project on the July 1965 decision process.

Several participants in that process commented on earlier drafts of the manuscript. While all of the principals are accountable for their actions in 1965, none bears any responsibility for errors in this book. George Ball, McGeorge Bundy, William Bundy, Gen. Andrew Goodpaster, Robert McNamara, Bill Moyers, Dean Rusk, and Gen. William Westmoreland took time from their busy schedules to read one or more drafts and provide important feedback.

Several colleagues provided detailed critiques of my manuscript. I am indebted to David Bonillo, Philip Dubois, Alexander George, George Herring, Walter LaFeber, Bruce Miroff, Richard Neustadt, Ken Oye, Charles Scribner, Byron Shafer, Larry Wade, and Aaron Wildavsky for their substantive contribution to and support for the project. It is a special pleasure to acknowledge the contribution of Fred Greenstein and Richard Immerman as collaborators and friends. They provided the tangible and intangible components to this book. Using their detailed knowledge of decision processes they challenged me to reformulate my ideas. Most important, they encouraged me to take temporary leave from our collaborative project in order to finish this book.

The book could not have been written without the generous support of the Russell Sage Foundation. I also benefited from a travel grant from my home institution, the University of California at Davis. Tina Lawson, Martin Elzy, E. Philip Scott, and Nancy Smith at the Lyndon Baines Johnson Library provided direction and manageability to the project. My respect and gratitude to these professional archivists goes well beyond these pages.

I was fortunate to have the best staff support at U.C. Davis. At one time or another, Cheryl Lytle, Vickie Zinner, and Brenda Petersen typed parts of the manuscript. Pat Johnson typed what I assured her was the final draft—and I then broke that promise. Robin Campbell then typed the whole book under conditions which made Dresden seem neat and tidy. Her typing and editorial skills saved the day. I want to thank Randolph Siverson, chairman of the U.C. Davis Political Science Department, for providing this staff support to finish the project, and Micki Eagle for handling all of the administrative aspects of a year's leave. My research assistant John Patton-Colella and his predecessors Paul Gold, Paul Fife, Brian Bethune, Patti Habel, and John Krein have my most sincere appreciation for a job well done.

I want to thank my publisher, George P. Brockway, for making this an exciting period in my life. His interest, advice, and responsiveness offered everything an author could ask from a publisher. And Frederick E. Bidgood had the unenviable task of maintaining editorial consistency between the two covers. He did a splendid job.

My wife and friend Janet deserves special acknowledgment. Despite her own professional demands, she carried more than her share of parenting so that I could sneak back to the office for one more night of work or off to Texas for another set of documents. She was always there to assure Scott and Lindsay that their dad would be home tomorrow. I cannot capture that contribution in words.

This book is dedicated to my mother Selma Berman and to the

memory of my father Irving Berman, who passed away just as I started the project. I wish I could have also shared this book with him. Late into the evening, early in the morning, during car rides, or simply at the dinner table our family would argue and debate the rights and wrongs of U.S. involvement in Vietnam. We represented two different generations who wanted a safe world for their children. I wish we knew then what my book shows about the tragic decision to take over the Vietnam War. We all might have redirected our energies to Washington, D.C.—where the burden of proof belonged.

Planning a Tragedy

I

Introduction: The Caligula
Syndrome

President-advisor relations constitute an integral component of the presidential decision-making process. While all presidents seek good advice, they do so differently and with varying degrees of success. Most analyses of Vietnam policy formulation concentrate only on the impact of President Johnson's personality on the quality of advice received. If Vietnam policy failed it was because Johnson scared his advisors into giving him what they thought he wanted, rather than the truth. To illustrate this point, most commentators cite Chester Cooper's description of National Security Council meetings: "During the process I would frequently fall into a Walter Mitty–like fantasy: when my turn came I would rise to my feet slowly, look around the room and then directly look at the President and say, very quietly and emphatically, 'Mr. President, gentlemen, I most definitely do *not* agree.' But I was removed from my trance when I heard the President's voice saying, 'Mr. Cooper, do you agree?' And out would come a 'Yes, Mr. President, I agree.' "[1]

Cooper's perspective is often used as prima facie evidence that Johnson's character traits produced a faulty process. Despite the president's own version of Cooper's fantasy—"I asked if anyone objected to the course of action I had spelled out. I questioned each

3

man in turn. Did he agree? Each nodded his approval or said 'yes' "[2] —Johnson's credibility was already too discredited by the war in Vietnam.

Lyndon Johnson, described so graphically by David Halberstam, was indeed "the elemental man, a man of endless, restless ambition . . . a politician the like of which we shall not see again in this country . . . a man of stunning force, drive and intelligence, and of equally stunning insecurity . . . he was, in that sense, the most human of politicians."[3] Johnson was also "his own worst enemy." According to his longtime associate and press secretary, George Reedy, "the man was driven by demons which no one else could locate and they drove him to frenzied action which often divided him from his warmest friends and delivered him into the hands of his foes. He could attract strong loyalties and bitter antagonisms—often among the same people and in that order. When he first entered the Presidency, he took the members of the White House press by storm. They adored him. Within one year, one of them told me: 'I once thought this man could walk on water. Now I wish he would try it and fall in and not come up.' The problem was simply that he did not regard a favorable attitude as sufficient. He wanted them to use *his* adjectives in describing *his* actions and when they did not do so, he decided they were in the pay of Bobby Kennedy, towards whom he was virtually paranoid. He treated them as inimical and they responded in kind."[4]

Johnson's operating style incorporated a preoccupation with secrecy, a need for controlling information both to and from the White House, an extreme sensitivity and tendency to overreact to written criticism, an emphasis on consensus and team play, and a tight rein on the White House staff. These components of style contributed, apart from objective reality, to negative perceptions of the advisory process.[5] The dominant variable in any advisory system is the personality of the president. Johnson's personality dominated his administration to such a degree, however, that assessments of the advisory process were often reduced to the impact of extremes in behavior on that process itself. The primary source documents provide a fascinating perspective on how Johnson's advisors viewed their own image problem. In mid-1965 Harry C. McPherson, special counsel to the president, wrote to President Johnson about a significant type of problem—the shadow which presidential personality cast over the entire surface level of advisory operations:

You said you wanted us to (1) praise each other to outsiders and (2) have a passion for anonymity. I realize these are not absolutely incompatible, and they are attributes every strong President has desired in his staff. *But coupled with the power and dominance of your personality the prescription does not appear to welcome the emergence of your staff as a distinguished collection of individuals. The public, if it thinks of us at all, thinks of docile calves hustling around at the will of a singular bull. . . .*

There was a mystique about the Kennedy staff, that it was a free-swinging, free-spirited collection of brilliant and independent intellects; each man became a personality, and oh what a good time they had running the government. On the other hand, we are rather bright, nice young men who lost our independence of mind the day we signed on. It wasn't true about the Kennedy staff, and it's not true about us, but it is a myth that dies hard.[6]

By February 1967 Alan Otten reported in the *Wall Street Journal* ("The Consenting Advisors") on the "degeneration in the quality of advice [Johnson] was getting from within his official family." Otten observed that most of the top staff were tired, overworked, and stretched thin by their boss. What Johnson needed were aides with "judgement and independence, a willingness to ask questions and argue."[7] The Otten article prompted McPherson to write, somewhat sarcastically, to Press Secretary George Christian with "two recommendations for stiffening the sycophantic spines of our staff and improving its image in the public prints:"

1. Stage a fist-fight between the staff and the President with full Rose Garden TV coverage. Special Assistants should background the columnists on the tactics they intend to use. The President's military aides, Cross and Robinson, together with Chief Rowley, can be expected to fight on his side. During the one-month training period preceding the fight, Watson, Jacobsen, Kintner, Rostow, and Califano will give up smoking cigarettes, Cater and McPherson cigars. Smoking is fatiguing and as Otten says, the staff is fatigued enough as it is.

2. Ask several former staff assistants to President Kennedy to come in and instruct our men on how to fight against a President. O'Donnell, Sorenson, Schlesinger, and Powers should describe their many vituperative encounters with President Kennedy, particularly during and after the Bay of Pigs affair. Their example should serve to strengthen our will,

and give us a better understanding of the ways in which independent-minded assertive assistants can promote the national interest by standing their ground against the temporary occupant of the White House.[8]

The material in this book shows that in 1965 presidential advisors were not "yesing" Lyndon Johnson. Nevertheless, several analysts have drawn just such a direct and linear line between Johnson's personality needs and advisory behavior for the July decision. Representative of such reductionism is John Stoessinger's analysis of Vietnam subtitled "Johnson's Personal War."[9] President Johnson "overwhelmed" his advisors with "the sheer force of his personality. They sensed what he wanted to hear and gave it to him." McNamara, Rusk, Taylor, and Bundy were bullied into submission. For proof, Stoessinger quotes David Halberstam's "juicy" example of loyalty Johnson-style: "I don't want loyalty. I want *loyalty.* I want him to kiss my ass in Macy's window at high noon and tell me it smells like roses. I want his pecker in my pocket."[10] This is, of course, delightful material for the lecture circuit or after-dinner hour, but offers no empirical evidence for explaining the actual dynamics of decision choice nor the cost-benefit calculus in various option trade-offs. Stoessinger argues that Johnson "did not have advisors to seek advice, but to elicit emotional support for his personal beliefs. And his advisors were indeed supportive."[11] It is undoubtedly true that advisors served the function of providing emotional support, particularly during the stressful decisions of 1965, but by no means is this the only or dominant explanation for decision choice. Moreover, the final point of reductionism is achieved when Stoessinger adopts Halberstam's description to explain the July decision as merely a response "to a personal challenge from Ho. If Ho wanted a challenge, a test of wills, then he had come to the right man. Lyndon Johnson of Texas would not be pushed around. . . . He was a man to stand tall when the pressure was there. To be counted. He would show Ho his mettle, show the toughness of this country."[12]

The primary source documents show that Lyndon Johnson *may* have staged the July deliberations as a smokescreen for buying time to ensure passage of domestic legislation through Congress. What appeared to the press, to attentive publics, and even to some advisors as a month of careful debate during which advisors advised and the president consulted, may have been the president's tactic for building consensus within the administration to legitimize a previously selected policy for political elites in Congress and subsequently to the American public. Lyndon Johnson's personality very probably played the dominant role in the president's undoing—but the reasons are much more complex and interdependent than a personal response to Ho Chi Minh. We need to start at the beginning, however, to understand just how and why the president made such fateful choices. In doing so I accept fully C. V. Wedgewood's warning that "history is lived forward but it is written in retrospect. We know the end before we consider the beginning and we can never wholly recapture what it was like to know the beginning only."[13]

II

The Road to July 1965

In an April 1965 speech at the Johns Hopkins University,[1] President Johnson cogently expressed the "whys" for United States involvement in Vietnam:

> We fight because we must fight if we are to live in a world where every country can shape its own destiny. And only in such a world will our own freedom be finally secure. . . . We are there because we have a promise to keep. Since 1954 every American President has offered support to the people of South Vietnam. We have helped to build and we have helped to defend. Thus, over many years, we have made a national pledge to help South Vietnam defend its independence. And I intend to keep that promise. To dishonor that pledge, to abandon this small and brave nation to its enemies, and to the terror that must follow, would be an unforgiveable wrong. We are also there to strengthen world order. Around the globe, from Berlin to Thailand, are people whose well-being rests, in part, on the belief that they can count on us if they are attacked. To leave Vietnam to its fate would shake the confidence of all these people in the value of an American commitment and in the value of America's word. The result would be increased unrest and instability, and even wider war. We are also there because there are great stakes in the balance. Let no one think for a moment that retreat from Vietnam would bring an end to conflict. The battle would be

renewed in one country and then another. The central lesson of our time is that the appetite of aggression is never satisfied. To withdraw from one battlefield means only to prepare for the next. We must stay in Southeast Asia—as we did in Europe—in the words of the Bible: "Hitherto shalt thou come, but no further." . . . Our objective is the independence of South Vietnam, and its freedom from attack. We want nothing for ourselves—only that the people of South Vietnam be allowed to guide their own country in their own way.

Johnson's rhetoric was wholly consistent with the policy statements of Presidents Truman, Eisenhower, and Kennedy in emphasizing that South Vietnam was a vital U.S. interest in the fight to contain communism. When Johnson assumed the presidency in November 1963, there was already a long institutional record of support for the applicability of the containment policy to Vietnam.* Indeed, three successive American presidents believed that the loss of Southeast Asia would threaten the security of the United States and the collectivity of Free World nations.

The view that South Vietnam was *vital* to U.S. security interests is best understood within the context of the falling domino thesis. In March 1950 President Truman's Economic Survey Mission to Vietnam reported that "Indochina is strategically important, for it provides a natural invasion route into the rice bowl of Southeast Asia should the Communists adopt this form of aggression. Moreover, it has great political significance, because of its potential influence, should it fall to the Communists, on Thailand, Burma, Malaya, and perhaps Indonesia."[3] In April 1954 President Eisenhower explained the basis for containment in Asia by using terms even a child could visualize: "You have a row of dominos set up, you knock over the first one, and what will happen to the last one is the certainty that it will go over very quickly."[4] In another speech President Eisenhower expanded on the domino reference: "Strategically South Vietnam's capture by the Communists would bring their power several hundred miles into a hitherto free region. The remaining countries in Southeast Asia would be menaced by a great flanking movement.

*In 1947, George Kennan, then a policy planner for the State Department, provided the rudiments for this policy: "the main element of any United States policy toward the Soviet Union must be that of a long-term, patient but firm and vigilant containment of Russian expansive tendencies."[2]

The freedom of 12 million people would be lost immediately and that of 150 million others in adjacent lands would be seriously endangered. The loss of South Vietnam would have grave consequences for us and for freedom."[5] Vietnam thus assumed a dual importance—not only was it strategically vital in terms of U.S. global policy, but the cost of "losing Vietnam" loomed as an ominous threat domestically and internationally.

United States economic support to Vietnam began in 1950 when President Truman provided France with $100 million (from funds previously earmarked in the Mutual Defense Program for "the general area of China") in an effort to prevent a Viet Minh victory in Indochina. If containment of communism constituted the cornerstone of American foreign policy, recent events had only reinforced President Truman's resolve that Vietnam not be lost to Communist aggression. The fall of Nationalist China, official recognition of Ho Chi Minh's régime by Communist China, the successful Soviet test of a nuclear device, and the outbreak of the Korean War all contributed to Truman's reluctant support of French colonialism in Vietnam. In December 1950 the United States joined France, Vietnam, Cambodia, and Laos in signing the Mutual Defense Assistance Agreement. The United States agreed to provide military supplies and equipment through an American Military Advisory Group, Indochina. This small contingent of U.S. advisors provided only limited logistical services since all supplies and equipment were dispensed through the French Expeditionary Corps.

On May 7, 1954, France "lost" Vietnam at Dien Bien Phu and shortly thereafter concluded the "Final Declaration of the Geneva Conference on the Problem of Restoring Peace in Indochina." The Geneva agreements primarily settled military and not political issues in provisionally dividing Vietnam at the Seventeenth Parallel pending free unifying elections in the North and South by July 1956. The accords prohibited reinforcement in troops or military equipment, created an International Control Commission to oversee the agreements, and provided conditions for refugee migration between the provisional zones north and south of the Seventeenth Parallel. In accepting these terms it was evident that Communist Viet Minh leaders anticipated the quick collapse of an economically devastated South Vietnam. In the event that South Vietnam did not fall, the Viet Minh left hidden in the South large amounts of arms and ammunition caches for future use. One State Department document identified the 1954–1956 period as one in which North Vietnam's leaders "hedged their bets."[6] Moreover, the Viet Minh "were willing to rely upon political means according to their own interpretation of the Geneva Accords. They left enough of their political and military apparatus in South Vietnam so as to weaken it from within and be able to take advantage of any elections should these come about. But they also were prepared to expand the apparatus in order to return to 'armed struggle' or an all-out military effort if the political gambit did fail."

The state of South Vietnam, although present at Geneva, was excluded from most discussions and therefore did not sign nor consider itself legally bound to the agreement by international law. The United States joined South Vietnam as a nonsignatory, not wanting to be associated with any further loss of territory to the Communists. Moreover, the Eisenhower administration was determined not to lose Vietnam as Truman had lost China. State Department spokesperson Walter Bedell Smith warned that while the United States would abide by the accords, it "would view any renewal of the aggression in violation of the aforesaid agreements with grave concern and as seriously threatening international peace and security."[7]

The United States was determined to pursue its own treaty commitments from allies in the Southeast Asia perimeter. On August 12, 1954, President Eisenhower convened his National Security Council in order to review U.S. policy in the Far East. NSC members agreed that the United States had already suffered a significant loss in prestige by backing France. Recouping such prestige was viewed as "inescapably associated with subsequent developments in Southeast Asia." NSC members were unanimous in their perceptions that the domino theory applied to areas directly adjacent to South Vietnam and to more remote areas such as the Philippines, Malaya, and Burma. The loss of Southeast Asia was viewed as "imperiling U.S. retention of Japan as a key element in the offshore island chain."[8]

The NSC meeting resulted in one of the most important "early" decisions leading toward war—the United States replaced France as the direct supplier of financial and military assistance to South Vietnam. The purpose of NSC 5429/2 (approved by President Eisenhower on August 20, 1954) was "to clarify and make formal, in a single document, U.S. policy on the Far East following the Geneva Conference of 1954."[9] This first post-Geneva statement of policy directly involved the United States in Vietnam: "The U.S. must protect its position and restore its prestige in the Far East by a new initiative in Southeast Asia, where the situation must be stabilized as soon as possible to prevent further losses to communism through (1) creeping expansion and subversion, or (2) overt aggression." The NSC paper concluded with a recommendation for a Southeast Asia collective security treaty and endorsed "covert operations on a large and effective scale in support of the foregoing policies."

NSC advisors were not alone in perceiving that containment of communism had been endangered by the French experiences in Vietnam and Geneva. An August 1954 CIA National Intelligence Estimate (NIE) on the post-Geneva prospects for Indochina concluded that the Communists would continue to pursue their revolutionary objectives in the South, that the Viet Minh would certainly win any election held in 1956, and that the future of a free Laos and Cambodia depended on developments in Vietnam.[10]

Secretary of State John Foster Dulles lost little time in trying to counter such predictions. In September 1954 the United States, the United Kingdom, France, Australia, New Zealand, Thailand, Pakistan, and the Philippines signed the Southeast Asia Collective Defense Treaty (which created SEATO). Each of the signatories accepted a rather ambiguous obligation to assist one another against "aggression by means of armed attack." Article IV, Paragraph 1 of the SEATO treaty provided the fundamental legal justification for the U.S. commitment to South Vietnam (a protocol state to SEATO along with Laos and Cambodia). Each party recognized that aggression by means of armed attack "would endanger its own peace and safety, and agrees that it will in that event act to meet the common danger in accordance with its constitutional processes." According to the BDM Study, "While Dulles wanted to put the communists on notice that aggression on their part would be vigorously opposed, the JCS insisted that US must not be committed financially, militarily or economically to unilateral action in the Far East and that US freedom of action must not be restricted. The two objectives conflicted and one cancelled out the other. Thus, the article of the SEATO treaty which was to provide the mechanism for collective action in the event of an enemy threat was diluted and was written so as not to pledge an automatic response to meet force with force. Instead, each signatory promised to 'act to meet the common danger in accord-

ance with its constitutional processes.' The US attempted to put teeth
into the SEATO pact through unilateral declarations of US readiness
to act. Secretary Dulles defined the obligations under the treaty as
being a clear and definite agreement on the part of the signatories,
including the US, to come to the aid of any member of the Pact who
under the terms of the treaty was being subjected to aggression.
However, he failed to instill the same dedication to instant intervention into the other SEATO member nations"[11]

Where SEATO involved multilateral relations, the United States
solidified its commitment in several bilateral agreements with South
Vietnam. The United States began sending military personnel for
purposes of training a South Vietnamese Armed Forces and mobile
civil guard. President Eisenhower initiated this commitment in a
letter to the president of South Vietnam, Ngo Dinh Diem.[12] The
letter included an explicit quid pro quo that U.S. foreign aid and
military assistance would be provided directly to South Vietnam so
long as there existed a legitimate and meritorious government:

> I have been following with great interest the course of development in
> Vietnam, particularly since the conclusion of the conference at Geneva.
> The implications of the agreement concerning Vietnam have caused
> grave concern regarding the future of a country temporarily divided by
> an artificial military grouping, weakened by a long and exhausting war
> and faced with enemies without and by their subversive collaborators
> within. Your recent requests for aid to assist in the formidable project
> of the movement of several hundred thousand loyal Vietnamese citi-
> zens away from areas which are passing under a de facto rule and
> political ideology which they abhor, are being fulfilled. I am glad that
> the United States is able to assist in this humanitarian effort. We have
> been exploring ways and means to permit our aid to Vietnam to be
> more effective and to make a greater contribution to the welfare and
> stability of the Government of Vietnam. I am, accordingly, instructing
> the American Ambassador to Vietnam to examine with you in your
> capacity as Chief of Government, how an intelligent program of Ameri-
> can aid given directly to your Government can serve to assist Vietnam
> in its present hour of trial, provided that your Government is prepared
> to give assurances as to the standards of performance it would be able
> to maintain in the event such aid were supplied. The purpose of this
> offer is to assist the Government of Vietnam in developing and main-
> taining a strong, viable state, capable of resisting attempted subversion
> or aggression through military means.

Critics of the U.S. intervention in South Vietnam would later cite this letter to support their claim that U.S. aid was *always* contingent on government legitimacy in the South.

President Eisenhower demonstrated his support for Diem by establishing the U.S. Operations Mission in 1955 as an adjunct to the U.S. embassy. The mission was charged with channeling advice and financial support to help Diem solve South Vietnam's economic problems. In 1955 alone the United States provided over $322 million in economic aid—"a larger amount than for any of the next nine years."[13] The United States also took an active role in establishing the National Bank of Vietnam (NBVN). Moreover, "more than 70% of the US economic aid funds supported the Commercial Import Program (CIP) which provided monies/credit for the importing of commodities and equipment considered essential to the functioning of the economy. The money generated by these transactions went into the 'counter-part funds' in the NBVN; jointly the US and GVN decided on the allocation of these funds. Additional revenue was generated by taxes imposed on the imported goods."[14]

By 1956 Diem's regime seemed to have made remarkable forward strides in rehabilitating the economy of South Vietnam. (Hans Morgenthau referred to the change between 1954 and 1956 as a "miracle.")[15] Moreover, Diem had also apparently succeeded in neutralizing internal opposition to his rule. At this time, Sen. John Kennedy's reflection on this period offers a valuable perspective: "Then, at last, in what everyone thought was the hour of total Communist triumph, we saw a near miracle take place. Despite the chaos, despite the universal doubts, a determined band of patriotic Vietnamese around one man of faith, President Diem, began to release and to harness the latent power of nationalism to create an independent, anti-Communist Vietnam."[16]

Nevertheless, despite these improvements in agricultural productivity and political stability, intelligence estimates predicted that Ho Chi Minh would win the 1956 all-Vietnam elections. Believing that conditions for free elections were impossible, Diem (encouraged by the United States) simply refused to hold them.[17] The decision received unanimous support from elites within the United States, as exemplified by Sen. John Kennedy's "plea that the United States never give its approval to the early nationwide elections called for by the Geneva Agreements of 1954. Neither the United States nor

Free Vietnam is ever going to be a party to an election obviously
stacked and subverted in advance, urged upon us by those who have
already broken their own pledges under the agreement they now
seek to enforce."[18]

In the process of consolidating Diem's power, his régime had become increasingly repressive and by 1957 popular dissatisfaction was
successfully exploited by the Communist underground. While Diem
had succeeded in establishing national authority, reorganizing the
armed forces, and increasing agricultural production, he had never
cultivated broad popular support. By his brazenly favoring Vietnam's Catholic minority with respect to political patronage and basic
freedoms, the larger Buddhist population soon came to hate Diem.
Diem's authoritarian techniques included the abolition of all opposing political parties, strictly enforced press censorship, and brutal
repression of the Buddhists. A Catholic by belief, Diem "had
little sympathy and no understanding for the plight of the peasants
whose station in life was one of unremitting toil, narrow political
views, and Buddhist upbringing."[19] Buttinger noted that "opposed
by the intellectuals, despised by the educated middle class, rejected by businessmen, hated by the youth and by all nationalists
with political ambitions, and totally lacking in mass support, the
Diem government had to rely for its survival on an apparatus of
coercion."[20]

In 1959 Hanoi committed its political and military apparatus in the
South to the struggle toward unification. Thousands of trained military leaders were sent into the South to build a political and military
apparatus for overthrowing the Diem government. These cadres
provided the core for the Viet Cong military. Infiltration into the
South increased substantially in 1959 and on September 10, 1960,
guidelines were established for what would become the National
Front for the Liberation of South Vietnam.

The increasing repressiveness of Diem's regime did nothing to
stop increases in U.S. assistance. Moreover, various joint U.S.–Vietnam communiqués provided public warning that this obvious
buildup of Communist forces was threatening the political independence of the South. An October 26, 1960, letter from President Eisenhower to President Diem provided additional assurances that "for so
long as our strength can be useful, the United States will continue to
assist Vietnam in the difficult yet hopeful struggle ahead."[21] But

Eisenhower's term was coming to an end and a new administration would inherit this still limited U.S. commitment. The Eisenhower administration had established certain tenets for its successor. The domino theory had provided sufficient justification for the United States to replace the French presence in Vietnam; the international and political stakes had been greatly elevated in public awareness; the government of Vietnam was now totally dependent on U.S. aid; and the United States would support *any* alternative to a Communist takeover—even Diem. None of this would be lost on John F. Kennedy. The recently declassified BDM study "The Strategic Lessons Learned in Vietnam" offers an interesting assessment of the transition period: "The progress made during this period was something of a success. This was especially true for South Vietnam in the early years of the US-supported Diem regime. The immediate US objective of preventing a communist takeover of the entire region had been accomplished through improvements in the domestic and economic stability of the anticommunist governments. Diem had promulgated a constitution, had a constituent assembly selected, put down dissident and divisive elements, and promoted social and economic reforms with much success. The situation inherited by President Kennedy when he took office was rich in rhetoric and momentum."[22]

The Kennedy Legacy: More Not Less

President Kennedy's first 100 days were filled with problems in neighboring Laos, not Vietnam—which for the moment remained a backburner issue. During a foreign policy briefing just one day prior to the inaugural, President Eisenhower did not even mention Vietnam to the president-elect. Instead, Eisenhower focused on Laos as the key domino threatening the security of Thailand, Cambodia, and the rest of Southeast Asia. Clark Clifford's memorandum of the meeting* provides a fascinating perspective on events of early 1961:

*The meeting was held in the Cabinet Room with the following men present: President Eisenhower, Secretary of State Christian Herter, Secretary of Defense Thomas Gates, Secretary of the Treasury Robert Anderson, and Gen. Wilton B. Persons. With President-elect Kennedy were the new secretary of state Dean Rusk, the new secretary of the treasury Douglas Dillon, and Clark M. Clifford.

President Eisenhower opened the discussion on Laos by stating that the United States was determined to preserve the independence of Laos. It was his opinion that if Laos should fall to the Communists, then it would be just a question of time until South Vietnam, Cambodia, Thailand and Burma would collapse. He felt that the Communists had designs on all of Southeast Asia, and that it would be a tragedy to permit Laos to fall. President Eisenhower gave a brief review of the various moves and coups that had taken place in Laos involving the Pathet Lao, Souvanna Phouma, Boun Oum, and Kong Le. He said that the evidence was clear that Communist China and North Vietnam were determined to destroy the independence of Laos. He also added that the Russians were sending in substantial supplies in support of the Pathet Lao in an effort to overturn the government. President Eisenhower said it would be fatal for us to permit Communists to insert themselves in the Laotian government. He recalled that our experience had clearly demonstrated that under such circumstances the Communists always ended up in control. He cited China as an illustration. . . . Secretary Herter stated, with President Eisenhower's approval, that we should continue every effort to make a political settlement in Laos. He added, however, that if such efforts were fruitless, then the United States must intervene in concert with our allies. If we were unable to persuade our allies, then we must go it alone.

At this point President Eisenhower said with considerable emotion that Laos was the key to the entire area of Southeast Asia. He said that if we permitted Laos to fall, then we would have to write off all the area. He stated that we must not permit a Communist take-over. He reiterated that we should make every effort to persuade member nations of SEATO or the ICC to accept the burden with us to defend the freedom of Laos.

As he concluded these remarks, President Eisenhower stated it was imperative that Laos be defended. He said that the United States should accept this task with our allies, if we could persuade them, and alone if we could not. He added that "our unilateral intervention would be our last desperate hope" in the event we were unable to prevail upon the other signatories to join us. . . .

The discussion of Laos led to some concluding general statements regarding Southeast Asia. It was agreed that Thailand was a valuable ally of the United States, and that one of the dangers of a Communist take-over in Laos would be to expose Thailand's borders. In this regard, it was suggested that the military training under French supervision in Thailand was very poor and that it would be a good idea to get American military instructors there as soon as possible so the level of military capability could be raised.[23]

The new president's reaction to the crisis in Laos bears consideration. The Communist Pathet Lao, with North Vietnamese backing and Soviet arms, were moving into the central Plaine des Jarres—seeking total control of Laos by reaching the Mekong River. Kennedy was determined to prevent a Communist victory, but wanted to avoid sending American troops. "Kennedy," according to Walt Rostow, "was not about to see Laos fall to the communists; but every experience of the situation in his first weeks of responsibility drove him to the conclusion that American forces should not engage there, if there was any way to avoid it: Laotians had little sense of national cohesion and limited military ability; the supply lines from Thai ports were long; the geography of the country decreed an extremely long front along the Mekong; the terrain, beyond the Mekong valley, was forbidding; Laos bordered on Communist China and American engagement there threatened to draw in Chinese forces, as had the movement toward the Yalu in Korea in 1950. But Kennedy's task, as he saw it, was to convince the communists that he would, in fact, fight if necessary to avoid a communist takeover while seeking a political settlement."[24]

During a March 23 press conference the new president called for a prompt end to the hostilities in Laos and the beginning of negotiations. "My fellow Americans, Laos is far away from America, but the world is small. Its two million people live in a country three times the size of Austria. The security of all Southeast Asia will be endangered if Laos loses its neutral independence. Its own safety runs with the safety of us all—in real neutrality observed by all."[25] Rostow recalled that "for the long pull, this was the occasion when Kennedy first impressed on the American people and the world his unambiguous commitment to the defense of Southeast Asia as a whole, as well as of Laos."[26]

Between March 23 and May 16 (the opening of the Geneva Conference on hostilities in Laos) Kennedy took several steps to convince the Communists that he meant business, but most important was an order which placed a contingent of U.S. Marines then at Okinawa on standby. "His action," recalled Rostow, "(much on Khrushchev's mind at Vienna) convinced Moscow that a cease-fire would have to be accepted; the Marines remained on Okinawa and the way was open for the fifteen months of diplomacy that yielded the Laos Accords of 1962."[27]

Even in the midst of the Laotian crisis Vietnam loomed ominously in Kennedy's plans. In late January the president read a situation report written by the legendary Brig.-Gen. Edward Lansdale which described the state of disrepair in Diem's South Vietnam and the potential for a Communist victory.[28] Lansdale recommended that the United States, despite Diem's liabilities, continue its support because the alternative was a Communist victory. Lansdale's account "clearly reflected the possibility, or even the likelihood, of major crisis in Vietnam in the coming year."[29] Turning to Walt Rostow, the president asked somewhat rhetorically, "This is the worst one we've got, isn't it? You know, Eisenhower never mentioned it. He talked at length about Laos, but never uttered the word Vietnam."[30]

In early April 1961 Rostow wrote a confidential memorandum urging that the president start "gearing up the whole Vietnam operation."[31] According to Rostow, the president had already decided "out of these first four months of experience, that if he had to engage American forces in Southeast Asia, he would do so in Vietnam rather than Laos. He wished, of course, to avoid any fighting, there or elsewhere. . . . Every aspect of Laos convinced Kennedy it was the wrong place to do battle, if it came to that. Vietnam appeared to have relative advantages, which Kennedy once tersely ticked off to me in these terms: relatively speaking, it was a more unified nation; its armed forces were larger and better trained; it had direct access to the sea; its geography permitted American air and naval power to be more easily brought to bear; there was the cushion of North Vietnam between South Vietnam and the Chinese border."[32]

On April 20 the president established an interagency task force headed by Deputy Secretary of Defense Roswell Gilpatric. The task force was given the mission of appraising "the communist drive to dominate South Vietnam" and "to recommend a series of actions (military, political and/or economic, overt/or covert) which, in your opinion, will prevent communist domination of that country."[33]

By May 6 the task force report reached the president's desk bearing the central theme that the United States must do whatever necessary to defend South Vietnam from Communist assault. On May 11 Kennedy approved National Security Action Memorandum 52 whereby 400 Special Forces troops (Green Berets) were dispatched to Vietnam and covert warfare (sabotage and harassment) against the North was endorsed. NSAM 52 fixed the U.S. objective "to prevent

Communist domination of South Vietnam,"[34] and authorized an increase in GVN forces from 170,000 to 200,000. In a joint U.S.–South Vietnam communiqué of May 13, 1961, President Kennedy reemphasized the U.S. commitment. "It is clear to the people of Vietnam and to the United States that the independence and territorial integrity of Vietnam are being brutally and systematically violated by Communist agents and forces from the north. It is also clear to both governments that action must be strengthened and accelerated to protect the legitimate rights and aspirations of the people of free Vietnam to choose their own way of life. The United States is also conscious of its responsibility and duty, in its own self-interest as well as in the interest of other free peoples, to assist a brave country in the defense of its liberties against unprovoked subversion and Communist terror. Free Vietnam cannot alone withstand the pressure which the Communist empire is exerting against it."[35] President Kennedy, however, went no farther than the situation required in adopting the restrained, wait-and-see policy of NSAM 52. Just two days later, Vice-President Johnson returned from a trip to Southeast Asia during which he reassured Diem that U.S. support could be counted on. Referring to Diem as "the Winston Churchill of the Orient," Johnson warned President Kennedy that "at some point we may be faced with the further decision of whether we commit major United States forces to the area or cut our losses and withdraw should our efforts fail. We must remain masters of this decision."[36]

By October 1961 mounting Viet Cong pressure led Diem to request additional military support from the United States—specifically, ground troops to bolster the South Vietnamese army. Kennedy hesitated and dispatched Gen. Maxwell Taylor and Walt Rostow (deputy special assistant to the president for national security affairs) to Vietnam to investigate the question of U.S. troop requirements. Following two weeks of survey work, Taylor cabled the president with a series of reports which confirmed the gloomy military situation. Taylor recommended that an 8000-man logistical task force of engineers, medics, and infantry be sent to the South for purposes of base security. Moreover, the task force would operate under the guise of providing such humanitarian effort as flood relief operations in the delta, but would really serve as a "visible symbol of the seriousness of American intentions."[37] General Taylor believed that these troops might "be called upon to engage in combat to protect themselves, their working parties, and the area in which they live. As a general reserve, they might be thrown into action (with US agreement) against large, formed guerrilla bands which have abandoned the forests for attacks on major targets." Taylor was unperturbed about "the risks of backing into a major Asian war" which were "present" but "not impressive." The report concluded with a recommendation that the United States pursue a "limited partnership" with the government of South Vietnam whereby the United States would "provide individual administrators for insertion into the governmental machinery in types and numbers to be worked out with President Diem." This shadow government would hopefully reform the Saigon bureaucracy and assist in implementing long-needed domestic programs.

The Taylor-Rostow report evoked a quick response from Secretary of State Rusk and Secretary of Defense McNamara. From Japan, Rusk first cabled the president with a warning that 8000 combat troops in Vietnam would violate the Geneva agreements and risk future U.S. escalation. Rusk viewed the problem as "whether Diem is prepared [to] take necessary measures to give us something worth supporting. . . . While attaching greatest possible importance to security in Southeast Asia, I would be reluctant to see us make [a] major additional commitment [of] American prestige to a losing horse."[38] Secretary McNamara and the Joint Chiefs supported the essentials of the Taylor report but argued that 8000 troops were not enough to "tip the scales decisively." Rather, 205,000 troops would be required to achieve U.S. goals. The secretary of defense recommended that President Kennedy *delay* action on the troop commitment in favor of an explicit U.S. policy directive on *the* "basic issue"—U.S. resolve to prevent a Communist takeover of South Vietnam. McNamara explained his reasoning to the president: "the domestic political implication of accepting the objectives are also grave. . . . it is our feeling that the country will respond better to a firm initial position than to courses of action that lead us in only gradually, and that in the meantime are sure to involve casualities."[39]

Three days later Rusk and McNamara joined forces in a memo to the president which recommended increased assistance (helicopters, communications equipment, naval equipment, reconnaissance aircraft) but opposed sending combat troops at this time. Rusk's biographer Warren Cohen wrote that the joint memo "read like a model of bureaucratic compromise."[40] According to George Ball, "Dean Rusk, I knew, had serious reservations about the commitment of American combat forces and recognized that, given the nature of the struggle, the political factor was fully as important—if not more so —than the military. But he did not want to get crosswise with McNamara. He never forgot that, during a long period when Secretary of State Dean Acheson and Secretary of Defense Louis Johnson were not on speaking terms, the machinery of decision had been badly crippled, and he was not going to let that happen again. Accordingly, no difference of view between them was ever likely to appear in public, nor would the President be often bothered by such differences; both Rusk and McNamara believed that they should— without compromising their convictions—try, so far as possible, to present the President with a common view, or, at least narrow the range of his options by doing their best to harmonize their opinions and thus save the President from painful choices."[41] For the moment Kennedy was advised to put off the troop decision in lieu of a major declaration of policy which again identified South Vietnam as a vital U.S. interest. The U.S. objective could be stated firmly as "preventing the fall of South Vietnam to communism." The Rusk-McNamara memo warned, however, "we recognize that the introduction of United States and other SEATO forces may be necessary to achieve this objective." This was soon evident in Secretary Rusk's November 15 telegram to Frederick Nolting, ambassador to South Vietnam, informing him of the president's decision to delay sending American troops to South Vietnam: "Very strictly for your own information, you should know that the Department of Defense has been instructed to prepare plans for the use of US combat forces in South Vietnam under the various contingencies that can be foreseen. . . . However, you should be entirely clear that it must be the objective of our policy to do all possible to accomplish our purpose with respect to GVN without the use of US combat forces."[42]

But external events soon threw the equation off balance. The cumulative toll of the Bay of Pigs, the Berlin Wall crisis, and Khrushchev's taunting of Kennedy in Vienna about how South Vietnam represented a Soviet laboratory for wars of national liberation all forced the Kennedy administration to make its stand in Vietnam— if only to save its domestic credibility. John Kenneth Galbraith recalled, "I heard him say many times. . . . There are just so many concessions that one can make to the Communists in one year and survive politically. And I remember his saying we, we just can't ... have another defeat this year in Vietnam."[43] As McGeorge Bundy recalled, "at this point we are like the Harlem Globetrotters. Passing forward, behind, sideways and underneath. But nobody has made a basket yet."[44] Vietnam now loomed as a test of the administration's inaugural commitment "to pay any price, to bear any burden, in the defense of freedom."

National Security Memorandum 111 titled "First Phase of Vietnam Program" represented Kennedy's decision to move from a relatively limited and restrained commitment to a significantly larger role in guaranteeing the maintenance of a non-Communist South Vietnam. "The US Government is prepared to join the Vietnam Government in a sharply increased joint effort to avoid a further deterioration in the situation in South Vietnam."[45] The NSAM incorporated much from the Taylor-Rostow report, but concluded that "the objective of our policy is to do *all possible* to accomplish our purpose *without use of US combat forces.*" The first goal may have precluded any possibility of the second. The NSAM authorized significant increases in military equipment (helicopters, light aviation, transport aircraft) "manned to the extent necessary by United States uniformed personnel and under United States operational control." To wit, American pilots would be flying bombing missions in the "execution of air-ground support techniques, and for special intelligence."[46] The NSAM also called on Diem to accept an American "share in the decision-making process in the political, economic and military fields as they effect the security situation." But Diem would ignore these policy mandates, and in so doing would contribute to his own downfall.

The Decision to Support the Overthrow of Diem

The United States continued to have a great deal of trouble dealing with Diem, who refused to implement the reforms mandated in NSAM 111. The situation was a genuine Catch-22. Diem lived on America's aid but ignored its advice because he *believed* that the United States viewed him as the only Vietnamese leader capable of rallying his country to defeat the Communists. Diem could not be forced into accepting American reforms since he believed that the United States would never invoke the ultimate sanction of withdrawing support. He also recognized, perhaps better than the Americans, that these very reforms might cause his government to fall.

The administration knew it was sitting on a keg of dynamite with Diem's increasingly authoritarian rule (really a family oligarchy consisting of his brother Ngo Dinh Nhu and his wife Madame Nhu, "the dragon lady"). During a May 8, 1963, celebration of Buddha's birthday in Hue, Diem's soldiers fired indiscriminately into a group of protestors who had violated orders forbidding the public display of flags. Eight Buddhists were killed and widespread demonstrations occurred throughout the country in protest of Buddhist repression and political discrimination. Not even the self-immolation of Buddhist monks would get Diem to acknowledge that a problem might exist. Madame Nhu's repulsive reference to the "bonze barbecue" fueled worldwide indignation at the Diem government *and* against the United States for supporting such a régime. Moreover, with pictures of Buddhist monks doused in gasoline dominating prime-time television news, "the American public at last started to glimpse the fact that something was amiss in Vietnam—and Kennedy . . . suddenly found himself burdened with a major political liability, in the presence of Diem."[47]

By July 13 the U.S. government was prepared to consider alternatives to Diem. A special National Intelligence Estimate entitled "The Situation in South Vietnam"[48] reported that international criticism was growing against the United States for supporting an "oppressive and unrepresentative régime." This CIA report speculated that should Diem be replaced, "there is a reasonably large pool of underutilized but experienced and trained manpower not only within the military and civilian sector of the present government but also, to some extent, outside. These elements, given continued support from the US, could provide reasonably effective leadership for the government and the war effort."

On August 21 (the eve of the arrival of the new American ambassador Henry Cabot Lodge in Vietnam), Diem's brother Ngo Dinh Nhu ordered a military assault by American-trained Special Forces units against Buddhist pagodas which resulted in the arrest of 1400 monks. Trying to protect his brother, Diem blamed the army for ordering the attack. Angry South Vietnamese generals went directly to the U.S. embassy and asked whether the United States would support a coup to remove Diem. When this news reached Washington, all of the principals were out of town or unavailable. The president was vacationing in Hyannisport; Secretary of Defense McNamara was mountain climbing; McNamara's deputy Roswell Gilpatric was spending the weekend at his farm in Virginia; Secretary of State Rusk was in New York at a baseball game; Maxwell Taylor was dining in a Washington restaurant; CIA Director John McCone was out of town. Averill Harriman finally located Undersecretary of State George Ball and U. Alexis Johnson at a public golf course in Washington. A cable was drafted by State Department personnel (Ball, Mike Forrestal, then on the White House staff, Harriman, and Roger Hilsman), was approved (by phone) by the president, and was sent to Henry Cabot Lodge. The new ambassador interpreted the cable as a "direct order to prepare for a coup against Diem."[49]

> U.S. Government cannot tolerate situation in which power lies in Nhu's hands. Diem must be given chance to rid himself of Nhu and his coterie and replace them with best military and political personalities available. ... We wish [to] give Diem reasonable opportunity to remove Nhu, but if he remains obdurate, then we are prepared to accept the obvious implication that we can no longer support Diem. You may tell appropriate military commanders we will give them direct support in any interim period of breakdown [of the] central government mechanism. ... Concurrently, with above, Ambassador and country team should urgently examine all possible alternative leadership and make detailed plans as to how we might bring about Diem's replacement if this should become necessary.[50]

With all of the principals reassembled in Washington the following Monday, a great deal of uncertainty surrounded the August 21 cable. Why had the United States reacted with such haste? Would a coup be detrimental to the progress of the war? Could Diem prevent the coup as he had in 1961? Who would succeed Diem? By August 29 the president had told his NSC staff that he still favored a coup so long as its success could be guaranteed.[51] The administration could not tolerate another CIA failure such as the Bay of Pigs. Ambassador Lodge then cabled Secretary Rusk:

> We are launched on a course from which there is no respectable turning back: the overthrow of the Diem government. There is no turning back in part because US prestige is already publicly committed to this end

in large measure and will become more so as the facts leak out. In a more fundamental sense, there is no turning back because there is no possibility, in my view, that the war can be won under a Diem administration, still less that Diem or any member of the family can govern the country in a way to gain the support of the people who count, i.e., the educated class in and out of government service, civil and military—not to mention the American people. In the last few months (and especially days) they have in fact positively alienated these people to an incalculable degree. . . . The chance of bringing off a Generals' coup depends on them to some extent; but it depends at least as much on us.[52]

The secretary responded with a notification to Lodge and Gen. Paul Harkins that the president "will support a coup which has a good chance of succeeding but plans no direct involvement of US armed forces."[53] Lodge was authorized to announce the suspension of aid to Diem at a time of his own choosing. "In deciding upon use of this authority, you should consider importance of timing and managing announcement so as to minimize appearance of collusion with Generals, and also to minimize danger of unpredictable and disruptive reaction by existing government."[54] Harkins was instructed to establish a "liaison with the coup planners and to review plans," but not personally to write such plans. Lodge was also instructed to do whatever necessary to "enhance the chances of a successful coup."[55] Nevertheless, in late August the generals questioned just how far the United States was committed to their cause and the coup was called off.

But the momentum for a coup could not be displaced. This was evident during an August 31 meeting of the National Security Council when Paul Kattenburg, a State Department officer and chairman of the Interdepartment Working Group on Vietnam, recommended withdrawing support for Diem. Kattenburg recreated the events of August 31, 1963:

> I was hurried without preparation by my old friend and then boss Assistant Secretary Roger Hilsman into a meeting of the executive committee of the National Security Council. I grew increasingly appalled as I listened to speaker after speaker, men at the top of our government like Rusk, McNamara, Taylor and Robert Kennedy who simply did not know Vietnam, its recent history, or the personalities and forces in contention. I concluded that under such leadership, and given the extremely difficult circumstances in Vietnam, we would never be

able to succeed there. I finally and imprudently for such meetings blurted out that I thought we should consider "withdrawal with honor." Dean Rusk and Lyndon Johnson's responses, cavalier dismissals of this thought, were indicative precisely of what I felt: that these men were leading themselves down a garden path to tragedy. We could not consider thoughts of withdrawal because of our will to "see it through," a euphemism once more hiding the fear of our top leadership that it might look weak—to Congress and the US public even more than to the Soviets.[56]

The administration was now committed—if not to getting in or out —to getting trapped. Between August and the November 1 coup two separate high-level fact-finding missions were sent to Vietnam—the Krulak-Mendenhall mission and the McNamara-Taylor mission.[57] The latter's October 2 report concluded that "the security of South Vietnam remains vital to United States security. For this reason, we adhere to the overriding objective of denying this country to communism and of suppressing the Viet Cong insurgency as promptly as possible." McNamara and Taylor recommended three options for the president:

1. Return to avowed support of the Diem regime and attempt to obtain the necessary improvements through persuasion from a posture of "reconciliation." This would not mean any expression of approval of the repressive actions of the regime, but simply that we would go back in practice to business as usual.

2. Follow a policy of selective pressures: "purely correct" relationships at the top official level, continuing to withhold further actions in the commodity import program, and making clear our disapproval of the regime. A further element in this policy is letting the present impressions stand that the US would not be adverse to a change of Government—although we would not take any immediate actions to initiate a coup.

3. Start immediately to promote a coup by high ranking military officers. This policy might involve more extended suspensions of aid and sharp denunciations of the regime's actions so timed as to fit with coup prospects and planning.[58]

During an October 2 NSC meeting the president selected option number 2. Economic sanctions against Diem would continue and the United States would support the plotting of a coup. On November

1, 1963, Diem was removed from office and murdered in the back of an American-built personnel carrier. While the coup was planned and implemented by RVNAF officers, Henry Cabot Lodge and the CIA were deeply involved. Lt.-Col. Lucien Conein, the advisor to Col. Le Quang Tung, was the CIA contact in Saigon. "Conein was present in the JGS headquarters building throughout the military actions against Diem. He was in constant communication with the US Embassy."[59]

Diem's death was followed by a period of great instability in Saigon. When Maxwell Taylor replaced Lodge as ambassador on July 2, 1964, he would deal with five different governments and five different prime ministers within the space of one year. Despite the revolving governments in Saigon, one constant remained—American complicity in the coup seemingly *tied* the United States to all succeeding régimes. Three weeks following the coup, President Kennedy was murdered in Dallas.

President Johnson's associates recall him as always believing that his predecessor's complicity in the overthrow of President Diem had been the worst error made by the United States during its involvement in Vietnam. The United States *became* responsible for the fate of successive governments in South Vietnam. Ambassador Taylor later reflected that "Diem's overthrow set in motion a sequence of crises, political and military, over the next two years which *eventually forced President Johnson in 1965 to choose between accepting defeat or introducing American combat forces.* There is no question but that President Kennedy and all of us who advised him bore a heavy responsibility for these happenings by having encouraged the perpetrators through the public display of our disapproval of Diem and his brother. That responsibility extends beyond the death of Diem—so bitterly regretted by President Kennedy—to the prolongation of the war and to the increased American involvement of later years, which were among the consequences of the events of this autumn of disaster. . . . The encouragement afforded the enemy by Diem's downfall found expression in a massive offensive, political and military, to exploit the removal of their mortal enemy. Taking into account all these effects, I would assess this episode as one of the great tragedies of the Vietnamese conflict and an important cause of the costly prolongation of the war into the next decade."[60]

The authors of the BDM Study reported: "few will argue against the fact that the role played by the US during the overthrow of Diem caused a deeper US involvement in Vietnam affairs. As efficient as the military coup leaders appeared, they were without a manageable base of political support. When they came to power and when the lid was taken off the Diem-Nhu reporting system, the GVN position was revealed as weak and deteriorating. And, by virtue of its interference in internal Vietnamese affairs, the US had assumed a significant responsibility for the new regime, a responsibility which heightened the US commitment and deepened the US involvement."[61] General Westmoreland's assessment was even more acute: "The young president, in his zeal, made the unfortunate mistake of approving our involvement in the overthrow of President Diem in South Vietnam. This action morally locked us in Vietnam. Political chaos prevailed in South Vietnam for over two years. Were it not for our interference in political affairs of South Vietnam and based on pragmatic consideration, we could in my opinion have justifiably withdrawn our support at that time in view of a demonstrated lack of leadership and unity in South Vietnam."[62]

Summary

In November 1961 the number of U.S. servicemen in Vietnam stood at 948; by January 9, 1962, there would be 2646, and by June 30, 5579. By the end of 1962 it rose to 11,300, and by the time of Kennedy's death in 1963, over 16,000 U.S. military personnel (double the number in the Taylor-Rostow report) would be in South Vietnam. Former Assistant Secretary of State William Bundy recalled that "President Kennedy took the decision to raise the ante through a system of advisors, pilots, and supplementary military personnel. . . . In effect, it was decided that the United States would take those additional actions that appeared clearly required to meet the situation, not knowing for sure whether these actions would in fact prove to be adequate, trying—despite the obvious and always recognized effect of momentum and inertia—not to cross the bridge of still further action, and hoping strongly that what was being taken would prove sufficient."[63]

We will never know "what might have been." We do know that Kennedy's decisions made Vietnam an *extraordinarily more difficult* problem for his successor. President Kennedy and his advisors never questioned whether or not Vietnam was really a vital interest. Communism had to be contained; Vietnam was defined as a pivotal domino in U.S. global policy. "He had," according to Arthur M. Schlesinger, Jr., "left on the public record the impression of a major national stake in the defense of South Vietnam against communism. He had left steadily enlarging programs of military and economic assistance. He had left national security advisors who for three years had been urging an American expeditionary force and a total commitment to the salvation of South Vietnam. On the other hand, he had consistently refused to send such a force or to make such a commitment. . . . And he had left private opposition, repeatedly and emphatically stated, to the dispatch of American ground forces."[64] The president had pursued a policy of doing just enough to satisfy the needs of the moment. "Whatever his fears or his ultimate intention," George Herring concluded, "he bequeathed to his successor a problem eminently more *dangerous* than the one he had inherited from Eisenhower."[65] It was dangerous because Johnson really believed his postassassination pledge "Let us continue." Whatever secret plans President Kennedy may have harbored for getting out, Johnson heard nothing of them when he asked Rusk, McNamara, and Bundy to stay because "I need you more than President Kennedy did."[66]

III

The Decisions of Early 1965:
Laying the Foundation for
a Major Commitment

The period following Diem's death in November 1963 and President Johnson's November 1964 election victory was one of political chaos in Saigon and doubt in Washington. Reporting from Saigon on December 21, 1963, Secretary McNamara noted that "the situation is very disturbing. Current trends, unless reversed in the next 2–3 months, will lead to neutralization at best and more likely to a communist-controlled state. The new government is the greatest source of concern."[1] The Joint Chiefs immediately recommended punitive bombing against the North as a means of controlling the insurgency in the South. South Vietnam was described as occupying "the pivotal position . . . in our world-wide confrontation with the communists,"[2] and bolder military action was viewed as a prerequisite for obtaining stability in the South.

Bombing the North had advocates within the administration. William Bundy, then assistant secretary of defense for international security affairs, wrote to the president on March 1, 1964, that bombing could be justified in support of political objectives in Vietnam.[3] Bombing would stop infiltration of supplies to the Viet Cong, stiffen the resolve of the GVN, and prove that the United States stood ready to halt the spread of communism. Under the heading "Best Action Possibilities," Bundy even recommended a blockade of Haiphong harbor because "this is a recognized military action that hits at the sovereignty of North Vietnam and almost inevitably means we would go further." The blockade would be followed by air attacks against key rail lines to Communist China, lines of communication, training camps, and key industrial complexes.

The momentum was clearly building in favor of an action decision or, for that matter, any decision which might change the political/military outlook in South Vietnam. On March 17, 1964, the administration issued National Security Action Memorandum 288 which reiterated the Truman-Eisenhower-Kennedy pledge that "we seek an independent, non-communist South Vietnam. . . . unless we can achieve this objective in South Vietnam, almost all of Southeast Asia will probably fall under Communist dominance."* Bundy warned the president that the types of military actions currently under consideration "would normally require a declaration of war under the Constitution. But this seems a blunt instrument carrying heavy domestic overtones and above all not suited to the picture of punitive and selective action only."[4] Johnson was advised to obtain a congressional resolution to support future military action in Southeast Asia. "Thus," the BDM study noted, "almost two months *before* the Tonkin Gulf crisis, the Johnson administration considered the possibility of bombing North Vietnam and obtaining a congressional resolution that would justify such action."[5]

Acting upon the recommendation of Secretary McNamara, President Johnson instructed the Joint Chiefs to prepare a contingency program of graduated military pressure against the North. The president also approved covert operations along the North Vietnamese coast. Operation Plan 34A was part of the "progressively escalating pressure" against the North. These 34A operations included U.S. patrol boat missions against North Vietnamese coastal installations. The U.S. Navy also began De Sota patrols by sending destroyers up the Gulf of Tonkin for intelligence-gathering purposes.[6]

---

*In June 1964 President Johnson changed the Country Team in South Vietnam. Maxwell Taylor became ambassador to South Vietnam, U. Alexis Johnson was appointed as Taylor's deputy, and Gen. William Westmoreland was promoted as commander of U.S. forces in Vietnam (MACV).

On August 2, 1964, the destroyer *Maddox* was returning from one of these electronic espionage missions when North Vietnamese torpedo boats fired on her. Rather than withdrawing U.S. ships from this danger zone, the president ordered another destroyer, the *C. Turner Joy*, to join the *Maddox* in the Gulf of Tonkin. Ambassador Taylor (an architect of the Joint Chiefs' contingency bombing plans) cabled Washington with a recommendation for immediate and severe bombing of the North. The president delayed any decision on Taylor's request. On August 4, both the *Maddox* and the *C. Turner Joy* reportedly came under attack. Considerable doubt exists as to whether this second "attack" ever took place. While there is little doubt that North Vietnamese gunboats were operating in the area, weather conditions were so bad and tensions aboard ship so high that Johnson later quipped, "For all I know, our Navy was shooting at whales out there."[7] But circumstantial evidence was all Johnson needed for ordering reprisals against the North.

The president later met with congressional leaders and sought assurance that his action would be supported. On August 10, 1964, Congress passed the Southeast Asia Resolution which provided Johnson with an awesome grant of power: "The Congress approves and supports the determination of the President, as Commander in Chief, to take all necessary measures to repeal any armed attack against the forces of the United States and to prevent further aggression. The United States regards as vital to its national interest and to world peace the maintenance of international peace and security in Southeast Asia . . . to take all necessary steps, including the use of armed force, to assist any member of protocol states of the Southeast Asia Collective Defense Treaty requesting assistance in defense of its freedom."[8]* With the election against Barry Goldwater less than three months away, however, President Johnson had no desire of being portrayed as planning for war. Instead, he left the rhetoric of war to Goldwater and the planning with his Joint Chiefs and Defense Department. "From a domestic political standpoint, Johnson's handling of the Tonkin Gulf incident was masterly. His firm but restrained response to the alleged North Vietnamese attacks won broad popular support, his ratings in the Louis Harris poll skyrocket-

*The White House files show that at least two months earlier a draft resolution was considered at an NSC meeting.

ing from 42 to 72 percent overnight."[9] All looked well until after the election when Johnson reached for his bombing plans.

Policy at a Crossroad

By late 1964 the Viet Cong were increasing their terrorist attacks and the first PLAF division-size battle of the war was underway at Binh Gia, forty miles east of Saigon. The Communists were clearly forcing the U.S. hand in order to determine how far the United States was really committed to South Vietnam. Only two days prior to the U.S. presidential election the Viet Cong attacked Bien Hoa airfield, killing four and wounding seventy-two Americans. President Johnson instructed an interagency working group (chaired by William Bundy) to canvass all "new" options and to forward their plans to the National Security Council. The interagency group formulated three options: first, a continuation of covert operations, money to the GVN, and controlled reprisals; the second was described as "fast/full squeeze"—controlled, rapid escalation against the North; and finally, "progressive squeeze and talk."[10] On December 1 the president approved the first option, but in doing so recognized that a clear provocation was necessary before proceeding with graduated reprisals.

By now the president understood that the war would never be won by air alone. Cabling Ambassador Taylor with the intent of "showing you the state of my thinking," President Johnson observed that "I am now ready to look with great favor on that kind of increased American effort [ground troops]."* Johnson went to unusual lengths in communicating with Ambassador Taylor on the question of a U.S. policy response to a deteriorating political situation:[11]

> Every time I get a military recommendation, it seems to me that it calls
> for a large scale bombing. I have never felt that this war will be won

---

*According to McGeorge Bundy, "This is an important cable. . . . [It] is an LBJ effort to get attention to well-designed ground action and it also shows clearly the temper of readiness to go further *inside South* Vietnam that he shows steadily from here on for 3 years in spite of all contrary counsel. Along with other indicators I take this to show he was never swayed on this basic issue by Ball or anyone else" (personal letter to the author).

from the air, and it seems to me that what is much more needed and would be more effective is a larger and stronger use of rangers and special forces and marines, or other appropriate military strength on the ground and on the scene. I am ready to look with great favor on that kind of increased American effort, directed at the guerrillas and aimed to stiffen the aggressiveness of Vietnamese military units up and down the line. Any recommendation that you or General Westmoreland take in this sense will have immediate attention from me, although I know that it may involve the acceptance of larger American sacrifices. We have been building our strength to fight this kind of war ever since 1961, and I myself am ready to substantially increase the number of Americans in Vietnam if it is necessary to provide this kind of fighting force against the Viet Cong.

President Johnson concluded with a strong show of support for his ambassador: "I know that you are the man on the spot and I know what a very heavy load you are carrying. I am grateful for it and I want you to know in turn that you have my complete confidence in the biggest and hardest job that we have overseas. *But in this tough situation in which the final responsibility is mine and the stakes are very high indeed, I have wanted you to have this full and frank statement of the way I see it.*" On January 6, Taylor cabled Johnson, "with regard to your feeling that this guerrilla war cannot be won from the air, I am in entire agreement, if we are thinking in terms of physical destruction of the enemy."[12]

Ambassador Taylor's New Year's gift for the president was a series of cables[13] bearing one central theme—"the situation in South Vietnam will continue to go downhill toward some form of political collapse unless new element or elements can be introduced." Ambassador Taylor now believed that even Diem had been better than the present chaos qua government of South Vietnam: "Until the fall of Diem and the experience gained from the events of the following months, I doubt that anyone appreciated the magnitude of the centrifugal political forces which had been kept under control by his iron rule. The successive political upheavals and the accompanying turmoil which have followed Diem's demise upset all prior U.S. calculations as to the duration and outcome of the counter-insurgency in SVN and the future remains uncertain today. There is no adequate replacement for Diem in sight."

The situation seemed so hopeless, the lack of leadership in Saigon so dire, that Ambassador Taylor actually raised the issue of withdrawing U.S. support when it appeared that General Khanh might assume power: "We are faced here with a seriously deteriorating situation characterized by continued political turmoil, irresponsibility and division within the armed forces, lethargy in the pacification program, some anti-US feeling which could grow, signs of mounting tensions by VC directly at US personnel and deepening discouragement and loss of morale throughout SVN. Unless these conditions are somehow changed and trends reversed, we are likely to face a number of unpleasant developments ranging from anti-American demonstrations, further civil disorders, and even political assassinations to the ultimate installation of a hostile government which will ask us to leave while it seeks accommodation with the national liberation front and Hanoi." Taylor concluded that since "we cannot expect anything better than marginal government," nor could the United States "change national characteristics, create leadership where it did not exist, nor raise additional GVN forces; should General Khanh gain control, we will have to do hard soul-searching to decide whether to try to get along with him again after previous failures or to refuse to support him and take the consequences—*which might entail ultimate withdrawal.*"*

Taylor nudged Johnson toward a favorable decision on air operations against the North. The ambassador recommended that the United States "look for *an occasion* to begin air operations just as soon as we have satisfactorily compromised the current political situation in Saigon."[15] For the president's protection, however, Taylor recommended "in order to assure yourself that we are missing no real bets in the political field, would you consider sending someone like Mac Bundy here for a few weeks." Bundy was the logical choice because he was "physically detached from the local scene" and pos-

---

*In his memoirs Taylor offered a perspective which is contradicted by the documents: "I have often been asked why, in view of the demonstrated inability of the South Vietnamese to pull themselves together in this critical period and cease the suicidal feuding among themselves with the enemy on the doorstep, I did not recommend that we give up and go home. We had made an honest effort to save this little country and had found it apparently incapable of self-defense and self-government. No one could charge us with failing an ally who seemed determined to fail himself. In response to this valid question, I must in honesty reply that it never occurred to me to recommend withdrawal. There were too many good reasons for not thinking about retreat."[14]

sessed a degree of objectivity which an "old Vietnamese hand would lack."

On January 7, 1965, Taylor received a direct reply from the president: "First, let me thank you for your 2052 and related messages. It is exceedingly helpful and thoughtful analysis of the situation, and *it gives me the clearest understanding I have had of the situation as you see it and of the reasoning behind your recommendations.*"[16] But the president was still not prepared to accept Taylor's proposal for a Phase II air campaign against the North. Reprinted below is a first draft of the cable to Taylor (written by McGeorge Bundy) which illustrates Washington's thinking during this crucial period:

> We concur in your judgement that large new American forces are *not* now desirable for security or for direct combat roles. . . .
>
> We concur in your view that any action against the North should be designed for political and psychological results. We want to avoid destruction for its own sake and to minimize risk of rapid escalation.
>
> We agree with your implicit assessment that strength and clarity of US commitment and determination are of major importance in political and even military balance in SVN.
>
> *We are not certain that any course of action now open to us can produce necessary turn-around in South Vietnam in coming months, but we are convinced that it is of high importance to try.*
>
> We are inclined to adopt a policy of prompt and clear reprisal, together with a readiness to start joint planning and execution on future military operations both within South Vietnam and against the North, but without present commitment as to the timing and scale of Phase II.
>
> Mac Bundy has reported your concern that CINCPAC be informed, and we agree that before final decisions are taken, he should be cut in. But recent leaks in Washington have redoubled my determination to make preliminary analyses and decisions privately, and for this reason this exchange of messages has been held in extraordinarily tight circle here. I want to hear your reactions before we enlarge the circle.[17]

On January 14 Taylor was informed that "immediately following the occurrence of a spectacular enemy action you would propose to us what reprisal action you considered desirable," so that Phase II bombing could begin.[18]

On January 27 Taylor cabled Bundy that another coup was underway, this one led by the Buddhist Institute leaders and General

Khanh: "The most sinister aspect of this affair is the obvious danger that the Buddhist victory may be an important step toward the formation of a government which will eventually lead the country into negotiations with Hanoi and the National Liberation Front. The Institute-Khanh combination is a union—albeit perhaps a temporary one—of two elements adverse to U.S. interests."[19]

The United States was not about to leave South Vietnam to its fate. Secretary of Defense McNamara and National Security Advisor McGeorge Bundy now saw the need to alter the basic U.S. policy directives toward Vietnam. Writing to the president, Bundy couched his observations within the framework of an advisory dilemma. Both he and McNamara "have reached the point where our obligations to you simply do not permit us to administer our present directives in silence and let you think we see real hope in them."* McNamara and Bundy had requested an 11:30 A.M. meeting in order to discuss these problems with the president.

> What we want to say to you is that both of us are now pretty well convinced that our current policy can lead only to disastrous defeat. What we are doing now, essentially, is to wait and hope for a stable government. Our December directives make it very plain that wider action against the Communists will not take place unless we can get such a government. In the last six weeks that effort has been unsuccessful, and Bob and I are persuaded that there is no real hope of success in this area unless and until our own policy and priorities change. The underlying difficulties in Saigon arise from the spreading conviction that the future is without hope for anti-Communist policy. Our best friends have been somewhat discouraged by our own inactivity in the face of major attacks on our own installations. The Vietnamese know just as well as we do that the Viet Cong are gaining in the countryside. Meanwhile, they see the enormous power of the United States withheld and they get little sense of firm and active U.S. policy. They feel that we are unwilling to take serious risks. In one sense, all of this is outrageous, in the light of all that we have done and all that we are ready

---

*"You should know that Dean Rusk does not agree with us. He does not quarrel with our assertion that things are going very badly and that the situation is unraveling. He does not assert that this deterioration can be stopped. What he does say is that the consequences of both escalation and withdrawal are so bad that we simply must find a way of making our present policy work. This would be good if it was possible. Bob and I do not think it is."

to do if they will only pull up their socks. But it is a fact—or at least so
McNamara and I now think. The basic directive says that we will not
go further until there is a stable government, and no one has much hope
that there is going to be a stable government while we sit still. The
result is that we are pinned into a policy of first aid to squabbling
politicos and passive reaction to events we do not try to control. Or so
it seems. Bob and I believe that the worst course of action is to continue
in this essentially passive role which can only lead to eventual defeat
and an invitation to get out in humiliating circumstances. We see two
alternatives. The first is to use our military power in the Far East and
to force a change of Communist policy. The second is to deploy all our
resources along a track of negotiation, aimed at salvaging what little can
be preserved with no major addition to our present military risks. Bob
and I tend to favor the first course, but we believe that both should be
carefully studied and that alternative programs should be argued out
before you. Both of us understand the very grave questions presented
by any decision of this sort. We both recognize that the ultimate responsibility is not ours. Both of us fully supported your unwillingness, in
earlier months, to move out of the middle course. We both agree that
every effort should still be made to improve our operations on the
ground and to prop up the authorities in South Vietnam as best we can.
But we are both convinced that none of this is enough and that the time
has come for harder choices.[20]

The memo was followed by a morning meeting during which the
president decided that Bundy should go to South Vietnam and confer with Taylor. Bundy later wrote to the president, "This is as good
moment as any to say how much Bob and I valued your comments
this morning in response to our memo, and how proud I am that you
are willing to entrust this particular mission to me."[21]

President Johnson soon cabled Taylor and thanked the ambassador
for "your very prompt and clear-headed account of the events of the
last 24 hours. We are inclined to share your judgement of the immediate meaning of these events [coup], and I have complete confidence in your judgement on the spot as you deal with this new
situation." The president then offered a clear picture of his thinking
in January 1965: *"I am determined to make it clear to all the world
that the US will spare no effort and no sacrifice in doing its full
part to turn back the communists in Vietnam. . . .* I am most eager
to have the closest possible sense of your own thinking on the

situation / on the spot. For this reason I am inclined now to take you up on your earlier suggestion that McGeorge Bundy come to Saigon."[22]

Bundy soon cabled Taylor with "preliminary thoughts for our talks."[23] Asking that Taylor avoid "extended organized briefings," Bundy wrote, "I think we need to compare our pictures of the existing situation. . . . Washington is assuming that the course of this contest has been generally unfavorable for more than a year and that in the absence of major changes it's likely to get worse." Indicative of the instability in Saigon, Bundy's visit coincided with yet another government coup and scheduled meetings had to be cancelled because government officials were now former officials. Bundy's correspondence with Taylor illustrated the awkwardness of the U.S. position: "President sees force of your argument that my visit should not come when there is no government to talk with. On the other hand, it looks to us as if General Khanh for better or for worse is the principal present power. *We see no early prospect of solid and stable administration no matter what happens in the next few days.*"[24] It was now obvious that Saigon could not achieve the precondition of stable government. U.S. decision-makers were in a real bind— finding no stable government, they were forced to lower their preconditions in order to justify policy.

When Bundy arrived in Saigon he met with General Khanh. Cabling the president, Bundy outlined the differences between himself and Taylor on support for the general:

> For immediate purposes—and especially for the initiation of reprisal policy, we believe that the government need be no stronger than it is today with General Khanh as the focus of raw power while a weak caretaker government goes through the motions. Such a government can execute military decisions and it can give formal political support to joint US/GVN policy. That is about all it can do. In the longer run, it is necessary that a government be established which will in one way or another be able to maintain its political authority against all challenges over a longer time than the governments of the last year and a half. The composition and direction of such a government is a most difficult problem, and we do not wholly agree with the mission in our estimate of its nature. *The mood of the mission with respect to the prospect of obtaining such a government is one of pessimism and frustration.* This is only natural in terms of the events of the past many

weeks. Two dominant themes predominate: a government headed by Khanh will be difficult if not impossible to deal with and, in any case would be short-lived; the Buddhists (or, more specifically, the few politically activist Bonzes) must be confronted and faced down (by military means if necessary) lest they maintain their power to unseat any government that does not bow to their every demand. *We tend to differ with the mission on both counts.* Specifically, we believe that General Khanh, with all his faults, is by long odds the outstanding military man currently in sight—and the most impressive personality generally. We do not share the conclusion of Ambassador Taylor that he must somehow be removed from the military and political scene. There are strong reasons for the Ambassador's total lack of confidence in Khanh. At least twice Khanh has acted in ways that directly disspelled Ambassador Taylor's high hopes for December. When he abolished the High National Council he undercut the prospect of the stable government needed for Phase II action against the North. In January he overthrew Huong just when the latter, in the Embassy's view, was about to succeed in putting the bonzes in their place. Khanh is not an easy man to deal with. It is clear that he takes a highly tactical view of the truth, although General Westmoreland asserts that Khanh has never deceived him. He is intensely ambitious and intent above all else on maintaining and advancing his own power. He gravely lacks the confidence of many of his colleagues—military and civilian—and he seems not to be personally popular with the public. He is correctly assessed as tricky. He remains able, energetic, perceptive and resilient, and in our judgment he will pursue the fight against the Communists as long as he can count on US help. (If he should conclude that the US was violently against him personally, he might well seek a way to power by some anti-American path, a path which would lead to disaster for both Vietnam and the United States.) But our principal reason for opposing any sharp break with Khanh is that we see no one else in sight with anything like his ability to combine military authority with some sense of politics.[25]*

*On January 31, 1964, former ambassador Frederick Nolting requested a visit with President Johnson. "Regarding Viet Nam, it seems to me that the situation there is now more susceptible to improvement, as the result of the recent shift of power. General Khanh, whom I know well, is in my opinion the ablest all-round Vietnamese leader on the scene at present and can be relied on, if we deal with him properly. He may well be able to rally support among the peasants (where he is not tarnished by complicity in Diem's assassination) as well as in the Army. But he is sensitive and will need careful handling. The allegiance of the younger officers will depend, I think, largely on how clear and firm the U.S. position is."[26]

The "commitment" to Khanh illustrated just how far Bundy and the president were willing to go in abandoning the original basis for U.S. support—stable and meritorious government in the South. When Ambassador Taylor recommended to Bundy that the United States not support a Khanh government and be prepared to "reduce advisory effort to policy guidance. Disengage and let the GVN stand alone," Bundy scribbled a question mark (?) in the margin.[27] Moreover, commitment to South Vietnam now took precedence over who represented the government of South Vietnam—the stakes were simply too high to permit a Communist victory.

But events soon vindicated Taylor. Khanh was removed from power in what Taylor joyfully described to the president as "the most tipsy-turvy week since I came to this post. A new government installed, a coup attempted against the commander-in-chief, the coup suppressed, the commander-in-chief deposed by those who put down the coup."[28] Taylor expressed relief that "Khanh, the troublemaker," had been replaced by a civilian prime minister, Dr. Phan Huy Quat.

Since there was no longer any doubt about "commitment," the only real question revolved around when graduated air strikes (as recommended by Taylor) would begin. The appropriate outrage finally occurred while Bundy was still in Vietnam at a "streetcar"[29] called Pleiku—where terrorist bombs struck the U.S. Army barracks, killing 9 and wounding 107 Americans. President Johnson immediately ordered the evacuation of all U.S. dependents and a series of tit-for-tat bombing raids (Flaming Dart) began between the U.S. and the DRV. The president preferred to describe the bombing as "prompt and adequate and measured," but Mac Bundy disagreed: "I believe that for a policy of continuing action the words 'adequate and measured and fitting' are better. 'Fitting' is the word we used at the time of Tonkin Gulf, and if we are going to continue actions in a situation in which there is no spectacular outrage like Pleiku, I think 'fitting' is a better word than 'prompt.' It may sound like mere semantics, but I think it is quite near the center of the problem of stating your desire precisely."[30]

Many secondary accounts suggest that the attack at Pleiku impacted greatly on the president's national security advisor. Yet, writing from the field, Bundy painted a bleak but not very different picture from the one he and McNamara had *already* endorsed.

Bundy concluded with a program recommendation for graduated and continuing air reprisals which "may fail and we cannot estimate the odds of success with any accuracy—they may be somewhere between 25% and 75%." Bundy provided the president with the following assessment of the situation in Vietnam:

The prospect in Vietnam is grim. The energy and persistence of the Viet Cong are astonishing. They can appear anywhere—at almost any time. They have accepted extraordinary losses and they come back for more. They show skill in their sneak attacks and ferocity when cornered. Yet the weary country does not want them to win. There are a host of things the Vietnamese need to do better and areas in which we need to help them. The place where we can help most is in the clarity and firmness of our own commitment to what is in fact as well as in rhetoric a common cause. *There is one grave weakness in our posture in Vietnam which is within our own power to fix—and that is a widespread belief that we do not have the will and force and patience and determination to take the necessary action and stay the course.* This is the overriding reason for our present recommendation of a policy of sustained reprisal. Once such a policy is put in force, we shall be able to speak in Vietnam on many topics and in many ways, with growing force and effectiveness. One final word. *At its very best, the struggle in Vietnam will be long.* It seems to us important that this fundamental fact be made clear to our people and to the people of Vietnam. Too often in the past we have conveyed the impression that we expect an early solution when those who live with this war know that no early solution is possible. It is our own belief that the people of the United States have the necessary will to accept and to execute a policy that rests upon the reality that there is no short cut to success in South Vietnam. *The situation in Vietnam is deteriorating, and without a new US action defeat appears inevitable*—probably not in a matter of weeks or perhaps even months, but within the next year or so. There is still time to turn it around, but not much. *The stakes in Vietnam are extremely high. The American investment is very large,* and American responsibility is a fact of life which is palpable in the atmosphere of Asia, and even elsewhere. *The international prestige of the United States, and a substantial part of our influence, are directly at risk in Vietnam.* There is no way of unloading the burden on the Vietnamese themselves, *and there is no way of negotiating ourselves out of Vietnam which offers any serious promise at present.* It is possible that at some future time a neutral non-Communist force may emerge, perhaps under Buddhist leadership, but no such force currently exists, *and any negotiated US withdrawal today would mean surrender on the installment plan.*[31]

Bundy's report raised doubts in the mind of at least one NSC staff member. Identifying his position as "one dove's lament," James Thomson argued that decision-makers were spending more time selecting bombing targets than on possible avenues for negotiations —"the only rational alternative"[32] to a major military commitment. Thomson argued against each of the themes in Bundy's February 7 memo: "It seems to me that we not lose our perspective: in South Vietnam we have slipped into a gross overcommitment of national prestige and resources on political, military and geographic terrain which should long ago have persuaded us to avoid such a commitment. Our national interest now demands that we find ourselves a face-saving avenue of retreat—that we marshal our imaginations and those of other powers—to discover such an avenue." Thomson argued that a policy of sustained reprisals was illogical:

I have assumed that the proposed policy of sustained reprisals seeks to achieve two objectives: (a) to stiffen the spine, morale, and sense of unity of the South Vietnamese and thereby induce greater political stability; and (b) to signal our determination, and our willingness to inflict increasingly heavy damage, to the Hanoi regime and its supporters. I have also sensed that where doubts might exist on the attainability of either one of these objectives, the reprisal track has been considered justifiable on the basis of the other objective alone. Thus, even though I have seen no intelligence estimates (including that of February 18th) which conclude that Hanoi would "call off its dogs" in response to a sustained reprisal track, I assume that the track has nonetheless commended itself to the Administration as a means to achieve stability through sustained euphoria in Saigon. I would judge that last night's coup attempt has seriously undermined our argument for the therapeutic effect in the South of air strikes against the North (although I suspect some may argue that the coup occurred as the result of our failure to make further air strikes earlier this week). Certainly the widespread public impression of air strikes as a desperation move—as a substitute for political stability in Saigon—will be compounded by this most recent power grab. I continue to believe that a policy of sustained reprisal against the North entails greater risks than we have any right to take in terms of our world-wide interests. Not so far down the track, given the factors of North Vietnamese and Chinese aircraft, US rules of engagement, Peiping's paranoia, and the Sino-Soviet Treaty, is the strong possibility of a ground war with China—a war in which we do not have the wherewithal to achieve any meaningful "victory" even if our people and our allies allowed us to take on the Chinese armies for a long ground struggle.

Thomson's rationale found little support among the principal foreign policy advisors to the president, who had already concluded that bombing the North was necessary to save South Vietnam. Moreover, most of them believed that an unwary provocation of China was not in itself a good argument against bombing the North. "It was," according to George Ball, "a Catch 22 and the quintessence of black humor. As though to demonstrate how harassed but ingenious men can turn logic upside down, my colleagues interpreted the crumbling of the South Vietnamese Government, the increasing success of the Viet Cong guerrillas, and a series of defeats of South Vietnamese units in the field not as one might expect—persuasive evidence that we should cut our losses and get out—but rather as proving that we must promptly begin bombing to stiffen the resolve of the South Vietnamese Government. It was classical bureaucratic casuistry. A faulty rationalization was improvised to obscure the painful reality that America could arrest the galloping deterioration of its position only by the surgery of extrication. Dropping bombs was a pain-killing exercise that saved my colleagues from having to face the hard decision to withdraw. Some gifted dialecticians carried the charade even one step further, arguing that we ourselves were responsible for the low state of morale in Saigon, since Ambassador Taylor had made Saigon's politicians nervous by demanding that the government shape up in a manner beyond its will to do so. Thus, it was argued, we must engage our power and prestige even more intensely since otherwise the South Vietnamese might fall apart, negotiate covertly with the Liberation Front of Hanoi, and ultimately ask us to leave."[33]

Vice-President Hubert Humphrey now joined Thomson and Ball in opposing the reprisal bombings. Humphrey's February 15 memo to the president resulted in the vice-president's banishment from future foreign policy meetings, a position he later described as being "in limbo."[34] George Ball, however, faced a different fate. He was

permitted, often encouraged, to dissent—a role in which Ball produced a series of brilliant and, as it turned out, prophetic memos to
the president. Most commentators focus on Ball as the institutional-
ized devil's advocate. But, according to Ball, "because the President
wanted, above all, to create the impression that there was no dissent
within the top circles, he adopted the practice of referring to me as
the 'devil's advocate' so as to provide an explanation if anyone outside the government expressed the suspicion that I was opposing our
Vietnam policy. Though it served in a measure as personal protection, I was later annoyed when academic writers naïvely suggested
that my long-continued efforts to extricate us from Vietnam were
merely a stylized exercise by an in-house 'devil's advocate.' Thus are
myths made. Not one of my colleagues ever had the slightest doubt
as to my intense personal convictions."[35]

Immediately following Bundy's recommendation for reprisal
bombing Ball joined forces with Ambassador Llewelyn Thompson in
drafting a memorandum which, with the concurrence of McGeorge
Bundy and McNamara, stated objectively the risks and possible
consequences of gradually mounting pressure against the North. "I
had hoped that by associating McNamara and Bundy (as well as
Thompson, for whose judgment the President had particular respect)
in a joint effort to point out the dangers of escalation, I could not only
shake up the President but smoke out my colleagues and try to
persuade them to agree, if not to extrication, at least to a more
cautious plan of action."[36] The memo noted that as U.S. bombs fell
closer to Hanoi, there was a greater likelihood that Chinese MIGs
would engage U.S. aircraft. This would create pressure for the United
States to bomb the major MIG base at Phuc Yen, near Hanoi, which
would almost certainly trigger a DRV ground force move into the
South, necessitating a probable U.S. troop effort of approximately
300,000 to stop them. Moreover, "the confrontation of Chinese
ground forces by American ground forces would induce debate in
the United States as to the need to use nuclear weapons—although
DOD [Department of Defense] does not believe there would be a
military requirement for such weapons. Recalling the Korean experience, some Americans would argue that United States ground forces
should not be asked to fight large numbers of Chinese troops without
resort to nuclear weapons, in which the United States has a clear
advantage. To use nuclear weapons against the Chinese would obvi-

ously raise the most profound political problems. Not only would their use generate probably irresistible pressures for a major Soviet involvement, but the United States would be vulnerable to the charge that it was willing to use nuclear weapons against non-whites only."[37]

Ball then reported what he *believed* were the major areas of disagreement between Bundy-McNamara and Ball-Thompson:

McNamara-Bundy Position

McNamara and Bundy believe that we must pursue a course of increasing military pressure to the point where Hanoi is prepared to agree not only to stop infiltration from the North, but effectively to call off the insurgency in the South and withdraw those elements infiltrated in the past.* To achieve this objective, they would accept the risks of substantial escalation, including the acceptance of ground warfare with Red China—although they believe it likely that we can achieve the desired objective without such a war. This view is shared by Maxwell Taylor.

Ball-Thompson Position

Ball and Thompson believe that—short of a crushing military defeat— Hanoi would never abandon the aggressive course it has pursued at great cost for ten years and give up all the progress it has made in the Communization of South Viet-Nam. For North Viet-Nam to call off the insurgency in South Viet-Nam, close the border, and withdraw the elements it has infiltrated into that country would mean that it had accepted unconditional surrender. . . .

Ball and Thompson have supported the air strikes that have so far taken place and they would support a program of gradually increasing military pressure. They believe that only in this way can the United States achieve a bargaining position that can make possible an international arrangement that will avoid a humiliating defeat to the United States. They do not believe, however, that we can realistically hope for an international arrangement that will effectively stop the insurrection in South Viet-Nam and deliver the entire country south of the Seventeenth Parallel to the government in Saigon free and clear of insurgency. They consider that the most we can realistically expect from any

*Ball's personal notes show that Bundy called Ball to correct this attribution. Bundy believed that since we did not know when this point would be reached, the U.S. objective could remain unformulated and therefore more flexible.[38]

international arrangement are measures to stop the infiltration so that we may be able, over time, to reduce our commitments. Hopefully the military actions preceding such an arrangement would have created a sufficient sense of unity in Saigon to make it possible for the South Vietnamese Government—with diminishing United States help—to clean up an insurgency that had become manageable by the shutting of the borders.

In all events, Ball and Thompson recommend that you must be prepared and alerted—whenever it appears that military conflict may have reached the level of intensity where Chinese ground intervention seems likely—to accept a ceasefire under international auspices short of the achievement of our total political objectives.[39]

When the president received Ball's memorandum, he showed no interest in these differences or, for that matter, in points of agreement between advisors. "The memorandum," Ball recalled, "accomplished nothing. Though I sent it to the President, he did not adhere to the pattern he followed with my later memoranda of reading it carefully, then holding a full-scale meeting to discuss it. Instead he met with Thompson, Bundy, and me, read the memorandum quickly, then asked me to go through it point by point. At the conclusion of the meeting, he thanked me and handed the memorandum back without further comment. Why he followed that uncharacteristic course I have never understood.[40]

Two weeks later Ball created a second chance. In October 1964 Ball had written a memo to Bundy, McNamara, and Rusk entitled "How Valid are the Assumptions Underlying our Vietnam Policies?"[41] Ball demanded proof from those who favored bombing that this policy preference could achieve its purported goals. But in October Johnson was too busy campaigning and he had left instructions that such papers were not to reach his desk. Now, on February 24, 1965, Ball believed that Johnson should read his memorandum. Ball invited Bill Moyers to lunch and showed him the document. "He was," Ball recalled, "struck by it and insisted—as I had assumed he would—on giving it to the President that afternoon. The following morning he called me to say that the President had read and reread my memorandum, had 'found it fascinating and wanting to know why he had not read it before.' I explained that I had prepared the memorandum five months earlier for McNamara, Rusk, and Bundy, but since it had made no dent in their firm convictions, I had left it up to them to decide whether to show it to the President."[42]

Why was Johnson so moved by Ball's argument? The undersecretary wrote from the premise that the political situation in Saigon was progressively deteriorating: "Even if that deterioration is checked, there seems little likelihood of establishing a government that can (a) provide a solid center around which the broad support of the Vietnamese people can coalesce or (b) conduct military operations with sufficient effectiveness to clean up the insurgency." Ball's purpose was to develop "a *prima facie* case for a possible alternative to intensifying our role in the Vietnamese war;"

1. Our *first* option is to continue the present course of action in an effort to strengthen the South Vietnamese effort, recognizing that at some point we shall probably either: a. Be forced to leave as a result of a neutralist coup or decision in Saigon; or b. Be forced to adopt one of the other options by the manifest hopelessness of the present course of action.

2. Our *second* option is to take over the war in South Vietnam by the injection of substantial U.S. ground forces operating directly under a U.S. chain of military command.

3. Our *third* option is to mount an air offensive against the North in the hope of bringing pressure on Hanoi that would either: a. Persuade the Hanoi Government that the game is not worth the candle and that it should cease direction and support of the insurgency in the South; or b. Improve our bargaining position in relation to Hanoi and Peiping so as to make possible an acceptable political solution through negotiation.

4. Our *fourth* option is to adopt a course of action that would permit a political settlement without direct U.S. military involvement under conditions that would be designed hopefully to: a. Check or at least delay the extension of Communist power into South Viet-Nam; b. Provide the maximum protection for Thailand, Malaysia, and South Asia; c. Minimize the political damage resulting to U.S. prestige in other Asian capitals, throughout the non-aligned world, and with our Western Allies.

The *first* option—to continue the present course of action—is not likely to lead to a clean-cut decision. To say this is not necessarily to condemn it. Yet if we are to seek a political solution without committing United States forces to direct military conflict by an air or ground offensive, it may be advantageous to set this process in train by an incisive decision under optimum circumstances rather than to let circumstances take their course.

The *second* option—*to take over the war by the injection of substantial U.S. ground forces—offers the worst of both worlds.* Our situation would in the world's eyes approach that of France in the 1950's. We would incur the opposition of elements in Viet-Nam otherwise friendly to us. Finally, we would find ourselves in *la guerre sale* with consequent heavy loss of American lives in the rice paddies and jungles.

The *third* option—to mount military pressure against the North primarily by an air offensive—is clearly preferable to the second. North Viet-Nam might well retaliate by ground action that would require the deployment of U.S. land forces. But there are obvious advantages in our initially choosing the offensive capability with which we have the unquestioned advantage.

In the last page of his cogent memorandum Ball argued, "what I am urging is that our Southeast Asian policy be looked at in all its aspects and in the light of our total world situation. It is essential that this be done before we commit military forces to a line of action that could put events in the saddle and destroy our freedom to choose the policies that are at once the most effective and the most prudent."

The president was deeply affected by Ball's argument—so much so that a February 26 meeting was scheduled to discuss its validity (or Ball's?). Ball recalled that "the debate was open and direct with no punches pulled. The President clearly showed that he had read the document, for he challenged specific points I had made, and even remembered the page numbers where those arguments occurred. Still my colleagues were fiercely opposed. Secretary McNamara produced a spectacular display of facts and statistics to show that I had overstated the difficulties we were now encountering and that the situation was much better than I represented—suggesting, at least by nuance, that I was not only prejudiced but ill-informed. Secretary Rusk made what I thought was a deeply felt argument about the dangers of not going forward. The meeting lasted a long while and, while I clung to the hope that I had forced some hard thinking (at least on the part of the President), it ended on an inconclusive note and I knew I had made no serious converts. Though I hoped by my memorandum to force a systematic analysis of our position that would reveal the folly of the course on which we were embarked, I did not succeed."[43]

The meeting revealed what would be a consistent pattern of behavior for the president—to place the burden of proof only on those who sought a way out of, and not into, the war. Johnson later cited such meetings as proof that Ball was indeed given his day in court. But Ball really never had a chance. In asking questions about upper limits, for example, Ball referred to the results of the Sigma II tests (September 8–11, 1964) conducted under the auspices of the Joint Chiefs. The tests asked "What is the most favorable result we could hope to achieve by military action against North Vietnam?" and concluded that even by exhausting all possible targets, this would not cripple Hanoi's capacity.[44] Those who favored escalation, a wider war, a larger commitment, were never required to provide assurance—moreover, they could not have done so—that their policy recommendation would achieve its goal. Slow and steady escalation was viewed as a safe policy because it required so little critical thinking about assumptions.

Ironically, bombing increased North Vietnam's resolve and determination. A June 29, 1965, State Department Intelligence Note on "The Effects of the Bombing of North Vietnam" concluded that "rather limited but quite uniform and convincing evidence indicates that the U.S. strikes against North Vietnam have had no significantly harmful effects on popular morale. *In fact,* the regime has apparently been able to increase its control on the populace and perhaps even to break through the political apathy and indifference which have characterized the outlook of the average North Vietnamese in recent years."[45] Moreover, the bombing certainly led to increased pressure for the United States to send ground troops—first to protect U.S. installations and later to accomplish what bombing could not. According to Paul Kattenburg, "bombing failed to achieve its aims either in bringing the DRV quickly to its knees or bolstering the situation on the ground in the South to a point where it would at least begin to improve. Instead, bombing brought about the massive, though gradual, introduction of PAVN troops into the South, while in the South itself the political-military situation was not improving. . . . Rolling Thunder was a fateful U.S. decision in Vietnam primarily because it brought about what its opponents feared, massive ground retaliation by the North Vietnamese, without bringing about what its proponents sought, the DRV to the conference table on terms then acceptable to the U.S."[46] By April 1965 Gen. Earle Wheeler wrote to Secretary McNamara with a dismal appraisal of air strikes against the North between February 7 and April 4, 1965. Wheeler informed McNamara that "the air strikes have not reduced in any major way the over-all military capabilities of the DRV. . . . I think it fair to state that our strikes to date, while damaging, have not curtailed DRV military capabilities in any major way. The same is true as regards the North Vietnamese economy. The North Vietnamese people exhibit an understandable degree of apprehension for the future. The Hanoi government continues to maintain, at least publicly, stoical determination."[47]

The First Troops Arrive

On February 21, 1965, General Westmoreland requested two battalions of marines to protect the U.S. air base at Danang from VC retaliation during Rolling Thunder missions.[48] The general estimated that there were approximately twelve enemy battalions totaling 6000 men within striking distance of Danang—the base for Rolling Thunder missions. On February 26 President Johnson approved Westmoreland's request. In his memoirs Westmoreland wrote, "I saw my call for marines at Danang not as a first step in a growing American commitment but as what I said at the time it was: a way to secure a vital airfield and the air units using it."[49] There is some doubt as to whether General Westmoreland really viewed his request as a stop-gap measure or as the first step in the implementation of a program for American combat troops to Vietnam. The *Pentagon Papers* analyst believed that "there seems to be sufficient evidence to conclude that General Westmoreland and his staff saw in the deployment of the Marines the beginning of greater things to come."[50] The MACV Command History noted on the day the marines landed, "thus step one in the buildup of forces had been taken and subsequent steps appeared to be assured."[51] Yet, according to General Westmoreland, "although I was skeptical of success, I hoped that it would work and wanted to give it every chance of success. It was not a 'foot in the door ploy' to the deployment of U.S. ground troops which I truly hoped to avoid. On the other hand, our mission was clear and I had to make plans to ask for whatever I deemed necessary to avoid defeat and accomplish our national objective. The *Pentagon Papers* jump to a false conclusion as to my orientation and are wrong. . . . As to the MACV Command History, the quoted comment was that of the historian, not mine. Yes, it was a 'first step,' but I did *not* consider the deployments to protect Danang Air Base to be an 'assured' step towards a 'build up of forces.' "[52]

Ambassador Taylor opposed Westmoreland's request, arguing as he had since early January that it would be "very difficult to hold the line on future deployments. . . . intervention with ground forces would at best buy time and would lead to ever increasing commitments until, like the French, we would be occupying an essentially hostile foreign country. . . . As I analyze the pros and cons of placing any considerable number of marines in Danang area beyond those presently assigned I develop grave reservations as to the wisdom and necessity of so doing. Such action would be a step in reversing long standing policies of avoiding commitment of ground combat forces in South Vietnam. *Once this policy is breached, it will be very difficult to hold the line.*"[53]

Nevertheless the momentum of the moment was in Westmoreland's favor and on March 8, 1965, 3500 U.S. Marines stormed ashore at Danang—the first time U.S. combat troops had been committed to the Asian mainland since Korea. The decision, in retrospect, involved very little planning. Westmoreland later recalled: "When the U.S. marines got word they were to land, it was like pulling the stopper from a bathtub. Any semblance of a low profile quickly disappeared. Under Admiral Sharp's direction rather than mine, the first of the two battalions stormed ashore near Danang on March 8 in full battle regalia as if re-enacting Iwo Jima, only to find South Vietnamese officials and U.S. Army advisers welcoming them and pretty Vietnamese girls passing out leis of flowers. One U.S. Army district advisory group composed of a captain, a lieutenant, and two sergeants greated the marines good naturedly with a sign painted on a sheet: WELCOME TO THE GALLANT MARINES. . . . I did urge on the marines one concession to an Embassy quibble: changing the name of the marine contingent from the 'Marine Expeditionary Force' to the 'III Marine Amphibious Force' lest the brigade be associated in Vietnamese minds with the French Expeditionary Corps."[54] Years later Taylor wrote, "it was curious how hard it had been to get authorization for the initiation of the air campaign against the North and how relatively easy to get the Marines ashore."[55] U.S. soldiers would soon be active combatants in Southeast Asia. The BDM study described this as an "amazing point" because the United States had *never* been officially invited to send these combat troops in March 1965.[56]

Inside the White House there appears to have been a presumption that troops would be sent regardless of Taylor's opposition. Six days before the marines landed, but two days after Westmoreland's request, President Johnson dispatched the army chief of staff, Gen. Harold K. Johnson, to Saigon with direct orders to confer with General Westmoreland and find out "what more can be done within South Vietnam."[57] Westmoreland recalled that, "disappointed in the lack of results from the bombing of the North, the President and some of his advisors were letting their frustrations show. As General Johnson descended in an elevator with the President, following breakfast in the family quarters, President Johnson, towering over the Chief-of-Staff, thrust an index finger in his breastbone, leaned his face close, and said: 'You get things bubbling, General.' "[58] General Johnson returned to Washington on March 14 with a "bubbling" twenty-one–point program, reviewed by the president on March 15. General Johnson's recommendations included proposals for increasing U.S. combat aid and logistical support, creation of an international force for an antiinfiltration role along the DMZ, and dispatching another army division to defend U.S. installations. The president approved more American military aid and combat support but took no action on logistical support nor on the international force along the DMZ. Westmoreland believed that this was "a cardinal error, for as long as any possibility existed of commiting US troops, logistical preparation should have been started."[59] Following General Johnson's departure, General Westmoreland initiated his own detailed study of the Vietnam situation, believing that "we might be about to make a most momentous decision, one not to be undertaken without the most careful deliberation and analysis."[60]

The movement toward commitment of offensive ground troops was now well underway. On March 16, 1965, McGeorge Bundy wrote to the president that "the existing situation in South Vietnam is bad" and the U.S. "eventual bargaining position will be improved and not weakened if the U.S. presence on the ground increases in coming weeks."[61] On March 16 Westmoreland sought Ambassador Taylor's concurrence for landing a third marine battalion at Phu Bai (per General Johnson's request) to protect a radio relay unit and airstrip. "Intrinsic in my proposal," Westmoreland later wrote, "was that American troops would be used in offensive operations. Whereas I saw the commitment as strategically defensive, aimed primarily at forestalling South Vietnamese defeat, the adage that a good offense is the best defense was as applicable in Vietnam as it had been elsewhere throughout history."[62] Ambassador Taylor recommended that U.S. troops be restricted to coastal enclaves, a strategy which General Westmoreland's staff study had already rejected as an "inglorious, static use of U.S. forces in overpopulated areas with little chance of direct or immediate impact on the outcome of events."[63] While Taylor agreed that the third division would stop any talk of U.S. withdrawal, the ambassador sided with the counterarguments:

> This proposal for introducing the battalion is a reminder of the strong likelihood of additional requests for increases in U.S. ground combat forces in South Vietnam. Such requests may come from the U.S. side, from the Vietnam side, or from both. All of us here are keenly aware of the Government of Vietnam trained military manpower shortage which will exist throughout 1965 and which probably can be rectified only in part by an accelerated mobilization. We will soon have to decide whether to try to get by with inadequate indigenous forces or to supplement them with third country troops, largely if not exclusively U.S. This matter was discussed with General Johnson during his recent visit who no doubt had raised it following his return to Washington. The introduction of a U.S. division obviously increases U.S. involvement in the counterinsurgency. . . . It is not desirable to introduce a U.S. division into South Vietnam unless there are clear and tangible advantages outweighing the numerous disadvantages, many of which have been noted above. Obviously, one division would make some contribution, but it remains to be proved that it will be sufficient to reverse the downward trend and give such a lift to the Government of Vietnam forces that they would perform better by the stimulation of the U.S. presence rather than worse in a mood of relaxation at passing the Viet Cong burden to the U.S.[64]

Ambassador Taylor was recalled to Washington for a series of NSC meetings to consider new courses of action. The ambassador "found the President and most of his top advisors close to a decision to commit more American troops, but still wavering."[65] Taylor's first meeting with the president was scheduled on March 31. Prior to that meeting Mac Bundy wrote to Johnson that "the three problems on Max's mind are these: (1) The timing and direction of the attack on the North; (2) the timing, size and mission of any U.S. combat deployments to Vietnam; and (3) the terms and conditions of a political resolution of the problem. He has done more thinking on (1) and (2) than on (3)—and so have we. I think that on (1) he is in reasonable agreement with our outline plans for the next 2 or 3 weeks. *But he is prepared to go toward Hanoi faster than McNamara.* You may want to probe him on this because *I sense that you are leaning a little ahead of Bob on this one.* (4) On US deployments, I think *Taylor and McNamara are very close together* in the notion of a coastal deployment of the remaining battalions of the Marine Expeditionary Brigade."[66]

Bundy added his own identification of the political/military situation in the South, prefacing his remarks with the comment that "I have deliberately put the political problems up near the front because they are the harder ones." Bundy reported that "Hanoi has shown no signs of give, and Peiping has stiffened its position within the last week." Bundy was excessively optimistic with regard to what American military resources could achieve. Bombing, combined with a U.S. military presence and other political/economic carrots, represented unplayed trump cards for dealing with Hanoi. "We want to trade these cards for just as much as possible of the following: an end to infiltration of men and supplies, an end of Hanoi's direction, control and encouragement of the Viet Cong, a removal of cadres under direct Hanoi control, and a dissolution of the organized Viet Cong military and political forces. We do not need to decide today just how we wish to mesh our high cards against Communist concessions. But we will need to be in such a position soon."[67]

The presidential policy review of April 1–2 resulted in NSAM 328 which, by order of the president, was not to be made public (until June 8 when a State Department official inadvertently referred to its instructions).[68] The policy directive authorized a modest 18,000- to 20,000-man increase of marine battalions and marked President Johnson's acceptance of General Westmoreland's strategy for offensive utilization of ground troops. The change in mission was presented very cautiously, perhaps implying that the president favored experimenting before a larger force commitment was made. The NSAM reported that "the President approved a change of mission for all Marine battalions deployed to Vietnam to permit their more active use under conditions to be established and approved by the Secretary of Defense in consultation with the Secretary of State." The decision to keep NSAM 328 from public disclosure was based on this explicit change in mission from advice and static defense to active combat operations against the VC. Johnson believed this had to be kept secret. NSAM 328 is quite clear in this regard: "The President desires that with respect to [these] actions . . . premature publicity be avoided by all possible precautions. The actions themselves should be taken as rapidly as practicable, but in ways that should minimize any appearance of sudden changes in policy, and official statement on these troop movements will be made only with the direct approval of the Secretary of Defense, in that these movements and changes should be understood as being gradual and wholly consistent with existing policy."

By denying any change in mission President Johnson helped to create conditions for the credibility gap which came to haunt him in later years. Reporters in the field could see that marines were not sitting tight in foxholes. American troops were, according to Westmoreland, "engaging in full-scale offensive operations. Yet, the White House chose to meet the press' allegations obliquely."[69] This was apparent in Taylor's cable to Secretary Rusk in which the ambassador explained that he and all U.S. mission representatives were restricting themselves to the Defense Department's language of "limited missions": "Under these circumstances we believe that the most useful approach to press problems is to make no, repeat, no special public announcement to the effect that U.S. ground troops are now engaged in offensive combat operations, but to announce such actions routinely as they occur. As the marines move from their present posture of securing the Da Nang airbase 'in depth' to actions which can be related only indirectly to Da Nang, military spokesman will be queried on whether the marine mission has changed and he will answer that, while we never discuss future, current operations speak for themselves. Eventually, of course, fact that marines or other ground troops are engaged in offensive combat will be officially confirmed. This low-key treatment will not, repeat, not obviate the political and psychological problems mentioned above, but will allow us to handle them undramatically, as a natural consequence of our determination to meet our commitments here. Our treatment, in short, should be patterned on the manner in which we presented the application of U.S. air power against the Viet Cong."[70]

Following the April 1 NSC meeting, CIA Director John McCone wrote to Rusk, McNamara, Bundy, and Taylor with specific questions about NSAM 328 and the overall rationale of U.S. military policy. While McCone and Ball represented two opposite policy extremes, both shared a common premise in challenging the logic of Rolling Thunder operations which "to date have not caused a change in the North Vietnamese policy of directing Viet Cong insurgency, infiltrating cadres and supplying material. If anything, the strikes to date have hardened their attitude." Moreover, while at the April 1 NSC meeting the decision had been made to change the mission of U.S. ground forces to active combat operations against the Viet Cong guerrillas, it was agreed that "we should continue roughly the present slowly ascending tempo of Rolling Thunder operations." McCone believed that such a constrained policy played directly into the hands of Hanoi strategists. "With the passage of each day," McCone warned, "and each week, we can expect increasing pressure to stop the bombing. This will come from various elements of the American public, from the press, the United Nations and world opinion. Therefore time will run against us in this operation and I think the North Vietnamese are counting on this." McCone concluded with cogent and prophetic advice:

> Therefore I think what we are doing is starting on a track which involves ground force operations which, in all probability, will have limited effectiveness against guerrillas, although admittedly will restrain some VC advances. However, we can expect requirements for an ever-increasing commitment of U.S. personnel without materially improving the chances of victory. I support and agree with this decision but I must point out that in my judgment, forcing submission of the VC can only be brought about by a decision in Hanoi. Since the contemplated actions against the North are modest in scale, they will not impose unacceptable damage on it, nor will they threaten the DRV's vital interests. Hence, they will not present them with a situation with which they cannot live, though such actions will cause the DRV pain and inconvenience.
>
> I believe our proposed track offers great danger of simply encourag-

ing Chinese Communist and Soviet support of the DRV and VC cause if for no other reason than the risk for both will be minimum. I envision that the reaction of the NVN and Chinese Communists will be to deliberately, carefully, and probably gradually, build up the Viet Cong capabilities by covert infiltration of North Vietnamese and, possibly, Chinese cadres and thus bring an ever-increasing pressure on our forces. In effect, we will find ourselves mired down in combat in the jungle in a military effort that we cannot win, and from which we will have extreme difficulty in extracting ourselves.

Therefore it is my judgment that if we are to change the mission of the ground forces, we must also change the ground rules of the strikes against North Vietnam. We must hit them harder, more frequently, and inflict greater damage. Instead of avoiding the MIG's, we must go in and take them out. A bridge here and there will not do the job. We must strike their air fields, their petroleum resources, power stations and their military compounds. This, in my opinion, must be done promptly and with minimum restraint.

If we are unwilling to take this kind of a decision now, we must not take the actions concerning the mission of our ground forces for the reasons I have mentioned above.[71]

In late April McCone conveyed his thoughts *directly* to the president, noting, "I attach a copy of my memorandum of April 2nd, which may not have come to your attention, since it argues this case in a little more detailed way." McCone believed that the limited scale of air action would lead inexorably to a demand for ground forces in a war the United States could not win. "As we deploy additional troops, which I believe necessary, we concurrently hit the North harder and inflict greater damage. In my opinion, we should strike their petroleum supplies, electric power installations, and air defense installations (including the SAM sites which are now being built)":

I am not talking about bombing centers of population or killing innocent people, though there will of course be some casualties. I am proposing to "tighten the tourniquet" on North Vietnam so as to make the Communists pause to weigh the losses they are taking against their prospects for gains. We should make it hard for the Viet Cong to win in the south and simultaneously hard for Hanoi to endure our attacks in the north.

I believe this course of action holds out the greatest promise we can hope for in our effort to attain our ultimate objective of finding a political solution to the Vietnam problem. This view follows logically, it seems to me, from our National Intelligence Estimate of 18 February 1965, which concludes that the Hanoi regime would be more likely than not to make an effort to "secure a respite" by some political move when and if, but not before, a sustained U.S. program of air attacks is damaging important economic or military assets in North Vietnam.[72]

Washington Takes Control

Taylor left Washington satisfied that a number of important issues had been resolved, primarily that the president was not about to move hastily into an Asian ground war. Yet nothing could have been further from reality. According to Taylor, "I first became aware of the President's new mood from a series of cables which began to arrive following my return. They indicated growing concern over the military situation and a desire to accelerate deployments beyond the schedule approved during my visit. There seemed to be an eagerness in some quarters to rush in troops now that the initial official reluctance had been breached."[73] On April 14 Taylor cabled Secretary of State Rusk, "recent actions relating to the introduction of US ground forces have tended to create an impression of eagerness in some quarters to deploy forces into SVN which I find difficult to understand. I should think that for both military and political reasons we should all be most reluctant to tie down Army/Marine units in this country and would do so only after the presentation of the most convincing evidence of the necessity."[74] The "quarters" belonged to Secretary McNamara. Admiral Sharp offered a third-party interpretation of the problem: "By the middle of April 1965 a considerable difference of opinion had developed between Washington and Saigon. In a series of messages, the Secretary of Defense expressed his desire to move ahead quickly with the introduction of U.S. and third-country ground forces and their deployment in a combat role. Ambassador Taylor became increasingly distressed by what he perceived to be an insistence on moving in a direction and at a pace which exceeded the actions authorized earlier in NSAM #328."[75]

These changes in "vibrations" from Washington were transmitted to Taylor in a series of cables between April 14 and 15. The April 15

Department of Defense cable noted that "highest authority believes the situation in South Vietnam has been deteriorating and that, in addition to actions against the North, something new must be added in the South to achieve victory." The cable included plans for counterinsurgency operations as well as sending a brigade for purposes of base security in the Bien Hao-Tau area and along the coast. According to Taylor, "these steps were viewed in Washington as experiments which, if successful, could justify requests for additional troops. The cable noted other possible innovations such as stiffening Vietnam military units with American soldiers, providing advisors to improve Vietnamese recruiting techniques, utilizing mobile U.S. medical dispensaries in the countryside, introducing U.S. Army civil affairs personnel into the provinces, and distributing food directly through American channels to Vietnamese military personnel and their families."[76]

In a dissenting memo to Bundy, Taylor asked "that all action on these matters be held in abeyance pending a discussion of them with McNamara, Wheeler, and Sharp in Honolulu." Taylor argued, "I am greatly troubled by [DOD 1523392, April 15]. . . . it shows no consideration for . . . decision taken in Washington during my visit. . . . it shows a far greater willingness to get into the ground war than I had discerned in Washington during my recent trip."[77] According to Taylor's perspective, the cables "were the product of Washington initiative flagged to a new level of creativity by a president determined to get prompt results. It was a reminder to us in Saigon that the conduct of U.S. policy would be taken over by Washington if we were not careful."[78] Prior to sending the cables, McGeorge Bundy wrote to the president anticipating Taylor's reaction to McNamara's initiatives: "My own judgment is that direct orders of this sort to Taylor would be very explosive right now because he will not agree with many of them and he will feel that he has not been consulted."[79] But Bundy was not overly concerned with Taylor's reservations because he believed that Taylor could soon be brought on board. In that same memo to the president, Bundy observed:

I am sure we can turn him around if we give him just a little time to come aboard, but I am not sure that you yourself currently wish to make a firm decision to put 10,000–15,000 combat troops in Vietnam today. As Taylor says, we were planning when he left to use the Marines already on the scene in combat roles and see how that worked. It is not clear that we now need all these additional forces. Your own desire for mixing our Marines with theirs is quite a different matter, and I think that should be pressed sharply. The net of this is that I would strongly recommend that you hold up on Bob's telegram tonight and take time to talk it over with Rusk, McNamara and me either after the meeting with the Senators or tomorrow morning.[80]

The appointment log shows that a meeting did occur, where it was decided that all the principals should meet in Honolulu to iron out their differences. At Honolulu the principals reached the consensus that 40,000 additional U.S. troops would be needed to convince the DRV/VC that they could not win the war—bringing the total authorized troop commitment to 90,000 by June. McNamara reported the views of the principals to the president:

1. North Vietnam cannot be expected to capitulate or to come to a position acceptable to us in less than six months. This is because the conferees believe that a settlement will come as much, or more, from a Viet Cong failure in the South as from inflicting pain on North Vietnam, and that it will take more than six months, perhaps a year or two, to demonstrate Viet Cong failure in the south.

2. With respect to strikes against the north, the conferees all agree that the present tempo is about right, that sufficient increasing pressure is provided by repetition and continuation. All envision a strike program continuing at least six months, perhaps a year or more, avoiding the Hanoi/Haiphong/Phuc Yen areas during that period. There might be fewer fixed targets, or more restrikes, or more armed reconnaissance missions. All believe that the strike program is essential to our campaign, both psychologically and physically, but that it cannot be expected to do the job alone. All consider it very important that strikes against the north be continued during any negotiation talks.

3. None of the participants foresees a dramatic improvement in the south in the immediate future. The strategy for achieving our objectives proposed by Ambassador Taylor, General Wheeler, Admiral Sharp, and General Westmoreland is to break the will of the North Vietnamese by denying them victory. Ambassador Taylor puts it in terms of a demonstration of Communist impotence, which will lead eventually to a political solution. The conferees see slow improvement in the south, but all emphasize the critical importance of

holding on and avoiding, for psychological and morale reasons, a spectacular defeat of South Vietnamese or U.S. forces. All suspect that the recent Viet Cong lull is but the quiet before the storm.[81*]

Bundy's prediction about bringing Ambassador Taylor on board was an accurate one, evidenced by Bundy's post-Honolulu memo to the president: "Max Taylor has made one reservation to Bob McNamara's statement of his views in Bob's memorandum of April 21, and I think you ought to know about it. . . . In essence, Max says that he thinks we can get a favorable settlement in a matter of months rather than in 'perhaps a year or two,' if we keep up our bombing and introduce substantial US and third-country forces."[83]

Despite George Ball's warning to the president that a "150 percent increase in our troop deployment in South Vietnam would multiply our dangers and responsibilities while limiting our freedom of maneuver,"[84] the Honolulu consensus was accepted by the president.†

By now, however, there was even doubt within the intelligence community that the Honolulu numbers would be sufficient. An April 30 report from the CIA Office of National Estimates confirmed that "the general outlook remains dreary and in some respects the dangers of the situation have increased." The report focused on the impending VC summer offensive and its effect on the political stability of Saigon:

> Within South Vietnam governmental weakness and the possibility of military coups will continue. Although a greatly enlarged U.S. presence

---

*According to Admiral Sharp, "The foregoing is, in fact, a distortion of the view I took at that conference. However, as with most conferences that Secretary McNamara attended, the published results somehow tended to reflect his own views, not necessarily a consensus."[82]

†During the last week of April and the first week of May, President Johnson's attention focused almost exclusively on events in the Dominican Republic. On April 24 rebel forces overthrew the ruling military junta, beginning two weeks of civil war in Santo Domingo. President Johnson, believing that the rebels (led by ex-President Juan Bosch) had been infiltrated by Communists, dispatched approximately 21,000 U.S. Marines to the Dominican Republic. The president's action was supported by the American public, and Johnson's success in the Caribbean probably shaded his expectation that the public would support similar moves against another Communist aggressor in Vietnam.

and involvement has thus far boosted South Vietnamese morale and combativeness, this will continue only if our efforts are demonstrably effective. There will be constant danger that the war weary people of South Vietnam will let the U.S. assume an even greater share of the fighting. There will also be danger that increased U.S. troop commitment will lead more South Vietnamese to accept the Communist line that U.S. colonialism is replacing French. This could turn increasing numbers of Vietnamese toward support of the Viet Cong effort to oust the U.S. . . . The Vietnam situation thus appears to be entering a critical phase. If, during the next few months, the Viet Cong can pull off one or more spectacular military victories, or if defeatism increases substantially in South Vietnam or if the political situation again deteriorates, the Communist effort in Vietnam would gain great momentum. If, on the other hand, a major Viet Cong military effort this summer is generally repulsed, the Viet Cong position would suffer substantially, with a corresponding increase in GVN morale and popular support. It is of course possible, though we believe it unlikely, that the Viet Cong will avoid a major engagement this summer because of supply difficulties and a desire to increase their build-up for combat at a later date.[85]

In May, Secretary Rusk requested an assessment of probable DRV/VC activities during the summer. Taylor cabled Rusk that Rolling Thunder had not weakened the DRV's "determination to continue directing and supporting Viet Cong and seeking further intensification of war in the South." In South Vietnam the "political situation is still basically unstable" and open to Communist manipulation. According to Taylor, "Vietnamese Communists have shown themselves to be a tough enemy, both physically and morally, and it is likely that they interpret our apparent reliance on air power and the restricted employment of U.S. ground forces and statements of certain U.S. leaders as indicating pretty clearly we are reluctant to engage in ground war."[86]

But the United States would not look reluctant for very long. On June 3 Ambassador Taylor cabled Secretary Rusk with a shocking perspective on the military and political situation.[87] No amount of bombing the North would cause Hanoi to give up the insurgency in the South. "Such a change in DRV attitudes can probably be brought about only when, along with a sense of mounting pain from the bombings, there is also a conviction on their part that the tide has turned or soon will turn against them in the South.* Obviously these two conditions have not yet been met and our job in the coming months will be to bring them about. This may take a long time and we should not expect quick results. . . . If our assumptions with respect to DRV reactions are correct, there is no strategy that can bring about a quick solution, but rather our strategy must be based upon a patient and steady increase of pressure following an escalating pattern while making maximum effort to turn the tide here in the South. *This does not mean that we must 'win' in the South to bring about a change in DRV attitudes, but rather the DRV must perceive that the tide has turned or is likely to turn. Hopefully at this point the DRV will seek to find some way out, and if and when it does, there could be a "bandwagon" effect that would so lower VC morale and so raise that of South Vietnam as to permit bringing major hostilities to a reasonably early conclusion."*[89]

McGeorge Bundy disagreed with Taylor's view of the military situation. Bundy wrote to the president, "what they [the mission] say in essence is that they would like to maintain and increase pressure by air attacks as well as by efforts in the South. They would avoid the Hanoi-Haiphong area except for an occasional selected target—*and they believe a little more than we do* that pain in the North will help bring a change of heart in Hanoi. *I share Bob McNamara's view* that we can readily frame a specific program over the next month that will be acceptable to the Embassy without unacceptable risks of escalation. *I myself am more attracted than Rusk and McNamara* by the notion of an occasional limited attack inside the Hanoi perimeter

---

*Taylor recalled that "all of us were in agreement that what we were doing would never have a decisive effect in itself; however, we felt that it should be continued for its value in bringing pressure to bear on Hanoi. While most of the Joint Chiefs of Staff favored a rapid increase in the scope and intensity of the bombing, the Honolulu conferees believed that if the already approved target system were only moderately extended to the north our available aircraft would have all they could do without going as far as the Chiefs' wishes. I felt that the extent of the target system was not so important in producing the desired psychological effect in Hanoi as an inexorable continuity of attack repeated day after day without interruption. I am afraid, however, that despite repeated efforts, I never convinced either the proponents of massive bombing or the partisans of frequent bombing pauses of the validity of this concept. As for the need for additional combat troops, we concluded after much discussion that they were necessary to give the required impetus to the ground campaign in South Vietnam where the decisive action lay."[88]

—probably in the Haiphong port area."[90]

On June 5, 1965, President Johnson received the U.S. mission's overall estimate of the political-military situation in South Vietnam (drafted by the Mission Intelligence Committee and concurred in by Ambassador Taylor, Ambassador Johnson, and General Westmoreland). The report is of particular interest as an assessment of overall prospects on the eve of what would become the purported debate on the U.S. commitment. In a covering memorandum McGeorge Bundy informed the president that "you may not wish to read it all, but the last two pages on the basic military balance are interesting, and also troubling."[91] Ambassador Taylor portrayed the "unsettled political situation" as a reflection of "the traditional divisive forces at work in South Vietnam (particularly the religious and regional cleavages), the inexperience of the Vietnamese with practical political processes, the frustrations of two decades of war without victory in sight, and the predominant weight of the Saigon 'intellectuals' in the 'political equation.' " Taylor believed that Prime Minister Quat was the *victim* of these factors, and like his predecessors, he had failed to neutralize or balance opposing forces "before they reached such proportions as to constitute a strong challenge to his government." According to Taylor, "Prime Minister Quat's performance in the current crisis has not been reassuring. He has not projected an image either as a forceful leader or as an astute politician." Moreover, "when faced with his first real challenge, Quat has been found to be indecisive—an almost fatal posture in the arena of jugular-vein politics in Saigon." Taylor then applied the Diem-Khanh et al. logic to Quat: "Having said this, any realistic assessment must admit that Quat and his close associates constitute perhaps the best group on the scene at present. No single leader stands out as a clear alternative and no group exists which shows promise of handling the affairs of state much better." Alas, the more things changed, the more they remained the same.

Taylor's view of the military situation was equally dismal. The Viet Cong had regrouped and equipped themselves for a major offensive. "To meet the shortage of ARVN reserves, it will probably be necessary to commit US ground forces to action." Moreover, the Communists had quickened the tempo of fighting, and since early May main force units had returned to the battlefield in increasing numbers. "The apparent aims of this campaign are to alter the balance of military forces in favor of the Viet Cong by inflicting maximum attrition on the government forces, including specifically the piecemeal destruction of regular ARVN ground combat units where possible." Taylor reported that the Viet Cong ground forces were being reinforced by PAVN troops in the South. "While the Viet Cong have suffered heavy losses, they have generally achieved their objectives in actions to date. . . . Taking advantage of terrain and weather conditions, the Viet Cong appear likely to achieve further successes."

Taylor's cable caused quite a stir in Washington and the ambassador was recalled from Saigon for a June 8 meeting. The president was alarmed with the bleakness of Taylor's report. If correct, Johnson would be forced to "save" South Vietnam much sooner than he expected.

Taylor's impending visit was the focus of a June 5 White House meeting (attended by McNamara, Ball, McGeorge Bundy, and William Bundy). But the discussion first centered on recent intelligence disclosures that the Soviet Union was shipping outdated but still functional IL-28 bombers to North Vietnam. An INR Intelligence Report suggested that the IL-28s were intended "to reinforce Soviet commitment, bolster morale of the North Vietnamese and constrain Chinese allegations [that] Soviets dragging feet."[92] The Joint Chiefs had recommended preemptive strikes against the IL-28s but all of those present rejected that proposal. Secretary Rusk believed that "whatever Soviet calculations and expectations may be, by shipping IL-28s, Soviet leaders must be judged to have accepted substantial new risks to themselves, and certainly to U.S.–Soviet relations."[93] In the middle of the discussion on possible U.S. response to the IL-28s the president arrived unexpectedly. One participant recalled the president's saying, "Lady Bird is away, I was all alone, and I heard you fellows were getting together, so I thought I'd come over." The remarkable informality of the meeting produced a candid conversation about Vietnam policy.[94] The president asked a series of piercing questions of his principal foreign policy advisors: "How do we get what we want? Is it possible? What will it cost?" Rusk, McNamara, and Ball offered similar diagnoses, but different treatments. For Rusk, Hanoi had to be convinced that it could not win by force. Once that point was reached, the enemy would view reunification as a lengthy project incorporating political not military tactics. Secretary McNamara acknowledged that Hanoi now believed it was winning the struggle. Only through increasing pain in the North and stalemate in the South could Hanoi be convinced otherwise. Ball argued that the struggle would be a very long one. The United States needed to provide the VC/DRV with a real and not token alternative for the bargaining table. None of the president's advisors provided an optimistic assessment. At its best the war would be lengthy and involve a major commitment of U.S. forces. In several years, after the death of thousands of U.S. soldiers, and many more Vietnamese, perhaps Hanoi could be forced to call off its dogs. The president left the meeting wondering just where events would next lead him.

On June 7 General Westmoreland ("acutely aware of the gravity of my conclusions") informed Washington that the current DRV/VC summer offensive spelled almost certain doom for ARVN's military capabilities. South Vietnam would fall unless the United States committed forty-four battalions to Southeast Asia.

> I believe that the DRV will command whatever forces it deems necessary to tip the balance and that the GVN cannot stand up successfully to this kind of pressure without reinforcements. Even if DRV/VC intentions are debatable, their capabilities must be acknowledged and faced. *. . . I see no course of action open to U.S. except to reinforce our efforts in SVN with additional U.S. or third country forces as rapidly as is practical during the critical weeks ahead.* Additionally, studies must continue and plans developed to deploy even greater forces, if and when required, to attain our objectives or counter enemy initiatives.[95]

Westmoreland's report forced decision-makers to confront what three previous administrations had sought to avoid. "I made up my mind," Westmoreland recalled, "that if the United States intended to achieve its goals of denying the enemy victory in South Vietnam, Washington had to face the task realistically. Without substantial American ground combat troops, I concluded the South Vietnamese would be unable to withstand the pressure from combined Viet Cong and North Vietnamese forces. . . . The enemy was destroying battalions faster than they could be reconstituted and faster than we planned to organize them under the ARVN's crash build-up program."[96] Westmoreland viewed the military crisis as a by-product of Saigon's internal political problems: "With governments coming and going as if Saigon was a revolving door, I could see little possibility of the South Vietnamese themselves overcoming the military crisis."[97]

Secretary of State Rusk was especially disturbed by Westmoreland's call for action, wondering whether or not the general was exaggerating the situation. He cabled Ambassador Taylor requesting an explanation for discrepancies between mission intelligence assessments which had *only* been gloomy compared to Westmoreland's report which "implies, though does not, repeat not, already state, that there is a serious danger of complete military collapse within relatively short period of time."[98] Given the extensive documentation of mission reports quoted earlier in this book, it is somewhat bewildering that Secretary Rusk should cross-examine mission intelligence estimates. "We have not, repeat not, received this impression from the totality of mission reporting, particularly the daily and weekly military reports and indeed REF TEL [referenced telegram] does not, repeat not, appear on the surface to describe any dramatic and unexpected development in the military situation during the past several months. We agree that performance by some ARVN units during past few weeks has been disappointing, but we lack information on current effectiveness and morale of ARVN as a whole."

Before Ambassador Taylor could even respond, the Joint Chiefs registered their support for General Westmoreland's requests.[99] General Wheeler wrote to Secretary McNamara that "there are significant indications that the Communists may be on the threshold of moving the conflict in Southeast Asia to a higher level of intensity." The Communists had clearly added a "new dimension to the situation in Vietnam" with recent deployments of jet fighters, light bombers, and surface-to-air missiles (SAM) in North Vietnam. Wheeler's memorandum was forceful in language and consistent in one basic premise: "In this unstable military situation, appropriate countermeasures are required. The Joint Chiefs of Staff consider that the ground forces situation requires a substantial further build-up of U.S. and Allied forces in the RVN, at the most rapid rate feasible on an orderly basis." Wheeler also recommended the intensification of air action against North Vietnam "necessary to reduce DRV, and further establish U.S. interest to prevent a Communist seizure of SVN." In his oral history Wheeler recalled that "in the summer of 1965 it became amply clear that it wasn't a matter of whether the North

Vietnamese were going to win the war; it was a question of when they were going to win it."[100]

When Ambassador Taylor arrived in Washington he found himself in the middle of a presidentially chaired debate on General Westmoreland's recommendation and not on Taylor's previous political-military assessment. There was no unanimity on Westmoreland's request. The general was asking for 150,000 ground troops; none of the president's civilian advisors was willing to go that far. Taylor favored an additional 8000 over the 90,000 authorized in Honolulu; McNamara withheld his complete endorsement and recommended a ceiling of 95,000, which Rusk and Taylor eventually supported. The president, still hesitant and suspicious of the military, sided with his civilian advisors.

But events in the South soon betrayed Johnson—vindicating Westmoreland's prediction that the monsoon onslaught was on.* A series of devastating ARVN military defeats forced Ambassador Taylor to cable the president that "It is clear that the primary objective of the Viet Cong is to chew up the regular forces of South Vietnam and to cause their attrition to a point where major geographic objectives can be taken and held for considerable periods of time. . . . General Westmoreland is thoroughly aware of the problem and is studying new tactics to cope with the Viet Cong."[102]

The president soon received Westmoreland's more detailed "Concept of Operations—Force Requirements and Deployments—South Vietnam."[103] Westmoreland began by showing displeasure with Secretary Rusk's questions concerning "my current estimate of the seriousness of the situation in South Vietnam." The general reemphasized the seriousness of the military situation by identifying recent

---

*On June 12, 1965, South Vietnam's generals peacefully took control of the government following a constitutional crisis involving Quat's legal authority in firing cabinet members. The generals formed a nineteen-member national leadership council with Nguyen Cao Ky installed as prime minister and Maj.-Gen. Nguyen Van Thieu as chief of state. Taylor wrote to Rusk: "I am disturbed by the selection of General Ky as Prime Minister. While he is a well-motivated, courageous, and patriotic officer who has matured considerably over the past two years, he is completely without the background and experience necessary for an assignment as difficult as this one. The American general officer closest to him describes him as 'a proud man and a fine military commander, although a naïve, inexperienced politician and civil affairs administrator. I believe he will do his absolute best to succeed in his new position, but he will require a lot of technical assistance, moral support and a normal amount of conscientious understanding.' We will do our best to provide these missing ingredients."[101]

battlefield losses and high desertion rates: "The South Vietnamese battlefield strength is declining in the face of North Vietnamese reinforcements and a Viet Cong offensive. *It is my considered opinion that the South Vietnamese armed forces cannot stand up to this pressure without substantial US combat support on the ground.* ... The Vietnamese Armed Forces Commanders do not believe that they can survive without the active commitment of US ground combat forces. The *only possible response* is the aggressive deployment of US troops together with Vietnamese general reserve forces to react against strong Viet Cong–North Vietnamese attacks."

Westmoreland based his recommendation on a significant point which I discuss in Chapter Four—the Communists were moving in for the kill in what General Giap had described as the climactic "Third Stage" of revolutionary warfare. "The VC are now maneuvering large forces up to reinforced regiments equipped with heavy weapons. Thus, we are approaching the kind of warfare faced by the French in the latter stages of their efforts here." Westmoreland has been accused of misleading Washington with undue optimism, but the general understood all too well that his request was "no force for victory but as a stop-gap measure to save the ARVN from defeat." On June 22, for example, he responded to General Wheeler's question "Would 44 battalions be enough to convince the VC/DRV that they could not win?" by reporting that "there was no evidence that the VC/DRV would alter their plans regardless of what the U.S. did in the next six months. The 44 battalion force should, however, establish a favorable balance of power by the end of the year. If the U.S. was to seize the initiative from the enemy, then further forces would be required into 1966 and beyond."[104]

Of particular interest is a June 10, 1965, "resumé of intelligence community"[105] views on Vietnam. U.S. objectives in Vietnam were identified as "the reduction of Viet Cong insurgency to manageable levels and, as part of this, forcing the DRV to cease promoting that insurgency." The intelligence document outlined four options: *First,* the United States could continue with essentially its present course and objectives by bombing selected targets in the DRV (but not population centers, economic targets, SAM sites, and jet-capable airfields in the Hanoi-Haiphong area), and build up its combat strength considerably in the South. "This will probably not permit us to impose our will on the enemy. The DRV would continue to reinforce the VC, and we doubt that US/ARVN forces could soon produce any

decisive improvement in the military situation. The most likely results would be heavy US casualties, an over-emphasis on the military
aspects of the conflict to the detriment of the political, and bogging
down of the war at higher levels of commitment and intensity, and,
perhaps ultimately, a petering out of GVN/ARVN determination
and intensity." *Second,* the United States could escalate the war by
increasing its forces to the extent necessary to defeat the Viet Cong.
This would include bombing all targets and imposing a naval quarantine of the North. "This would risk convincing the Communists that
the US intended to destroy the DRV regime and thus bring us close
to the 'flash-point' of Chinese Communist intervention. If they
judged that the Hanoi regime was losing control of the country, they
would probably enter the DRV unilaterally and might engage US air
forces with their own." *Third,* the United States could cease bombing in the North, hold on in the South, and seek to negotiate as good
a Vietnam settlement as it could get. The objective would be to settle
for a Laos-type "neutralist" solution—guaranteed by other powers.
The CIA believed that such "overtures for negotiation would probably be rejected and the enemy, scenting a weakening in US determination, would probably fight on, while raising his terms. Also, a sudden US turning in this direction, without punishing the DRV above
present levels, would have a seriously dispiriting effect upon non-
Communists in Southeast Asia." The *fourth* option found support
from the CIA: the United States should increase the weight of attack
on the DRV; increase ground forces up to authorized levels; and
stress a major program of political, social, and economic action in
South Vietnam "in order to prevent a collapse in South Vietnam
morale and military capabilities." The plan "would involve the deployment of substantial US ground forces in the South—a prime
requirement for the immediate future." But the CIA did not believe
such a buildup would affect *VC/DRV determination to prosecute the
struggle:* "The arrival of US forces in these numbers (150,000) would
not change the Communists' basic calculation that their staying
power is inherently superior to that of Saigon and Washington." The
real test would come in *combat* and the CIA intelligence paper was
brutally frank in its admission that "we do not know how the test of
combat would come out at the level of US involvement now being
considered." Moreover, a 150,000-man force level would *not* impact
on Hanoi's resolve. Rather, the test would come in the jungles of
South Vietnam, exactly where McNamara said it would *not* be. No-

where in the CIA paper can there be found Westmoreland's assumption that the VC/DRV would move, or were moving, into the Third Stage. In fact, the paper maintained that "the Communists would probably hold to their present strategy of attrition and subversion, although at a significantly increased scale. They would still seek to defeat the GVN through exhaustion and internal collapse without letting US/GVN forces engage them in decisive battle."

The time for decision was fast approaching. Within the White House George Ball had already decided to make his move. In a fascinating attempt to influence President Johnson's future ability to control events, Ball titled his June 18 memo "Keeping the Power of Decision in the South Vietnam Crisis."[106] He began by quoting Ralph Waldo Emerson, "Things are in the saddle, and ride mankind." Ball argued that the United States was on the threshold of a new war. "In raising our commitment from 50,000 to 100,000 or more men and deploying most of the increment *in combat roles* we are beginning a new war—the United States *directly* against the Viet Cong. The President's most difficult continuing problem in South Viet-Nam is to prevent 'things' from getting into the saddle—or, in other words, to keep control of policy and prevent the momentum of events from taking command. The best formula for maintaining freedom of decision is (a) to limit our commitments in time and magnitude and (b) to establish specific time schedules for the selection of optional courses of action on the basis of pre-established criteria."

The president needed to understand the effect of losing control: "Perhaps the large-scale introduction of American forces with their concentrated fire power will force Hanoi and the Viet Cong to the decision we are seeking. On the other hand, we may *not* be able to fight the war successfully enough—even with 500,000 Americans in South Viet-Nam—to achieve this purpose. Before we commit an endless flow of forces to South Viet-Nam we must have more evidence than we now have that our troops will not bog down in the jungles and rice paddies—while we slowly blow the country to pieces. A review of the French experience more than a decade ago may be helpful. The French fought a war in Viet-Nam, and were finally defeated—after seven years of bloody struggle and when they still had 250,000 combat-hardened veterans in the field, supported by an army of 205,000 South Vietnamese. To be sure, the French were fighting a colonial war while we are fighting to stop aggression. But when we have put enough Americans on the ground in South Viet-

Nam to give the appearance of a white man's war, the distinction as to our ultimate purpose will have less and less practical effect. . . . Yet *the more forces we deploy in South Viet-Nam—particularly in combat roles—the harder we shall find it to extricate ourselves without unacceptable costs if the war goes badly.* With large forces committed, the failure to turn the tide will generate pressures to escalate. There will be mounting domestic demands that we expand our air attacks on the North so as to destroy Hanoi and Haiphong. Yet if our air attacks threaten the total destruction of the North Vietnamese economy, Red China can hardly help but react. And our best Soviet experts do not believe that the Soviet Union could stand down in the event that we became involved directly with the Chinese."

Ball urged the president to act cautiously—make the necessary commitment to the 100,000 level—*but no more.* The summer would then be used as a test of U.S. performance and South Vietnam's resolve: "We cannot be sure how far the cancer has infected the whole body politic of South Viet-Nam and whether we can do more than administer a cobalt treatment to a terminal case." The president was advised to instruct his top advisors—"limited in this case, for security reasons, to the Secretaries of State and Defense (and possibly also the Chairman of the Joint Chiefs): (a) that you are *not* committing US forces on an open-ended basis to an all-out land war in South Viet-Nam; (b) that instead you are making a *controlled commitment* for a *trial period* of three months; (c) that on the basis of our experience during that trial period we will then appraise the costs and possibilities of waging a successful land war in South Viet-Nam and chart a clear course of action accordingly; (d) that, during the test period, in publicly stating American aims and purposes, American spokesmen should emphasize our willingness to stay in South Viet-Nam *so long as we are wanted* (a qualification that has tended to become submerged in recent months); and (e) that, in carrying out this limited decision, your advisers should— during the three-months period—press the war on the ground in South Viet-Nam as vigorously as possible, while seeking quietly and effectively to avoid those longer-term actions and commitments that would reduce your freedom of decision at the end of the period. *Direct* your top advisers to prepare the following plans: (a) A plan for continuing the land war in South Viet-Nam on a stepped-up basis; (b) A plan for conducting a vigorous diplomatic offensive designed to bring about a political settlement; and (c) Plans for bringing about a military or political solution—short of the ultimate US objectives—that can be attained without the substantial further commitment of US forces. These last should be regarded as plans for cutting losses and eventually disengaging from an untenable situation."

Ball was clearly trying to push the burden of proof onto those who favored escalation—believing that any reevaluation of policy would result in a plan for cutting U.S. losses. But he was also asking that Johnson use staff resources to prepare a plan for the politics of getting out—something which the president never did. It could and should have been done. For the next month Ball pushed hard for a systematic analysis of those "unwilling" to think in terms of getting out. The undersecretary pulled no punches with the president: "The technique of cutting our losses requires intensive study. *No one has yet looked at the problem carefully since we have been unwilling to think in those terms.*" Ball concluded his memorandum with a realistic assessment of the U.S. position in June 1965: "Since we cannot yet be sure that we will be able to beat the Viet Cong without unacceptable costs, we would be prudent to undertake an additional study of the political means to achieve less than a satisfactory solution—or, in other words, a solution involving concessions on our side as well as the Viet Cong."

The president read Ball's memo at Camp David and was deeply affected by the undersecretary's analysis. For one moment, at least, the president seemed to question whether or not he should go ahead with the major commitment. Ball had presented an impassioned but persuasive argument for controlling the U.S. commitment. But on the other side were those who warned that the cost of losing South Vietnam was too great to pay. In the balance stood Australia, New Zealand, the Philippines, NATO, and India. The president then made an important action decision: he directed *both* McNamara and Ball, with staff assistance, to produce studies on the Vietnam situation with specific policy options. He gave each of the parties one week to develop their reports and ordered Ball and McNamara to limit knowledge of this project to as few as possible. *Each was promised his day in court.*

But events in Saigon again literally flew out of control and Johnson was quickly losing the power of decision. On June 28, 1965, Taylor reported to Rusk that he had just met with General Ky and Thieu.

"They were all sober-faced and depressed. . . . Ky went straight to his principal point—the need for additional US ground combat forces. He is sensing for the first time the difficulty which we have anticipated for some time of fielding sufficient combat-ready South Vietnamese units to cope with growing numbers of Viet Cong units during the next few months. He is impressed with the need for injection of additional US (or other third country) forces to tide over the monsoon offensive period, and to take off Viet Cong pressure while mobilization measures are being taken and—to use his expression—'while rear is being cleaned up.' "[107]

That same week the Viet Cong executed Sgt. Harold Bennett, a U.S. prisoner of war, and later bombed a Saigon riverboat restaurant near the U.S. embassy, killing forty-four persons including twelve Americans. Hanoi claimed that Bennett's execution was in retaliation for South Vietnam's recent execution of a convicted VC terrorist. The National Liberation Front radio broadcast of June 25 acknowledged that "Bennett has now paid for his crimes," and informed the United States that a VC death list also included the names of Ambassador Taylor, Deputy Ambassador U. Alexis Johnson, and General Westmoreland.

Taylor immediately cabled the president with the recommendation for a quick bombing reprisal in the Hanoi-Haiphong area. Describing these events as "the bloodiest Viet Cong atrocity which we have suffered,"[108] Taylor argued that executions were likely to continue *"since they [VC] are well aware we place higher value on human life than they do"* (a remarkable statement from an old Vietnamese hand). Taylor was adamant that "we cannot permit ourselves to be placed in position of paying blackmail for lives of US prisoners in form of preventing GVN from executing terrorists who are tried and convicted of violating Vietnamese civil law. If not sternly repressed, terrorism is likely to become a VC tactic of increased proportions."

But also writing to the president was McGeorge Bundy, who reported that *Rusk, McNamara, and Bundy all disagreed* with Taylor's reprisal recommendation. Bundy wrote, "We do not believe that important escalation should be attached to a single episode *at this stage*. McNamara and I do think however, that if terror and executions continue, we should substantially increase weight of Rolling Thunder attacks probably including oil supplies in Haiphong area. Rusk is less certain. We are considering usefulness of leaflet drops on

Hanoi-Haiphong area which would say that if these outrages continue, necessary further action will be taken. Meanwhile you should
know of Taylor's recommendation in case you wish to take his judgment and overrule Washington doves."[109]

The problem now facing President Johnson *was* different from
that which had faced his predecessors. Within a matter of weeks
South Vietnam would fall to the Communists without a substantial
ground commitment by the United States. Was the United States
committed to saving South Vietnam, preventing a Communist takeover, or saving face? Writing to the president, Senate Majority
Leader Mansfield (pursuant to an evening phone conversation) noted
that "there is *not* a government to speak of in Saigon. In short we
are now at the point where we are no longer dealing with anyone
who represents anybody in a political sense. We are simply acting to
prevent a collapse of the Vietnamese military forces which we pay
for and supply in any event and who presumably are going in the
same direction we are going. That reality is not going to be lost on
any government—friend or foe anywhere in the world."[110] The reality was certainly not lost on George Ball who, writing to the president, now described South Vietnam "as a country with an army and
no government."[111]

In the month of July the president would face crucial choices about
the selection and implementation of policy. The consensus among
the president's senior advisors was that major new action should be
part of a whole policy and not in response to a particular outrage.
Bundy reported that "we don't all agree as to when and how it will
be necessary to hit targets in Hanoi-Haiphong area. We do all agree
that this is a major decision which should be made in a wider context
than these atrocities."* And so it would be. President Johnson had
already instructed McGeorge Bundy and Secretary McNamara to
"find more dramatic and effective action in SVN."[113] The "whole
policy" was being written by Secretary McNamara. The secretary's

---

*When Taylor learned of Washington's decision not to accept his recommendation
for retaliatory strikes, the ambassador cabled the president directly: "It seemed to us
that the enemy had escalated and by the rules of the game we should respond—
otherwise we would seem to accept this kind of thing as an inevitable new way of life.
I have not yet received an indication of the countervailing reasons which led to the
contrary decision in Washington but hope to receive them in due course."[112] Taylor
would be replaced within the month by Henry Cabot Lodge, returning for a second
tour as ambassador.

responsiveness was documented by a June 26 (revised on July 1, 1965) memo to the president under the title "Program of Expanded Military and Political Moves with Respect to Vietnam." These recommendations initiated a series of policy debates *within* the administration that established the context as well as the timetable for the July 28 decision. But Lyndon Johnson would be very careful in determining just how such a consensus should develop and, even more central to his purpose, how such a consensus would be *perceived* by political elites and the general public.

IV

The Advisory Process at Work:
Framing Issues or Framed Advisors?

By the end of June the president had provisionally authorized a 95,000-man force level to South Vietnam. Meanwhile both Secretary McNamara and Undersecretary Ball were developing their program recommendations. On June 26 McNamara decided to circulate a first draft of his proposals to the principals.[1] Writing from the premise that the Viet Cong were clearly winning the war, McNamara admitted that "the tide almost certainly cannot begin to turn in less than a few months and may not for a year or more; the war is one of attrition and will be a long one." Moreover, for the United States the term "winning" had a rather limited definition since "our objective is to create conditions for a favorable settlement by demonstrating to the VC/DRV that the odds are against their winning. Under present conditions, however, the chances of achieving this objective are small—and the VC are winning now—largely because the ratio of guerrilla to anti-guerrilla forces is unfavorable to the government." Secretary McNamara developed three options for the president: (1) cut U.S. losses and withdraw with the best conditions that can be arranged; (2) continue at about the present level, with U.S. forces limited to about 75,000, holding on and playing for the breaks while recognizing that the U.S. position will probably grow weaker; (3)

expand substantially the U.S. military pressure against the Viet Cong in the South and the North Vietnamese in the North. At the same time launch a vigorous effort on the political side to get negotiations started.

McNamara unequivocally supported the third option—a series of expanded military moves as prerequisites for a negotiated settlement on U.S. terms. The secretary recommended that US/GVN ground strength should be increased to *whatever* force levels were necessary to show the VC that they "cannot win." The increases would bring U.S. and third-country troop levels to forty-four battalions and be accomplished by a call-up of 100,000 reserves. McNamara's military recommendations (which are central to the evaluation of later option trade-offs) included a quarantine on the movement of all war supplies into North Vietnam, the mining of DRV harbors, the destruction of all rail and highway bridges from China to Hanoi, armed reconnaissance of communication lines from China, destruction of all war-making supplies inside of North Vietnam, and destruction of all air-fields and SAM sites.

In estimating the chances of success for this expanded military program, McNamara now admitted that turning the tide depended "on whether the South Vietnamese hold their own in terms of numbers and fighting spirit; and on whether the US forces can be effective in a quick-reaction reserve role, a role in which they *have not* been tested." Moreover, "since troops once committed as a practical matter cannot be removed, since US casualties will rise, since we should take call-up activities to support the additional forces in Vietnam, the test of endurance may be as much in the US as in Vietnam."

Explicit in McNamara's memorandum was the sense of emergency and impending doom for South Vietnam if the United States did not move quickly in its commitment of troops. The Communists were changing their military tactics from guerrilla to conventional warfare. Much of the justification for additional deployments was based on the reasoning that U.S. troops would *not* be engaged in jungle warfare. McNamara emphasized this point by writing that "the number of US troops is too small to make a difference in the traditional 10–1 government–guerrilla formula, but it is not too small to make a significant difference in the kind of war which seems to be evolving in Vietnam—a 'Third Stage' or conventional war in which it is easier to identify, locate and attack the enemy."[2] Later in his memo

McNamara reiterated that "the VC, especially if they continue to take high losses, can be expected to depend increasingly upon the PARVN forces as the war moves into a more conventional phase."* Reduced to its fundamentals, the McNamara plan was one of action, not restraint. In facing the impending Communist takeover of the South, McNamara stood ready to raise the ante significantly by Americanizing the war.

This expanded military campaign was viewed as a prerequisite for any effective bargaining between the United States and Hanoi. McNamara identified several possible political initiatives which could be tried but probably rejected—at least until the tide had turned. On closer examination, however, these political initiatives were little more than token gestures to sanctify the military campaign. McNamara recommended, for example, that the United States "should press the Chinese to bring the aggression against the South to an end." The United States might also place a high-level representative in contact with Moscow in order to "reiterate that US objectives are limited but at the same time we have a firm determination to achieve them. . . . we would press the Soviets to avoid any deeper involvement. We would emphasize that continuation of the military phase can only be harmful to the communist cause and urge the Soviets to step in (perhaps with British co-chairman) to move the situation away from war and toward a peaceful settlement." Other political initiatives (all likely to be rebuffed) included bringing the Vietnam question before the United Nations,[4] and a Geneva conference on the subject "Peace in Southeast Asia."

In the overall evaluation of his proposed military program, McNamara exuded confidence that the United States would persevere. "Even though casualties will increase and the war will continue for some time, the United States public will support this course of action because it is a combined military-political program designed and likely to bring about a favorable solution to the Vietnam problem."[5] McNamara seriously underestimated, however, just how long

*This is especially interesting when compared with the secretary's April 25 statement, "the infiltration of the North Vietnamese battalion does not suggest that the Viet Cong may be trying to move into the Third State of insurgency. The Viet Cong have had battalions operating in the South heretofore but . . . sent as individuals into the South with consequent implications as to their manpower problems rather than operational tactics."[3]

a democracy would tolerate a costly and inconclusive war. He also underestimated the degree to which President Johnson would hide the nature of the military-political program *from* the American people.

In a *Top Secret* memo (perhaps the most interesting document to be declassified) to the Secretary of Defense, McGeorge Bundy criticized McNamara's first draft for its "grave limitations."[6] Bundy informed McNamara that at this particular stage of the deliberative process he was primarily interested in getting the secretary to "raise questions . . . and I am afraid it [my memo] may sound unhelpful." The memo shows that from the White House staff level, perhaps the *only* way of affecting particular choices of tactics in Vietnam was to argue with McNamara—clearly *primus inter pares* among the principals—at this key time. Bundy opposed the recommended doubling of the U.S. land commitment and warned McNamara that "our troops are entirely untested in the kind of warfare projected." Bundy was critical of tripling the U.S. air effort "when the value of the air action we have taken is sharply disputed." It was also preposterous to consider mining "at a time when nearly everyone agrees the real question is not in Hanoi, but in South Vietnam." Bundy minced few words in his assessment of McNamara's idea: "My first reaction is that this program is rash to the point of folly." Bundy then took positions on several issues which, in principal, placed him on the side of George Ball. Bundy rejected McNamara's emphasis on the Third Stage: "I see no reason to suppose that the VC will accommodate us by fighting the kind of war we desire. . . . I think the odds are that if we put 40–50 battalions with the missions here proposed, we shall find them only lightly engaged and ineffective in hot pursuit."

Bundy then raised the types of questions which are rarely attributed to the quality of decision-making during the period. The president's national security advisor was extremely critical of McNamara's deployment figures, arguing that a 200,000-man level was based "simply on the increasing weakness of Vietnamese forces. But this is a *slippery slope* toward total US responsibility and corresponding fecklessness on the Vietnamese side." Sounding even more like George Ball, Bundy noted that McNamara's paper "omits examination of the upper limit of US liability." Bundy asked, "If we need 200 thousand men now for these quite limited missions, may we not need 400 thousand later? Is this a rational course of action? Is there

any real prospect that US regular forces can conduct the anti-guerrilla operations which would probably remain the central problem in
South Vietnam?"* Bundy concluded by criticizing McNamara's
"hurry" to make a decision which involved such grave implications:
"It is not at all clear that we should make these kinds of decisions
early in July with the very fragmentary evidence available to us now
on a number of critical points: the tactics of the VC, the prospects
of the Ky government, and the effectiveness of US forces in these
new roles. *Any expanded program needs to have a clear sense of its
own internal momentum.* The paper does not face this problem. If
US casualties go up sharply, what further actions do we propose to
take or not to take? More broadly still, what is the real object of the
exercise? If it is to get to the conference table, what results do we
seek there? *Still more brutally, do we want to invest 200,000 men to
cover an eventual retreat? Can we not do that just as well where we
are?"*

In retrospect there was a remarkable astuteness to Bundy's queries
—the types of questions which *should* have dominated analysis for
the next month. The secretary of defense stood prepared to Ameri-
canize the war by committing more than 200,000 troops to the mainland. What would constitute the upper limits of a U.S. investment?
Could 400,000 men win a guerrilla war? Would it even be a guerrilla
war or a main-force engagement? What did contingency plans look
like for six months or one year down the road? What if the United
States had made a strategic error in its estimate of Chinese or Soviet
response? If the anticipated results were not achieved, what then?
Escalate? Negotiate a way out? Withdraw first? Dig in? What if Hanoi
did come to the conference table? What would a postsettlement U.S.
involvement look like? The principals went out of their way *not* to
ask these questions—preferring instead to demand proof from
George Ball why Thailand would not be the next domino.

---

*Yet Bundy was not a closet dove. He urged McNamara to consider alternatives
which included even "more drastic warning to Hanoi than any we have yet given."
In developing the "big stick" reasoning, Bundy wrote: "If General Eisenhower is right
in his belief that it was the prospect of nuclear attack which brought an armistice in
Korea, we should at least consider what realistic threat of larger action is available to
us for communication to Hanoi. A full interdiction of supplies to North Vietnam by
air and sea is a possible candidate for such an ultimatum. These are weapons which
may be more useful to us if we do not have to use them."

Bundy was not alone in criticizing McNamara's proposals. CIA Director William Raborn agreed with the general premise that some type of increased U.S. military role was necessary "to avoid the real risk of a major political-military defeat in the next several months."[7] Acknowledging that the "VC may now be winning. They certainly believe they are," Raborn doubted that any tide could be turned without a much larger commitment from the United States: "We cannot realistically hope 'to prove to the VC that they cannot win in SVN and therefore to turn the tide of the war' except by actually beginning to turn the tide against the VC. Obviously we cannot do this if US/GVN forces sustain a series of shattering setbacks during the next few weeks. To have any hope of turning the tide we must, at a minimum, avoid defeat and, under present conditions, some actions along the lines recommended in the presentation [McNamara's] are patently essential if defeat is to be avoided. *If we succeed in not losing the war* during the monsoon season (through October, say) what we will have won is the chance to settle down to a protracted struggle to contain communist pressures from the North and help build a stable, viable independent South Vietnam."

The CIA director expressed grave reservations, however, about McNamara's assumptions. The U.S. objective "to force the DRV to the conference table" was "very limited." Raborn even asked "whether it was intended actually to narrow previously stated US objectives or whether the formulation is simply a foreshorted statement?" Moreover, the CIA defined U.S. objectives as a combination of halting the insurgency in the South plus the equally formidable task of building a political/military apparatus strong enough to survive once the United States curtailed its extraordinary commitment. The CIA director echoed Bundy's point that Secretary McNamara was probably incorrect with regard to the Third Stage assumption: "It should not be expected, however, that the Viet Cong will necessarily stand and fight against superior forces. Rather they may drop backward a step to smaller-scale harassment and hit-and-run raids in which they do not encounter superior U.S. combat units. Not until they themselves are being hounded, harassed and hurt in many areas without prospect of relief will there be a likelihood of the VC/DRV seeking a respite via the conference table or by any other device."[8]

Raborn was least sanguine concerning McNamara's charade of political gestures intended to show a willingness to negotiate. Most of the initiatives had already been attempted and all were useless until the DRV/VC believed it could not win in Vietnam. The Communists, according to Raborn, would abandon their insurgency *only* when they were convinced that there was absolutely no possibility for early victory and when North Vietnam was under constant punitive attack: "So long as the Communists think they scent the possibility of an early victory (which is probably now the case) we believe that they will persevere and accept extremely severe damage to the North. Conversely, if North Vietnam itself is not hurting, Hanoi's doctrinaire leaders will probably be ready to carry on the Southern struggle almost indefinitely. . . . We stand to gain by keeping the doors open, as we have, but not by over-stressing our anxiety to confer." Raborn then focused on an often-overlooked problem—how would South Vietnam be able "to stand successfully against the Communists in the event that a negotiated settlement could be reached and the bulk of US forces withdrawn? It is certain that, in the wake of any such settlement, the Communists would continue their efforts against the Saigon government, either by political means or through outright violation of agreements. There is little point in spending US lives and treasure to obtain a conference or settlement which, in the absence of a viable non-Communist state, must lead either to US re-intervention or a subsequent Communist takeover."

The significance of the Bundy and Raborn critiques rested in their number and the status of those involved. It is generally assumed that except for George Ball's "tolerated" dissent, relative unanimity existed among the principals. The evidence shows, however, that very early in the deliberative process the president's special assistant for national security and the CIA director raised tough and realistic questions of McNamara's program. Moreover, neither individual was a "dove," nor did either favor a negotiated surrender. Rather, both believed that if the United States was about to embark on a major war commitment, answers were needed for the most basic types of questions. Both believed that the situation required, at the very least, a careful review of strategy, if not basic assumptions.

Undersecretary of State George Ball believed that the answers from such a systematic review would lead the United States away from war. On June 28 Ball wrote to the principals with his frequently quoted "Plan for Cutting Our Losses in South Vietnam."[9] Writing from the same premise as McNamara, Westmoreland, Bundy, and

Raborn "that we are losing the war in Vietnam," Ball demanded proof from those who favored escalation. There was no assurance that the United States could achieve its political objectives by expanding the bombing, nor was there any guarantee that its military objectives could be achieved with a substantial increase in combat forces. "On the contrary, we would run grave risks of bogging down an indeterminate number of American troops in a protracted and bloody conflict of uncertain outcome. This group is so great, in fact, that those who advocate this course must sustain the burden of proof that commitment of American forces to combat will assure our objectives at an acceptable cost."

Given the uncertainty in various outcomes, Ball argued that the United States should either extricate itself from Southeast Asia or reduce its defense perimeters in South Vietnam to accord with a limited U.S. deployment. This was really the last chance for getting out. If the United States proceeded with the proposed commitment, a substantial number of Americans would be killed. By developing a careful plan for withdrawal, the United States could extricate itself with only temporary loss of prestige. "We should maintain our present levels of deployment while we seek to get out of the quagmire and cut our losses." Ball concluded with prophetic advice for the president:

> The position taken in this memorandum does not suggest that the United States should abdicate its leadership in the cold war. But any prudent military commander carefully selects the terrain on which to stand and fight, and no great captain has ever been blamed for a successful tactical withdrawal.
>
> From our point of view, the terrain in South Vietnam could not be worse. Jungles and rice paddies are not designed for modern arms and, from a military point of view, this is clearly what General de Gaulle described to me as a "rotten country."
>
> Politically, South Vietnam is a lost cause. The country is bled white from twenty years of war and the people are sick of it. The Viet Cong —as is shown by the Rand Corporation Motivation and Morale Study— are deeply committed.
>
> Hanoi has a government and a purpose and a discipline. The "government" in Saigon is a travesty. In a very real sense, South Vietnam is a country with an army and no government.
>
> *In my view, a deep commitment of United States forces in a land war*

in South Vietnam would be a catastrophic error. If ever there was an occasion for a tactical withdrawal, this is it.

Ball recommended that President Johnson reemphasize President Eisenhower's original commitment to President Diem: U.S. assistance was contingent upon a government which truly represented the people of South Vietnam, and such a government had to maintain adequate standards of performance to receive support. South Vietnam's military leaders needed to be given an ultimatum—they had one month to put together a Government of National Union under civilian leadership; otherwise the United States would be forced to reconsider its commitment: "Moreover," Ball warned, "if no such willingness prevails in Saigon, we cannot take over the war ourselves."

In rebuttal to McNamara's memo, Ball argued that expansion of the bombing into North Vietnam would have only negligible results because the VC would not be scared into quitting: "So long as victory in the South appears possible, Hanoi's determination can probably be broken only by the total devastation of North Vietnam and its occupation by US forces—and this is not in the cards." Substantial damage to the civilian economy and disruption of communication lines between North Vietnam and China would "be far more likely to precipitate reactions by China and Russia than to diminish the fighting power of the Viet Cong in South Vietnam." Ball then returned to a familiar theme: "No one has yet shown that American troops can win a jungle war against an invisible enemy." Ball quoted extensively from the memoirs of Gen. Matthew Ridgway who in 1954 had urged Eisenhower not to intervene on behalf of the French at Dien Bien Phu:

I sent out to Indo-China an Army team of experts in every field: engineers, signal and communications specialists, medical officers, and experienced combat leaders who know how to evaluate terrain in terms of battle tactics.

The land was a land of rice paddy and jungle—particularly adapted to the guerrilla-type warfare at which the Chinese soldier is a master. This meant that every little detachment, every individual, that tried to move about that country, would have to be protected by riflemen. Every telephone lineman, road repair party, every ambulance and every rear-area aid station would have to be under armed guard or they would be shot at around the clock.

We could have fought in Indo-China. We could have won, *if we had been willing to pay the tremendous cost in men and money that such intervention would have required—a cost that in my opinion would have eventually been as great as, or greater than, that we paid in Korea.*

As I have pointed out earlier in this narrative, when the day comes for me to face my Maker and account for my actions, the thing I would be most humbly proud of was the fact that I fought against, and perhaps contributed to preventing, the carrying out of some hare-brained tactical schemes which would have cost the lives of thousands of men. *To that list of tragic accidents that fortunately never happened I would add the Indo-China intervention.*[10]

Ball's recommendations were immediately questioned by NSC staff member Chester Cooper. Writing to McGeorge Bundy, Cooper argued that Ball's view was, "God help us, perhaps a realistic account of what we confront in Vietnam. A more ebullient artist might have cast the situation in somewhat less somber tones, but there is not much point here in determining how dark a grey or how deep a black to use."[11] But Cooper was unwilling to swallow Ball's medicine— even when concurring in the diagnosis. Cooper even accepted Ball's premise that "the situation is grave, the local prospects dubious, the overall outlook dangerous," but differed from Ball in his belief that the United States should take "the initiative in discussion with the DRV (the Ball paper leaves this to the GVN, although it contemplates talks at some point between the US and the Chi Coms). My concept of the scenario, in either the short or the longer run would be to work out some kind of deal with Hanoi (cutting Moscow in as desirable), keep the Chinese out of it, and have the GVN work out a modus vivendi with a disarmed VC." Cooper also believed that McNamara's program would probably not work. He admitted to "a queasy feeling . . . that the force levels contemplated in some quarters assume either that the ARVN will cave in (in which case we've had it, whatever we do), or that more ambitious military objectives can be attained (which, with all deference, I doubt)." Still there was a light at the end of the tunnel: "On the ground in South Vietnam we face a tough summer, but *if* we can come out of it in the fall with a situation in which the VC is not much better off than it was in May, *we may be over the hump.* Can this fairly limited objective be accomplished with the forces already in South Vietnam? I wouldn't presume to say." In the short run it was easier, and certainly cognitively satisfying, to "hope" that policy would take you over the hump. For many of the participants excessive optimism replaced critical analysis of Ball's thesis.

Ball's own thinking culminated in his July 1, 1965, memorandum, "A Compromise Solution for South Vietnam,"[12] where he *changed tactics* from cutting losses to holding on long enough to lose through negotiations. Ball wrote to the president "the South Vietnamese are losing the war to the Viet Cong. No one can assure you that we can beat the Viet Cong or even force them to the conference table on our terms, no matter how many hundred thousand white, foreign (US) troops we deploy." U.S. conventional forces could not win a guerrilla war and President Johnson now faced *the* crucial question —"should we limit our liabilities in South Vietnam and try to find a way out with minimal long-term costs?" Failure to conclude a negotiated settlement would mean "protracted war, involving an open-ended commitment of US forces, mounting US casualties, no assurance of a satisfactory solution, and a serious danger of escalation at the end of the road." Ball echoed McGeorge Bundy's reservations concerning the internal momentum once a decision to escalate was made: "Once we suffer large casualties, we will have started a well-nigh irreversible process. Our involvement will be so great that we cannot—without national humiliation—stop short of achieving our national objectives. Of the two possibilities I think humiliation would be more likely than the achievement of our objectives—even after we have paid terrible costs."

With McNamara's memorandum still providing the lightning rod, Assistant Secretary of State William Bundy wrote a *Top Secret* memo recommending "A Middle Way Course of Action in South Vietnam."[13] Bundy, who had originally provided staff assistance to Ball in the last week of June, was unable to agree with the undersecretary's conclusion. Instead the assistant secretary went back to his office and drafted the "Middle Way" memo—located between the extremes of McNamara and Ball. The "middle way" was not a "compromise solution." Bundy's basic theme was one of holding the line until U.S. troops could be tested in their new offensive roles. According to Bundy, "in essence, this is a program to hold on for the next two months, and test the military effectiveness of US combat forces and the reaction of the Vietnamese army and people to the increased US role."

Bundy recommended the completion of all scheduled marine deployments which would bring U.S. combat strength to eighteen battalions and 85,000 men. Bundy was rather explicit in what he did *not* favor, disagreeing with several parts of the defense secretary's recommendations. The United States should avoid bombing any urban areas near Hanoi and Haiphong because "hitting these cities would not *now* lead Hanoi to give in but might on the contrary toughen it. It would almost certainly lose us the support of such key governments as the UK and Japan. Above all, it would inevitably intensify the Soviet commitment and probably remove the chance of the Soviets exerting restraint in the fall." Bundy recommended putting off any decision to mine North Vietnam's harbors or destroy rail and road lines from China to North Vietnam: "The harbor operation would tend to throw North Vietnam into the arms of Communist China and diminish Soviet influence. . . . Whatever we think the chances are now of making the effort in the South really costly to Hanoi, the present deployment of major added US forces gives no real promise of helping the chances of this kind of success." Bundy then warned the president that Ball's scenario "would be an abandonment of the South Vietnamese at a time when the fight is not, and certainly does not appear to the world and to Asian countries to be, *going all that badly.* Such an abandonment would leave us almost no leverage as to South Vietnam, and would create an immediate and maximum shock wave for Thailand and the rest of Asia. . . . There may come a time when the South Vietnamese really have shown they have abandoned the struggle, that time is by no means here now." (Here Bundy's assessment of the situation was probably more unrealistic than any of the principals.)[14]

Bundy believed that his plan, politically as well as militarily, represented the safest course. "The middle way avoids clear pitfalls of either of the major alternatives. It may not give us quite as much chance of a successful outcome as the major military actions proposed in the McNamara memo, but it avoids to a major extent the very serious risks involved in this program in any case, and the far more disastrous outcome that would eventuate if we acted along the lines of the McNamara memo and still lost South Vietnam." Moreover, "the program rejects withdrawal or negotiating concessions in any form [Ball] and equally rejects a present decision to raise our forces level above 85,000 [McNamara]. The latter appears unwise because (a) we have not tested whether our forces can really find and hit the VC. This program gives us enough reserves to give a fair test. (b) we simply do not know, *and probably cannot know,* whether raising the US force level and combat involvement would (1) cause the Vietnamese government and especially the army to let up; (2) create adverse public reactions to our whole presence on 'white men' and 'like the French' grounds."

There was an important difference between the Ball and Bundy options. Where Ball hoped that delay would buy time for adverse events, Bundy believed that the president needed to "reckon the Congressional and public opinion problems of embarking now on what might appear clearly to be an open-ended ground commitment." Bundy's memo illustrates just *how much* uncertainty prevailed in the decision-making environment. Bundy maintained that "there is a point of sharply diminishing returns and adverse consequences that may lie somewhere between 70,000 and 100,000 US forces in total, and a fairly limited number of combat battalions who actually get into the countryside to fight in case of need." There was no need to rush into a decision: "what we need now is to test; perhaps, these fears will be groundless, but we lose little by waiting, compared to the risks. And these risks are affected by pace and timing; we might be readily accepted if we moved gradually; but arouse the worst fears and adverse reactions if we move fast."

By now input to the president included McNamara, Ball, and Bundy: A secretary of defense and two subordinates to the secretary of state. Three advocates, three plans, three choices, three quite unequal players: (1) get out with loss to honor and prestige—a tactical withdrawal based on the fact that U.S. forces could not win an Asian land war; (2) a limited commitment with option selection to follow a summer test period—a test of military effectiveness as well as public opinion acceptance; (3) a military buildup to save South Vietnam from collapse and deny Hanoi a victory—based on the fact that South Vietnam was central to U.S. strategic interests.

Johnson next heard from his secretary of state, Dean Rusk. In a rare personal memorandum to the president which had not been circulated to the other principals, Rusk argued that "the central objective of the United States in South Vietnam must be to insure that

North Vietnam not succeed in taking over or determining the future of South Vietnam by force. We must accomplish this objective without a general war if possible."[15] The war aim of the United States was not and could not be concerned with hypothetical issues such as what the South Vietnamese people would do if left alone: "The sole basis for employing US forces is the aggression from the North." If this aggression was removed, the U.S. forces would also leave. Rusk rejected Ball's position by noting "there can be no serious debate about the fact that *we have a commitment** to assist the South Vietnamese to resist aggression from the North. . . . *The integrity of the US commitment* is the principal pillar of peace throughout the world. If that commitment becomes unreliable, the communist world would draw conclusions that would lead to our ruin and almost certainly to a catastrophic war." Rusk never wavered in his resolve that the VC could be denied a victory, telling the president, "it is said that we are 'losing'; this means that we are not making headway, but rather falling behind, in the effort to stop the infiltration and to pacify the country. But that does not mean the Viet Cong are 'winning'; they have the power to disrupt, but they are not capable of occupying and organizing the country or any major part of it. *The Viet Cong can be denied a victory, even if complete pacification will be a long and tortuous prospect.*"

Rusk was willing, however, to accept the very constraints which would prevent what he most wanted: "Our problem, therefore, is to deny to Hanoi success in South Vietnam without taking action on our side which would force the other side (China, Russia) to move to higher levels of conflict." Standing logic on its head or ignoring at

---

*The question of U.S. treaty commitment had been debated within the administration. Responding to a request from the president, Ball prepared a memorandum on June 23, 1965, entitled "United States Commitments Regarding the Defense of South Vietnam." The report was forwarded to the president on June 27 with McGeorge Bundy's covering memorandum: "George asked me to say that he himself does not think the legal arguments about support for Vietnam are decisive. The commitment is primarily political and any decision to enlarge or reduce it will be political. My own further view is that if and when we want to shift our course and cut our losses in Vietnam we should do so because of a finding that the Vietnamese themselves are not meeting their obligations to themselves or to us. This is the course we started on with Diem, and if we got a wholly ineffective or anti-American government we could do the same thing again. With a 'neutralist' government it would be quite possible to move in this direction."[16]

least ten years of experience with Diem and his successors, Rusk favored getting tough with Ky and Thieu—both had to understand that U.S. support could not be taken for granted (but it would still be given and taken). Rusk's view illustrated the Catch-22 of U.S. policy. Words like "commitment," "promise," and "freedom" were used within a context which made any action *other* than escalation seem like cowardice or betrayal of a deserving ally. But once the decision was made to save South Vietnam, decision-makers accepted constraints imposed by possible Chinese and Soviet actions. The president committed the United States to fight a limited war against an enemy totally committed to revolutionary war.

An important insight into how the advisory process operated within the White House is evidenced by a previously unavailable memo from McGeorge Bundy to the president regarding the position of various principals. Writing to Johnson on July 1,[17] Bundy reported that "the positions within the government are roughly as follows: McNamara and Ball honestly believe in their own recommendations, though Bob would readily accept advice to tone down those of his recommendations which move rapidly against Hanoi by bombing and blockade. Dean Rusk leans toward the McNamara program, adjusted downward in the same way. The second level men in both State and Defense are not optimistic about the future prospects in Vietnam and are therefore very reluctant to see us move to a 44 battalion force with a call up of reserves. So they would tend to cluster around the middle course suggested by my brother. They would like to see what happens this summer before getting much deeper in. The Joint Chiefs are strongly in favor of going in even further than McNamara. Specifically, they want to take out the SAM sites, the IL-28s, and the MIGs in the Hanoi area."

Bundy then stated his own preference to the president. The memo is perhaps one of the most significant to be released under recent declassifications:

> *My hunch is that you will want to listen hard to George Ball and then reject his proposal. Discussion could then move to the narrower choice between my brother's course and McNamara's.* The decision between them should be made in about ten days. . . . I think you may want to have pretty tight and hard analyses of some *disputed questions* like the following:

1. What are the chances of our getting into a white man's war with all the brown men against us or apathetic?

2. How much of the McNamara planning would be on a contingency basis with no decision until August or September?

3. What would a really full political and public relations campaign look like in both the Bundy option and the McNamara option?

4. What is the upper limit of our liability if we now go to 44 battalions?

5. Can we frame this program in such a way as to keep very clear our own determination to keep the war limited? (This is another way of stating question 4.)

6. Can we get a cold, hard look at the question whether the current economic and political situation in Vietnam is so very bad that it may come apart even before this program gets into action? (I don't believe that it is that bad, but no one seems to be really sure of the facts today.)

Bundy reminded the president that the July 2 meeting "is not, repeat not, for decision, but for shaping of the issues that you want studied." Here is the evidence which shows that important questions about disputed evidence were indeed brought to Johnson's attention in *early* July. But information processing was soon relegated to a choice between the William Bundy and McNamara options—and not analysis of the basic assumptions which underlay each of the proposals. Moreover, McGeorge Bundy's questions were precisely the type which should have been asked and then staffed out. But the person asking them had just committed himself to a scaled-down McNamara program with a recommendation for a presidential decision by July 12. There would be discussion, but not analysis; and the only staff work would be for getting into the war as quietly as possible. The president had already signaled his special assistant for national security that he was to get in line behind McNamara's program.

Framing the Advisory Debate

In *The Vantage Point* Johnson selectively recalled, "I was not about to send additional men without the most detailed analysis. . . . I knew we faced a crucial question, one that was at the heart of our treaty commitment to Southeast Asia. If necessary, would we use substantial US forces on the ground to prevent the loss of that region to aggressive forces moving illegally across international frontiers?"[18] The president decided to send Secretary McNamara to Saigon purportedly to assess the impact that such a broadened U.S. role would have on the war. According to Taylor, "the primary purpose of this visit, obviously not made public, was to discuss troop requirements for the remainder of 1965 and the expectations from them if provided."[19] On July 7, 1965, McNamara wrote a *Top Secret* memorandum to Taylor concerning his mission.[20] "The main purpose of our visit will be to receive from you *your recommendations for the number* of US combat battalions, artillery battalions, engineering battalions, helicopter companies, tactical aircraft, and total military personnel to be assigned to South Vietnam between now and the end of this year; the time schedule on which such forces are required; *the results which we can expect to achieve with such force levels compared to alternative programs;* the probable requirements for additional forces next year; and the program of political contacts which you propose as a complement to your military actions." McNamara posed two basic questions which had not yet been satisfactorily answered with regard to the expansion of the U.S. role in South Vietnam: 1) "What assurance do we have that with the resulting force level we can prove to the Viet Cong they cannot win, and thereby force them to a settlement on our terms? 2) Will large increases in the number and involvement of U.S. combat units and military personnel in South Vietnam cause the Vietnamese Government, and especially the Army, to let up; will it create adverse popular reactions to our presence in the country?" The secretary then included a list of twenty-five additional questions, primary among which were:

1. How did you determine the number of US and ARVN battalions required to effectively counter the current or prospective Viet Cong forces?

2. Where do you propose to station US combat units and where and how will they be used; what casualties do you expect?

3. How long do you think it will take with your recommended forces (a) to seize the initiative, (b) to prove to the Viet Cong that they

cannot win, and (c) thereby to force them to a settlement on our terms?

4. Would it be wise to withdraw GVN military and para-military forces from certain outlying or exposed positions in order to concentrate in positions of strength and to reduce the penalties of the serious shortage of Government troops?

5. What reaction to the expansion of US and third-country forces do you expect from the VC and the DRV? . . .

8. What command arrangements do you propose for the expanded US force when engaged in combat?

9. What program of military pressure (bombing, mining, etc.) against North Vietnam, in terms of the types of targets, level of effort, etc., do you propose for the next six months as a complement to your plan of action in the South?

10. How effective has been the bombing of the Laotian infiltration routes; what Laotian bombing program do you recommend for the future in terms of specific targets and level of effort?

11. How effective have been the B-52 strikes; assuming 800 B-52 sorties are available each month, what bombing program do you recommend for the future in terms of specific targets and level of effort?

12. Exclusive of B-52 sorties, how many strike sorties and how many reconnaissance sorties per month do you recommend against targets in South Vietnam during the next six months; are all of your current requirements being met; if not, why not; should we be planning on additional airfields for South Vietnam and if so, by what date are they required and where should they be placed?

13. What has been the trend of each of the major indicators (population control, area control, desertions, weapons losses, terror incidents, price level, etc.) of the success or failure of the counterinsurgency campaign over the past year?

14. How does the freedom of movement today over the railroads and the major highways and waterways compare with that of a year ago?

15. What measures do we have of the success or failure of our efforts to prevent infiltration of men and equipment by sea; has the recently expanded program reduced such infiltration; if not, why not; are additional forces required?

16. Outline and appraise the effectiveness of alternative plans (including a barrier across the 17th Parallel) for the use of US troops in Laos for the purpose of preventing infiltration of men and equipment through that country into South Vietnam.

17. If you think it is possible militarily to cut off or very substantially cut down the infiltration of North Vietnamese personnel and material from the North to the South, when do you believe it will begin to have an important effect on VC activities and how decisive will that effect be? . . .

19. Outline the original plan for the expansion of the GVN military, paramilitary and police forces; the progress to date against the plan; and changes, if any, which you propose for the future. . . .

21. How important is the monsoon to military operations and to the military balance, and how should we expect military prospects to change when the monsoon ends? . . .

23. After the deployment of the recommended US forces, how would the GVN react to an extended pause (six or eight weeks) in the bombing of the DRV?

24. Should we consider the imposition of press censorship after the expansion of US forces?

25. What contacts do the South Vietnamese now have with the NLF and the DRV; what additional contacts would you recommend that they or the US have with those parties or the Soviets; how should such US contacts be initiated and with what notice to the GVN?

With McNamara scheduled to depart for Saigon, Ambassador Taylor cabled the president with perhaps his most negative evaluation of the situation in South Vietnam: "The combination of GVN/US military resources within SVN *is not presently sufficient to turn the tide against the VC and thus convince the DRV/VC leadership that there is no hope for victory in South Vietnam.* Similarly, the weight and duration of our air attacks in North Vietnam have been insufficient to produce tangible evidence of any willingness on the part of Hanoi to come to the conference table in a reasonable mood. *It is our overall conclusion that before we can expect to have an atmosphere conducive to an acceptable negotiated settlement we must raise the level of our joint efforts* both against the VC formations in SVN and against bombing target systems in North Vietnam and maintain the increased pressure for an indeterminate period."[21]

On July 16, 1965, Secretary McNamara, Henry Cabot Lodge (the announced successor to Taylor whose term expired by the end of July),* General Wheeler, and General Goodpaster arrived in Saigon.† General Thieu first assessed the political climate in South Vietnam. Noting that the new government had been in power for only three weeks, "the GVN has perhaps not succeeded in producing spectacular results; however, by the firm stand the GVN has taken, the religious and political groups appear to endorse the GVN program and are quiescent."[24] Thieu reiterated the new government's intention vigorously to prosecute the war and revitalize the economy. He also made clear that the new GVN wanted to hear what the United States planned to do in the way of a more serious commitment to the GVN. Johnson wrote in *The Vantage Point* that "when McNamara asked for their estimate of how many might be needed, the Vietnamese leaders said they thought that in addition to the forty-four battalions

*By the end of June McGeorge Bundy was pressing hard for Johnson to move up from September 1 to August 1 Henry Cabot Lodge's takeover as U.S. ambassador. Writing to the president on June 30, Bundy reported: "It is extraordinarily clear that any further action turns on what we can get the Ky government to do. In this situation, the quality and energy of our team in Saigon becomes decisive. Max Taylor is heavily preoccupied with the military situation, and the rest of his team is not geared to a full-steam operation with the new cabinet. So I begin to wonder if it would not be wise to settle hard on the plan for a Lodge-Sullivan team, and plan to get them out there together as soon as Lodge is briefed and Sullivan's successor is chosen. I have already told my brother Bill that Sullivan is the generally preferred choice for his job, and that he should accordingly find the right man quickly for Vientiane. But the decision on the timing of the Taylor-Lodge change is obviously one which only you can make. The more I think about it, the more I think the time of Lodge's takeover should be nearer 1 August than 1 September."[22]

†Chester Cooper recalls, "Deputy Ambassador Alexis Johnson arranged a small shirt-sleeves dinner with the new government leaders on the night of our arrival. The Vietnamese arrived somewhat late and Ky made a spectacular entrance. He walked in breezily, wearing a tight, white dinner jacket, tapered, formal trousers, pointed, patent leather shoes, and brilliant red socks. A Hollywood central casting bureau would have grabbed him for a role as a sax player in a second-rate Manila night club. McNamara, who definitely would not have gotten the part, seemed momentarily dazed and bemused at his first sight of Vietnam's new leader. (Somebody standing near me muttered, "At least no one could confuse him with Uncle Ho!") General Thieu wore a conservative business suit and seemed content, or at least resigned, to have Ky remain in the spotlight—a position Ky appeared eager to hold."[23]

they already had requested, there should be another combat division. Their total estimate called for about 200,000 American men in all categories."[25]

But while in Saigon purportedly to get answers for some rather basic questions, McNamara suddenly received a cable from his deputy, Cyrus Vance, which reported that *President Johnson had decided to go ahead with the forty-four–battalion request.* Johnson ordered McNamara back home and instructed the secretary to complete his program recommendations immediately.[26] As Westmoreland later wrote, *"Our July discussion turned out, in a way, to be moot."* Thus, the "debate" over the forty-four battalions never occurred. This is particularly bewildering because, according to Taylor's recollection, "the answers which McNamara got from us were not always precise or completely reliable, as the mission members who produced them were quick to concede."[27] Moreover, in answer to the fundamental question posed by McNamara, would the requested increase force the Viet Cong to a settlement on our own terms, Taylor answered negatively, because one guerrilla was equal to four to eight soldiers and the Viet Cong "could always make compensatory increases."[28] Westmoreland also admitted "it was virtually impossible to provide the secretary with a meaningful figure."[29]

With Secretary McNamara on his way to Washington, Ambassador Taylor cabled the president that "the only report worth your reading this week is the one which Bob McNamara is carrying back on the plane to you tonight. . . . [His recommendations] have the full concurrence of [Alexis] Johnson, Westmoreland and me."[30] Writing on the subject "Vietnam Planning at the Close of Business, July 18 (Sunday)," Mac Bundy suggested that the "timing of the message to the Congress is really the D-Day for the whole operation. If McNamara reports to you on Wednesday (July 21), *you probably do not wish to give the appearance of great haste* in reaching a decision, and for that reason I would recommend against going to the Hill before the first of the week (July 26). But a delay beyond *Monday* (July 26) would seem to me to create too wide a gap between McNamara's return and the point of decision."[31]

If the president had decided on the forty-four–battalion request, why do most of the principals maintain that McNamara's fact-finding mission touched off a serious debate within the administration? Why did it take another ten days before the president announced his decision? Was this a cover-up by advisors, or possibly by the president over his own advisors? The president had already decided that the forty-four battalions were needed to save South Vietnam—but he was unsure how to implement that decision. Should he accept McNamara's recommendation to call up the National Guard and Reserves or was there another way of meeting manpower needs? Moreover, were the needs and interests of political leadership compatible with McNamara's military program? If not, what compromise could be developed? How would the president then sell it to his advisory group and ultimately to the American people? These were the pressing questions which faced Lyndon Johnson as he awaited McNamara's return from Saigon.

On July 20 Secretary McNamara forwarded his final program recommendations to the president.[32] In a now-familiar theme McNamara wrote that "our objective in Vietnam is to create conditions for a favorable outcome by demonstrating to the VC/DRV that the odds are against their winning. We want to create these conditions, if possible, without causing the war to expand into one with China or the Soviet Union and, in a way which preserves support of the American people and, hopefully, of our allies and friends." Noting that "a hard VC push is now on to dismember the nation and to maul the army," McNamara reported "the situation in South Vietnam is worse than a year ago (when it was worse than a year before that)." The inflation-wracked economy was on the verge of collapse and "the odds are less than even that the Ky government will last out the year. . . . The DRV/VC seem to believe that South Vietnam is on the run and near collapse; they show no signs of settling for less than a complete takeover." On the military front, Viet Cong main and local forces were inflicting serious defeats on ARVN forces. The GVN was quickly losing its ability to protect and safeguard its people. McNamara admitted that "ARVN overall is not capable of successfully resisting the VC initiatives without more active assistance from more US/Third Country ground forces than those thus far committed. Without faster outside help, the ARVN is faced with successive tactical reverses, loss of key communication and population centers particularly in the highlands, piecemeal destruction of ARVN units, attrition of RVNAF will to fight, and loss of civilian confidence. *Early commitment of additional US/Third Country forces in sufficient quantity, or general reserve and offensive roles, should stave off GVN defeat."*

The secretary emphasized that the government to Viet Cong ratio "over-all is now only a little better than 3-to-1, and in combat battalions little better than 1.5–1. Some ARVN units have been mauled; many are understrength and therefore 'conservative.' Desertions are at a high rate, and the force build-up has slipped badly. The VC, who are undoubtedly suffering badly too (their losses are very high), now control a South Vietnamese manpower pool of 500,000 to 1 million fighting-age men and reportedly are trying to double their combat strength, largely by forced draft (down to 15-year-olds) in the increasing areas they control. They seem to be able more than ever to replace their losses."

McNamara reported that U.S. aid had thus far produced only negligible results: "There are no signs that we have throttled the inflow of supplies for the VC, or can throttle the flow while their material needs are as low as they are; indeed more and better weapons have been observed in VC hands, and it is probable that there has been further build-up of North Vietnamese regular units. . . . Nor have our air attacks in North Vietnam produced tangible evidence of willingness on the part of Hanoi to come to the conference table in a reasonable mood."

McNamara's memorandum combined the picture of military and political disrepair with the seeds of action. The secretary of defense outlined three options for the president, each involving different probabilities, outcomes, and costs:

(a) Cut our losses and withdraw under the best conditions that can be arranged—almost certainly conditions humiliating the United States and very damaging to our future effectiveness on the world scene.

(b) Continue at about the present level, with the US forces limited to say 75,000 holding on and playing for the breaks—a course of action which, because our position would grow weaker, almost certainly would confront us later with a choice between withdrawal and an emergency expansion of forces, perhaps too late to do any good.

(c) Expand promptly and substantially increase the US military pressure against the Viet Cong in South and maintain the military pressure against the North while launching a vigorous effort on the political side* to lay the groundwork for a favorable outcome by clarifying our objectives and establishing channels of communication. This alternative would stave off defeat in the short run and offer a good chance of producing a favorable settlement in the longer run; at the same time it would imply a commitment to see a fighting war clear through at considerable cost in casualties and material and would make any later decision to withdraw even more difficult and even more costly than would be the case today.

In endorsing option C McNamara recommended raising the ante from the sixteen maneuver battalions presently deployed to forty-four (thirty-four U.S., nine Korean, one Australian) plus an important change in mission for these troops—to search and destroy. In evaluating the probability of success, McNamara returned to the conventional phase assumption: "The success of the program from the military point of view turns on whether the Vietnamese hold their own in terms of numbers and fighting spirit, and on whether the forces can be effective in a quick-reaction reserve role, a role in which they are only now being tested. The number of US troops is too small to make a significant difference in the traditional 10–1 government-guerrilla formula, but it is not too small to make a significant difference in the kind of war which seems to be evolving in Vietnam—a 'Third Stage' of conventional war in which it is easier to identify, locate and attack the enemy. . . . The overall evaluation is that the course of action recommended in this memorandum—if the military and political moves are properly integrated and executed with continuing vigor and visible determination—stands a *good chance* of achieving an *acceptable outcome* within a *reasonable time* in Vietnam."

A good chance, an acceptable outcome, a reasonable time? What was McNamara referring to? The secretary identified nine elements which would constitute an acceptable outcome for the United States: "(1) VC stops attacks and drastically reduces incidents of terror and sabotage. (2) DRV reduces infiltration to a trickle, with some reasonably reliable method of our obtaining

---

*"Ambassador Lodge states 'any further initiative by us now [before we are strong] would simply harden the Communist resolve not to stop fighting.' Ambassadors Taylor and Johnson would maintain discreet contacts with the Soviets but otherwise agree with Ambassador Lodge."

confirmation of this fact. (3) US/GVN stop bombing of NVN. (4) GVN stays independent (hopefully pro-US, but possibly genuinely neutral). (5) GVN exercises governmental functions over substantially all of SVN. (6) Communists remain quiescent in Laos and Thailand. (7) DRV withdraws PAVN forces and other NVNese infiltrators (not regroupees) from SVN. (8) VC/NLF transform from a military to purely political organization. (9) US combat forces (not advisors or AID) withdraw." McNamara believed that "a favorable outcome could include also arrangements regarding elections, relations between North and South Vietnam, participation in peace-keeping by international forces, membership for North and South Vietnam in the UN, and so on. The nine fundamental elements can evolve with or without an express agreement and, except for what might be negotiated incidental to a cease-fire, are more likely to evolve without an express agreement than with one. *We do not need now to address the question whether ultimately we would settle for something less than the nine fundamentals; because deployment of the forces recommended . . . is prerequisite to the achievement of any acceptable settlement, and a decision can be made later,* when bargaining becomes a reality, whether to compromise in any particular."[33]

McNamara warned the president (based on Westmoreland's advice) that the forty-four battalions (175,000–200,000 men) would be enough *only* through 1965—"it should be understood that the deployment of more men (perhaps 100,000) may be necessary in early 1966, and that the deployment of additional forces thereafter is possible but will depend on developments." According to Westmoreland, "In the end I told him [McNamara] only that I thought twenty-four more battalions in addition to the forty-four under consideration, plus more combat support and logistical troops, would put us in a position to begin the 'win phase' of our strategy. That meant about 175,000 American troops at the start, followed by about 100,000. Yet, I warned that VC and North Vietnamese actions well might alter the figures, which they did any number of times."[34]

McNamara recommended that the president authorize the call-up of approximately 235,000 Reserves and National Guard. "This number—approximately 125,000 Army, 75,000 Marines, 25,000 Air Force and 10,000 Navy—would provide approximately 36 maneuver battalions by the end of this year. The call-up would be for a two-year period; but the intention would be to release them after one year, by which time they could be relieved by regular forces if conditions permitted."* The secretary also recommended "that the regular armed forces be increased by approximately 375,000 men (approximately 250,000 Army, 75,000 Marines, 25,000 Air Force and 25,000 Navy). This would provide approximately 27 additional maneuver battalions by the middle of 1966. The increase would be accomplished by increasing recruitment, increasing the draft and extending tours of duty of men already in the service. I recommend that a supplemental appropriation of approximately $X for FY 1966 be sought from the Congress to cover the first part of the added costs attributable to the build-up in and for the war in Vietnam. A further supplemental appropriation might be required later in the fiscal year."[35] McNamara's bottom line must have stunned the president: "It should be noted that in mid-1966 the United States would, as a consequence of the above method of handling the build-up, have approximately 600,000 additional men (approximately 63 additional maneuver battalions) as protection against contingencies."

After reading McNamara's report, NSC staff member Chester Cooper offered some cogent insight to the secretary: *"Will the President be able to settle for something less than a clear cut military victory (or at least something that can be creditably passed off as one) after committing forces of the contemplated scale?"* Cooper believed the forces would "hopefully stop the erosion of security, at some point push the VC back into the jungle, and, sooner or later, make them more amenable to a political settlement." Cooper asked, "would a much larger force which provided a greater chance for a 'military victory' be easier for him to live with than the contemplated force which might break the back of the main force, but not necessarily cut deeply into the VC capability for substantial guerrilla activity?" Moreover, Cooper asked, "should the report explicitly state that the forces contemplated may very well turn out to be significantly less than what may have to be committed not only in Vietnam but elsewhere, as we raise the ante here?" This was followed by a more blunt question:

---

*McNamara wrote to me that "because of what I considered to have been the essential role of the Reserves in resolving the 1961 Berlin crisis, I strongly favored calling them up in 1965."

"After the commitment of even the contemplated level of US forces, will *we* be able to settle for a political settlement involving anything less than the VCs turning in their suits altogether?"[36]

What started in 1963 as the inheritance of a still-limited commitment with heavy symbolic overtones, now loomed as a major Asian land war. Half a million American soldiers fighting in Southeast Asia by 1966 was a staggering figure for the president who wanted to build a Great Society. Lyndon Johnson's day of reckoning had arrived. It was now time to turn in his chips.

The Deliberative Process at Work?

In *The Vantage Point* Johnson wrote that he "wanted to go over [McNamara's] proposal with the greatest care. I realized what a major undertaking it would be. The call-up of large numbers of reserves was part of the package. This would require a great deal of money and a huge sacrifice for the American people. I summoned my top advisors to the White House on July 21, the day after McNamara returned."[37] What followed is a remarkably documented discussion of alternatives to McNamara's recommendations. To some, like Jack Valenti, "those who sat in on all the meetings over the week-long torment knew that Lyndon Johnson listened carefully to every new point. . . . It was as if he were determined to dredge up every piece of information that might have even the barest relevancy to the decision."[38] Yet to Chester Cooper "we were now in too deep to back out and it was a foregone conclusion, as the President had already warned, that major new deployments would be made. The only questions revolved around the size of the new forces to be committed and how they were to be raised and supported."[39] The first session* to discuss McNamara's report was scheduled for July 21. Before the president arrived, McNamara reviewed his program recommendations with the group. After three quarters of an hour

---

*Those attending included Rusk, Ball, William Bundy, Lodge, and Unger from the State Department; McNamara, Vance, and McNaughton from Defense; Wheeler representing the Joint Chiefs; Rowan and Marks from USIA; McGeorge Bundy, Valenti, Busby, and Cooper from the White House.

the president arrived and asked a series of questions (the questions really do appear as staged for purposes of consensus building; *Johnson already had the answers and the policy*):*[40] "What I would like to know is what has happened in recent months that requires this kind of decision on my part. What are the alternatives? I want this discussed in full detail, from everyone around this table." Johnson continued, "Have we wrung every single soldier out of every country that we can? Who else can help us here? Are we the sole defenders in the world? Have we done all we can in this direction? What are the compelling reasons for this call-up? What results can we expect? Again, I ask you what are the alternatives? I don't want us to make snap judgments. I want us to consider all our options." The discussion which followed was an extremely important one. According to George Ball, "This meeting was special only in that, once the decision under consideration was accepted, the United States would commit thousands of its young men not just to passive defense missions but to aggressive combat roles. The war would then become unequivocably our own. There would be no turning back for months, perhaps years—and that would not occur until we had suffered horrible casualties, killed thousands of Vietnamese and raised the level of national anxiety and frustration above the threshold of hysteria."[42] In reproducing the discussion in its entirety, I alert my readers to William Bundy's recollection that "at the first meeting (July 21) the President went through this, 'Is it right? What are the alternatives? George Ball, tell me what you think the alternatives are? What is the case? That case?' *It was a bit of a set piece, though, I have to say.* I don't feel that this was where the decision was being made in all honesty—that I think McNamara had already reported at dawn to the President and gave him it—*you felt it had been staged to a degree.*"[43]

GEORGE BALL: Isn't it possible that the VC will do what they did against the French—stay away from confrontation and not accommodate us?

GENERAL WHEELER: Yes, that is possible, but by constantly harassing them, they will have to fight somewhere.

---

*According to McGeorge Bundy, "McNamara's report poses real questions to [President Johnson]. But they're not, to him, the Ball questions. They are the reserve call-up and similar questions. That's why some found the following discussions real and some not. It depended where you were in your perception of what was really on his mind."[41]

MCNAMARA: If the VC doesn't fight in large units, it will give the ARVN a chance to resecure hostile areas. We don't know what VC tactics will be when the VC is confronted by 175,000 Americans.

RABORN: We agree. By 1965's end, we expect NVN to increase its forces. It will attempt to gain a substantial victory before our build-up is complete.

THE PRESIDENT: *Is there anyone here of the opinion we should not do what the memorandum says? If so, I want to hear from him now, in detail.*

BALL: Mr. President, I can foresee a perilous voyage, very dangerous. I have great and grave apprehensions that we can win under these conditions. But let me be clear. If the decision is to go ahead, I am committed.

THE PRESIDENT: But, George, is there another course in the national interest, some course that is better than the one McNamara proposes? We know it is dangerous and perilous, but the big question is, can it be avoided?

BALL: There is no course that will allow us to cut our losses. If we get bogged down, our cost might be substantially greater. The pressures to create a larger war would be inevitable. The qualifications I have are not due to the fact that I think we are in a bad moral position.

THE PRESIDENT: Tell me then, what other road can I go?

BALL: Take what precautions we can, Mr. President. Take our losses, let their government fall apart, negotiate, discuss, knowing full well there will be a probable take-over by the Communists. This is disagreeable, I know.

THE PRESIDENT: I can take disagreeable decisions. But I want to know can we make a case for your thoughts? Can you discuss it fully?

BALL: We have discussed it. I have had my day in court.

THE PRESIDENT: I don't think we can have made any full commitment, George. You have pointed out the danger, but you haven't really proposed an alternative course. We haven't always been right. We have no mortgage on victory. Right now, I am concerned that we have very little alternatives to what we are doing. I want another meeting, more meetings, before we take any definitive action. We must look at all other courses of possibility carefully. Right now I feel it would be more dangerous to lose this now, than endanger a great number of troops. But I want this fully discussed.

RUSK: What we have done since 1954 to 1961 has not been good enough. We should have probably committed ourselves heavier in 1961.

CARL ROWAN: What bothers me most is the weakness of the Ky government. Unless we put the screws on the Ky government, 175,000 men will do us no good.

LODGE: There is not a tradition of a national government in Saigon. There are no roots in the country. Not until there is tranquility can you have any stability. *I don't think we ought to take this government seriously. There is simply no one who can do anything. We have to do what we think we ought to do regardless of what the Saigon government does.* As we move ahead on a new phase, we have the right and the duty to do certain things with or without the government's approval.

THE PRESIDENT: George, do you think we have another course?

BALL: I would not recommend that you follow McNamara's course.

THE PRESIDENT: Are you able to outline your doubts? Can you offer another course of action? *I think it's desirable to hear you out, truly hear you out, then I can determine if your suggestions are sound and ready to be followed, which I am prepared to do if I am convinced.*

BALL: Yes, Mr. President. I think I can present to you the least bad of two courses. What I would present is a course that is costly, but can be limited to short-term costs.

THE PRESIDENT: Alright, let's meet again at 2:30 this afternoon to discuss George's proposals.

The morning meeting highlighted just how far *from* logic decision-makers had traveled. In order to achieve military victory against the North, Ambassador Lodge recommended that the GVN should be ignored. The United States now had a "right" to fight Communist aggression regardless of the government structure in the South. Yet the burden of proof was still directed at Ball, who dared suggest that the "least bad" scenario would be to let the government fall and negotiate an agreement—well aware that the Communists would ultimately take over. When Ball raised the crucial point that 175,000 Americans could not fight effectively in the jungle terrain, General Wheeler quickly retorted that "search and destroy" would achieve the necessary end. Ball's final day in court came that afternoon when he faced the president and peers for well over an hour of cogent but fruitless analysis. He never had a chance. Johnson simply used the occasion to let everyone believe that all sides had been considered.

BALL: We cannot win, Mr. President. The war will be long and protracted. The most we can hope for is a messy conclusion. There remains a great danger of intrusion by the Chinese. *But the biggest problem is the problem of the long war.* The Korean experience was a galling one. The correlation between Korean casualties and public opinion showed support stabilized at 50 percent. As casualties increase, the pressure to strike at the very jugular of North Vietnam will become very great. I am concerned about world opinion. If we could win in a year's time, and win decisively, world opinion would be alright. However, if the war is long and protracted, as I believe it will be, then we will suffer because the world's greatest power cannot defeat guerrillas. Then there is the problem of national politics. Every great captain in history was not afraid to make a tactical withdrawal if conditions were unfavorable to him. The enemy cannot even be seen in Vietnam. He is indigenous to the country. I truly have serious doubts that an army of Westerners can successfully fight Orientals in an Asian jungle.*

THE PRESIDENT: This is important. Can Westerners, in the absence of accurate intelligence, successfully fight Asians in jungle rice paddies? I want McNamara and General Wheeler to seriously ponder this question.

BALL: I think we all have underestimated the seriousness of this situation. It is like giving cobalt treatment to a terminal cancer case. I think a long, protracted war will disclose our weakness, not our strength. The least harmful way to cut losses in SVN is to let the government decide it doesn't want us to stay there. Therefore, we should put such proposals to the GVN that they can't accept. Then, it would move to a neutralist position. I have no illusions that after we were asked to leave South Vietnam, that country would soon come under Hanoi control. What

---

*Following the meeting, Chester Cooper wrote to McGeorge Bundy that the discussion had focused on two rather disturbing military outcomes which might result from a substantial increase in U.S. forces: "(a) the VC main forces will be forced by US forces into reverting back to guerrilla warfare; (b) the VC main forces will choose not to confront our units head-on and voluntarily revert to guerrilla actions." Cooper warned that "either way, it would appear that we and the GVN will be faced with the problem of guerrilla rather than positional warfare. The fact that this may mean that the VC cannot achieve a military victory offers small comfort; neither we nor the GVN have as yet demonstrated that we can win this kind of war."44

about Thailand? It would be our main problem. Thailand has proved a good ally so far, though history shows it has never been a staunch ally. If we wanted to make a stand in Thailand, we might be able to make it. Another problem would be South Korea. We have two divisions there now. There would be a problem with Taiwan, but as long as the Generalissimo is there, they have no place to go. Indonesia is a problem, as is Malaysia. Japan thinks we are propping up a lifeless government and are on a sticky wicket. Between a long war and cutting our losses, the Japanese would go for the latter. My information on Japan comes from Reischauer (the American ambassador to Japan).

THE PRESIDENT: But George, wouldn't all these countries say that Uncle Sam was a paper tiger, wouldn't we lose credibility breaking the word of three presidents, if we did as you have proposed? It would seem to be an irresponsible blow. But I gather you don't think so?

BALL: No sir. The worse blow would be that the mightiest power on earth is unable to defeat a handful of guerrillas.

THE PRESIDENT: Then you are not basically troubled by what the world would say about our pulling out?

BALL: If we were actively helping a country with a stable government, it would be a vastly different story. Western Europeans look upon us as if we got ourselves into an imprudent situation.

THE PRESIDENT: But I believe that the Vietnamese are trying to fight.

BALL: Thieu spoke the other day and said the communists would win the election.

THE PRESIDENT: I don't believe that. Does anyone believe that? (All expressed views contrary to Ball.)

MCNAMARA: Ky will fall soon. He is weak. We can't have elections there until there is physical security, and even then there will be no elections because as Cabot said, there is no democratic tradition.

MCGEORGE BUNDY: *To accept Ball's argument would be a radical switch in policy without visible evidence that it should be done.* George's analysis gives no weight to losses suffered by the other side. The world, the country, and the Vietnamese people would have alarming reactions if we got out.

RUSK: If the communist world found out that the United States would not pursue its commitment to the end, there was no telling where they would stop their expansionisms.

LODGE: I feel there is greater threat to start World War III if we don't go in. *Can't we see the similarity to our indolence at Munich?* I simply can't be as pessimistic as Ball. We have great seaports in Vietnam. We don't need to fight on roads. We have the sea. Let us visualize meeting the VC on our own terms. We don't have to spend all our time in the jungles. If we can secure our bases, the Vietnamese can secure, in time, a political movement to, one, apprehend the terrorists, and two, give intelligence to the government. The procedures for this are known. I agree the Japanese agitators don't like what we are doing, but Sato is totally in agreement with our actions. The Vietnamese have been dealt more casualties than, per capita, we suffered in the Civil War. The Vietnamese soldier is an uncomplaining soldier. He has ideas he will die for.

UNGER: I agree that this is what we have to do. We have spotted some things we want to pay attention to.

THE PRESIDENT: I think we have said enough today. Let us adjourn for now.

Following the meeting, McGeorge Bundy wrote the president referring to "rising pressure in the coming days" and recommended a fireside or formal message within the next five days. "We really cannot get an orderly and well considered decision made before that, but I doubt if we can hold the fort any longer. . . . I think it makes good sense for your government to deliberate for three days on an issue of this magnitude."[45] To wit, Ball had been heard and disposed of. But now Johnson had other "advocates" to neutralize—the Joint Chiefs.

The following day Johnson met with the Joint Chiefs to hear their responses to McNamara's program.* The dialogue offers a fascinating perspective for understanding the dilemmas which confronted Johnson—and his advisors. The Joint Chiefs, for instance, soon found themselves in the same position as Ball—they were passionate advocates of a policy option which would bring the war to a conclusion,

*Present at the meeting were McNamara; Vance; Gen. Earle Wheeler; Gen. Harold K. Johnson, chief of staff of the army; Gen. John P. McConnell, chief of staff of the air force; Admiral D. L. McDonald, chief of naval operations; Gen. Wallace M. Greene, Jr., commandant of the marine corps; Secretary of the Air Force Harold Brown; Secretary of the Navy Paul Nitze; Secretary of the Army Stanley Resor; McGeorge Bundy; Jack Valenti; and Clark Clifford.

but at unacceptable costs to political leadership. There was a remarkable difference between Johnson's questions of the Joint Chiefs and his set-up of Ball. The president sounds almost panic-stricken in his substantive "tell me it ain't so" queries. In this one meeting the president asked every "right" question—but the questions were not intended to make a difference in option selection. Rather, their purpose was to legitimize a previously selected option by creating the illusion that other views were being considered. The master of consensus was at his best in these forums:

THE PRESIDENT: I asked Secretary McNamara to invite you here to counsel with you on these problems and the ways to meet them. I want you to hear from the chiefs the alternatives open to you and then recommendations on those alternatives from a military point of view. The options open to us are: one, leave the country, with as little loss as possible; two, maintain present force and lose slowly; three, add 100,000 men, recognizing that may not be enough and adding more next year. The disadvantages of number three option are the risk of escalation, casualties high, and the prospect of a long war without victory. I would like you to start out by stating our present position as you see it, and where we can go.

ADMIRAL MCDONALD (CHIEF OF NAVAL OPERATIONS): Sending in the Marines has improved the situation. I agree with McNamara that we are committed to the extent that we can't move out. If we continue the way we are now, it will be a slow, sure victory for the other side. But putting more men in it will turn the tide and let us know what further we need to do. I wish we had done this long before.

THE PRESIDENT: But you don't know if 100,000 men will be enough. What makes you conclude that if you don't know where we are going —and what will happen—we shouldn't pause and find this out?

ADMIRAL MCDONALD: Sooner or later we will force them to the conference table.

THE PRESIDENT: But if we put in 100,000 men won't they put in an equal number, and then where will we be?

ADMIRAL MCDONALD: Not if we step up our bombing. . . .

THE PRESIDENT: Is this a chance we want to take?

ADMIRAL MCDONALD: Yes, sir, when I view the alternatives. Get out now or pour in more men.

THE PRESIDENT: Is that all?

MCDONALD: Well, I think our allies will lose faith in us.

THE PRESIDENT: We have few allies really helping us now.

MCDONALD: Take Thailand for example. If we walk out of Vietnam, the whole world will question our word. We don't have much choice.

PAUL NITZE: In that area not occupied by US forces, it is worse, as I observed on my trip out there. We have two alternatives, Mr. President. Support the Vietnamese throughout their country or stick to the secure positions we do have. We need to make it clear to the populace that we are on their side. Then gradually turn the tide of losses by aiding the ARVN at certain points.

THE PRESIDENT: What are our chances of success?

NITZE: If we want to turn the tide, by putting in more men, it would be about sixty-forty. If we gave Westmoreland all he asked for, what are our chances? I don't agree that the North Vietnamese and China won't come in. Expand the area we could maintain. In the Philippines and Greece it was shown that guerrillas can lose.

THE PRESIDENT: Would you send in more forces than Westmoreland requests?

NITZE: Yes sir. It depends on how quickly the. . . .

THE PRESIDENT: How many? Two hundred thousand instead of 100,000?

NITZE: We would need another 100,000 in January.

THE PRESIDENT: Can you do that?

NITZE: Yes, sir.

MCNAMARA: The current plan is to introduce 100,000 men with the possibility of a second 100,000 by the first of the year.

THE PRESIDENT: What reaction is this going to produce?

GENERAL WHEELER: Since we are not proposing an invasion of the North, the Soviets will step up material and propaganda, and the same with the Chicoms. The North Vietnamese might introduce more regular troops.

THE PRESIDENT: Why wouldn't North Vietnam pour in more men? Also, why wouldn't they call on volunteers from China and Russia?

WHEELER: First, they may decide they can't win by putting in force they can't afford. At most they would put in two more divisions. Beyond that, they strip their country and invite a countermove on our part. Second, on volunteers—the one thing all North Vietnam fears is the Chinese. For them to invite Chinese volunteers is to invite China taking over North Vietnam. The weight of judgment is that North Vietnam may reinforce their troops, but they can't match us on a buildup. From a military viewpoint, we can handle, if we are determined to do so, China and North Vietnam.

THE PRESIDENT: Don't you anticipate retaliation by the Soviets in the Berlin area?

WHEELER: You may have some flare-up but the lines are so tightly drawn in Berlin, that it raises the risk of escalation too quickly. Lemnitzer* thinks there will be no flare-up in Berlin. In Korea, if the Soviets undertook operations, it would be dangerous.

MCDONALD: Yes, sir. First, supply the forces Westmoreland has asked for. Second, prepare to furnish more men, 100,000, in 1966. Third, commence building in air and naval forces, and step up air attacks on North Vietnam. Fourth, bring in needed reserves and draft calls.

THE PRESIDENT: Do you have any ideas of what this will cost?

MCNAMARA: Yes, sir, twelve billion dollars in 1966.

THE PRESIDENT: Do you have any idea what effect this will have on our economy?

MCNAMARA: It would not require wage and price controls in my judgment. The price index ought not go up more than one point or two.

GENERAL MCCONNELL: If you put in these requested forces and increase air and sea effort, we can at least turn the tide to where we are not losing anymore. We need to be sure we get the best we can out of the South Vietnamese. We need to bomb all military targets available to us in North Vietnam. As to whether we can come to a satisfactory solution with these forces, I don't know. With these forces properly employed, and cutting off the VC supplies, we can surely do better than we are doing.

THE PRESIDENT: Do we have results of bombing actions and have they, in your judgment, been as fruitful and productive as we anticipated?

*Lyman Lemnitzer, chairman of the Joint Chiefs of Staff (October 1961 to July 1962) and supreme Allied commander, Europe (January 1963 to June 1969).

MCCONNELL: No, sir, they haven't been. They have been productive in South Vietnam, but not as productive in the North because we are not striking the targets that hurt them.

THE PRESIDENT: Are you seriously concerned when we change targets we escalate the war? They might send more fighters down. Can you be certain it won't escalate efforts on the ground? Would it hurt our chances at a conference if we killed civilians in this bombing, though of course we will take utmost precautions not to?

MCDONALD: We need to minimize all we can the killing of civilians.

THE PRESIDENT: Would you go beyond Westmoreland's recommendations?

MCDONALD: No, sir.

THE PRESIDENT: How many planes have we lost thus far?

MCDONALD: About 106 of all types. This is a small percentage of our total.

THE PRESIDENT: How many do we have out there?

MCDONALD: One hundred and forty-six combat. We have lost 54 combat.

THE PRESIDENT: How many Navy planes have we lost?

MCDONALD: It's in the thirties. We have about 125 Navy combat planes.

THE PRESIDENT: *Doesn't it really mean that if we follow Westmoreland's requests we are in a new war? Isn't this going off the diving board?*

MCNAMARA: If we carry forward all these recommendations, it would be a change in our policy. We have relied on the South to carry the brunt. Now we would be responsible for satisfactory military outcome.

THE PRESIDENT: *Would we be in agreement, that we would rather be out of there and make our stand somewhere else?*

GENERAL JOHNSON: The least desirable alternative is getting out. The second least is doing what we are doing. The best alternative is to get in and get the job done.

THE PRESIDENT: *But I don't know how we are going to get the job done. There are millions of Chinese.* I think they are going to put their stack in. Is this the best place to do it? We don't have the allies we had in Korea. Can we get our allies to cut off supplying the North?

MCNAMARA: No, sir, we can't prevent Japan, Britain, and the others from chartering ships to Haiphong.

THE PRESIDENT: Have we done anything to stop them?

MCNAMARA: No, we haven't put the pressure on them as we did in Cuba. But even if we did, it wouldn't stop the shipping.

BROWN: It seems that all of our alternatives are dark. I find myself in agreement with the others.

THE PRESIDENT: Is there anything to the argument that the South government will fail, and we will be asked to leave? If we try to match the enemy will we be bogged down in a protracted war and won't the government ask us to leave?

BROWN: Our lines of communication are very long, sir.

THE PRESIDENT: How long?

BROWN: About 7,000 miles from the west coast, but not too much greater than China's. The biggest weakness of the political situation is the lack of security they can offer their people.

THE PRESIDENT: Are we starting something that in two or three years we simply can't finish?

BROWN: It is costly to us to strangle slowly. But the chances of losing are less if we move in.

THE PRESIDENT: Suppose we told Ky of the requirements we need, and he turns them down. And then we have to get out and make our stand in Thailand.

BROWN: The Thais will go with the winner.

THE PRESIDENT: Well, if we don't stop in Thailand, where would we stop?

MCNAMARA: Laos, Cambodia, Thailand, Burma surely affect Malaysia. In two to three years the communist domination would stop there, but ripple effect would be great, in Japan, in India. We would have to give up some bases. Ayub would move closer to China. Greece, Turkey would move to neutralist positions. Communist agitation would increase in Africa.

GENERAL GREENE: Situation is as tough as when it started. But not as bad as it could be. Marines in the first corps areas are an example of the benefits that come to us. Here are the stakes as I see them. One, the national security stake; it is a matter of time before we would have to go in some place else. Two, there is the pledge we have made. Three, there is our prestige in the world. If you accept these stakes, there are two courses of action. One, get out. Two, stay in and win. Now, how to win in the North and in the South? The enclave concept will work. I would like to introduce enough Marines to do this. Two Marine divisions and one air wing. We have 28,000 out there now. We need an additional 72,000.

MCNAMARA: Mr. President, General Greene suggests these men over and above the Westmoreland request.

THE PRESIDENT: Then you are saying you will need 80,000 more Marines to carry this out?

GREENE: Yes, I am convinced we are making progress with the South Vietnamese, in food and construction. We are getting evidence of intelligence from the South Vietnamese. In the North, we haven't been hitting the right targets. We should hit pol (petroleum) storage, which is essential to their transportation. Also, we must destroy their airfields, their MIGs and their IL-28s.

THE PRESIDENT: What would they do?

GREENE: Nothing. We can test it by attacking pol storage. Then we should attack the industrial complex in the North. Also, they can be told by pamphlet drop why we are doing this. Then we ought to blockade Cambodia, and stop supplies from coming through there. *How long would it take? Five years, plus 500,000 troops. I think the American people would back you.*

THE PRESIDENT: How would you tell the American people what the stakes are?

GREENE: The place where they will stick by you is the national security stake.

GENERAL JOHNSON: We are in a face-down. The solution, unfortunately, is long-term. Once the military problem is solved the problem of political solution will be more difficult.

THE PRESIDENT: *If we come in with hundreds of thousands of men and billions of dollars, won't this cause China and Russia to come in? No one has given me a satisfactory answer to that.*

GENERAL JOHNSON: No, sir, I don't think they will.

THE PRESIDENT: MacArthur didn't think they would come in either.

GENERAL JOHNSON: Yes, sir, but this is not comparable to Korea.

THE PRESIDENT: But China has plenty of divisions to move in, don't they?

GENERAL JOHNSON: Yes, they do.

THE PRESIDENT: Then what would we do?

GENERAL JOHNSON: If so, we have another ball game.

THE PRESIDENT: But I have to take into account they will.

GENERAL JOHNSON: I would increase the buildup near North Vietnam, and increase action in Korea.

THE PRESIDENT: If they move in thirty-one divisions, what does it take on our part?

MCNAMARA: Under favorable conditions they could sustain thirty-one divisions and assuming the Thais contributed forces, it would take 300,-000 plus what we need to combat the VC.

THE PRESIDENT: *But remember they are going to write stories about this like they did in the Bay of Pigs. Stories about me and my advisors. That is why I want you to think carefully, very, very carefully about alternatives and plans.* Looking back on the Dominican Republic, General, would you have done anything differently?

GENERAL JOHNSON: I would have cleaned out part of the city and gone in, with the same numbers.

THE PRESIDENT: Aren't you concerned about Chinese forces moving into North Vietnam?

GENERAL JOHNSON: Sir, there is no evidence of forces, only teams involved in logistics. It could be they are investigating areas which they could control later.

THE PRESIDENT: What is your reaction to Ho's statement he is ready to fight for twenty years?

GENERAL JOHNSON: I believe it.

THE PRESIDENT: What would you describe as Ho's problems?

GENERAL JOHNSON: His biggest problem is doubt about what our next move will be. He's walking a tightrope between the Reds and the Chicoms. Also, he is worrying about the loss of caches of arms in the South.

THE PRESIDENT: Are we killing civilians in these Viet Cong areas?

GENERAL WHEELER: Certain civilians accompanying the Viet Cong are being killed. It can't be helped.

STANLEY RESOR (SECRETARY OF THE ARMY): Of the three courses the one we should follow is the McNamara plan. We simply can't go back on our commitment. Our allies are watching carefully.

THE PRESIDENT: *Do all of you think the Congress and the people will go along with 600,000 people and billions of dollars being spent 10,000 miles away?*

RESOR: The Gallup poll shows people are basically behind our commitment.

THE PRESIDENT: But, if you make a commitment to jump off a building and you find out how high it is, you may want to withdraw that commitment. I judge though that the big problem is one of national security. Is that right? Well, then, what about our intelligence. How do they (the VC) know what we are doing before we do it? What about the B-52 raid; weren't the Viet Cong gone before we got there?

MCNAMARA: They get it from infiltration in the South Vietnamese forces.

THE PRESIDENT: Are we getting good intelligence out of the North?

MCNAMARA: Only reconnaissance and technical soundings, we have none from combat intelligence.

It was now clear to the president that this would be a long war. The dialogue was without optimism or short-run terms of reference. The president's military advisors emphasized that it would take hundreds of thousands of men and several years to achieve military stalemate. The Joint Chiefs urged Johnson to seek public support on national security grounds. The president was advised to call up the Reserves and National Guard and *commit* the United States to winning the war. The president, however, seemed more concerned about stories people would write—about what history would say.

Prior to the meeting with the Joint Chiefs, Johnson had asked

McGeorge Bundy to write a paper which focused on criticism the
administration *could* expect *if* McNamara's proposals were adopted.
At the meeting Johnson told the Chiefs that "some congressmen and
senators think we are to be the most discredited people in the world.
What Bundy will now tell you is *not his opinion nor mine,* but what
we hear. I think you ought to face up to this too." But really the
argument they were about to hear was George Ball's. If ever there
occurred a "domestication of dissent"[46] the Bundy memorandum is
it. Bundy read from his paper: "The argument we will face is one, for
ten years every step we have taken has been based on a previous
failure and caused us to take another step which failed. As we get
further into the bag, we get deeply bruised. Also we have made
excessive claims we haven't been able to realize. Two, also after
twenty years of warning about war in Asia, we are now doing what
MacArthur and others have warned us about. We are about to fight
a war we can't fight and win as the country we are trying to help is
quitting. Three, there is a failure on our own to fully realize what
guerrilla war is like. We are sending conventional troops to do an
unconventional job. Four, how long—how much? Can we take casualties over five years—aren't we talking about military solution when
the solution is really political? Why can't we interdict better? Why
are our bombings so fruitless? Why can't we blockade the coast? Why
can't we improve our intelligence? Why can't we find the VC?"
Bundy was correct—*others,* not administration advisors, were serious about these questions. But when cast as comments by outsiders,
the queries assumed far *less* significance than if a McNamara,
Rusk, or Bundy had raised them. During a period of great stress
and uncertainty decision-makers were probably comforted by
Bundy's presentation—they may have even felt good upon hearing it.

The meeting with the Joint Chiefs was followed by smaller and
more informal meetings with Rusk, McNamara, Ball, Wheeler,
Bundy, Clifford, John McCloy, and Arthur Dean. As the decision time
approached, the group dwindled in size. The evening at Camp David
was spent with only McNamara, Arthur Goldberg, and Clark Clifford.
During this meeting the president's trusted friend Clark Clifford
repeated the warnings of a May 17 letter[47] in which he argued that
U.S. ground troops should be kept to a minimum because "a substantial buildup of US ground troops would be construed by the Communists, and by the world, as a determination on our part to win the war

on the ground. *This could be a quagmire. It could turn into an open-ended commitment on our part that would take more and more ground troops, without a realistic hope of ultimate victory."* At Camp David, Clifford continued this earlier line of reasoning: "I don't think we can win in South Vietnam. If we send in 100,000 men, the North Vietnamese will meet us. If North Vietnam runs out of men, the Chinese will send in volunteers. Russia and China don't intend for us to win the war. I can't see anything but catastrophe for my country."* Clifford's warning was heard but ignored. There was now too much momentum, too many advocates of escalation to stop the buildup. One important decision still remained, "how" would the United States raise the necessary manpower?

The Decision

Before dispatching McNamara to Saigon the president sent up several trial balloons regarding the mobilization of Reserves and National Guard. During a July 9 press conference Johnson warned: "Whatever is required I am sure will be supplied. We have met and taken action to meet the requests made by General Westmoreland, and as other needs appear, we will promptly meet them. We committed our power and our national honor, and that has been reaffirmed by three Presidents. I have neither a rosy nor a gloomy report to make. It will require understanding and endurance and patriotism. We have suffered 160,000 casualties since World War II, but we did not allow Greece or Turkey or Iran or Formosa or Lebanon or others to fall to aggressors, and we don't plan to let up until the aggression ceases."[48]

*A former White House official wrote me that "you quote Clark Clifford's scrutinizing [letter] of that fateful summer; he warned against the forthcoming involvement in a brilliant manner and I'm sure he was honest. But I remember that in private sessions both he and Abe Fortas of the 'Kitchen Cabinet' believed strongly the President could not 'cut and run' in Vietnam or even diminish our commitment. It isn't disingenuous of Clifford or anyone being hypocritical—just the effect on a man of sitting alone committing his ideas to paper and then in the presence of the President formulating them differently not because of intimidation but because face-to-face it is impossible not to consider the human factor, including the pressures upon the man before you that are easy to ignore in the solitude of your own study."

Four days later at a July 13 news conference (with McNamara and Lodge leaving the next day for Saigon) the president referred to the possible mobilization of National Guard and Reserve units:

> It is quite possible that new and serious decisions will be necessary in the near future. Any substantial increase in the present level of our efforts to turn back the aggressors in South Viet-Nam will require steps to insure that our reserves of men and equipment of the United States remain entirely adequate for any and all emergencies. . . .
>
> Our national honor is at stake. Our word is at stake. And it must be obvious to all Americans that they would not want the President of their country to follow any course that was inconsistent with our commitment or with our national honor. . . .
>
> As I said in my opening statement, the aggression has increased. The forces that are pursuing that aggression have greatly increased in number. It will be necessary to resist that aggression and, therefore, to have substantially larger increments of troops which we have been supplying from time to time.
>
> I do not think that anyone can tell at this date any special figure that will be required, but I think that following Ambassador Lodge and Secretary McNamara's trip, we will have a better estimate of what the rest of the year will hold for us.[49]

In the end President Johnson's political instincts played the determining role. Despite a lengthy report from the attorney-general which confirmed the president's legal authority to commit the Reserves *without* congressional authorization, *President Johnson did not want a great national debate on the war.* The rank-heavy Reserves would cost at least two billion dollars and take one year to train, pay, and equip for war. The president feared that a call-up would signal Hanoi and the Soviet Union that we were ready for war (just what McNamara believed was tactically necessary), and this only raised the risk of a major superpower confrontation. The president preferred the soft-sell approach but he needed a new plan. While that plan was being devised, however, Johnson realized that it was in *his* interest to keep the Reserves issue open for *public* discourse. Meanwhile Secretary McNamara was sent "back to the drawing-board" because the president, according to William Bundy, "had looked in the eye the consequences of a course of action involving taking the matter, on you might say a decisive and great debate basis, to the Congress at that particular moment of time." By the July 27 meeting "the upshot was a resubmission of the same decision, but in a form that didn't require a great debate, and just put a different cast on it. And that the presidential statement would do the work, and there would not be a great debate."[50] The change in plans was evident in a memo which McGeorge Bundy wrote to the president following the July 21 meeting: "Bob is carrying out your orders to plan this whole job with only $300–400 million in immediate new funds. But I think you will want to know that he thinks our posture of candor and responsibility would be better if we ask for 2 billion to take us through the end of the calendar year, on the understanding that we will come back for more, if necessary. Bob is afraid we simply cannot get away with the idea that a call-up of the planned magnitude can be paid for by anything so small as another few hundred million. Cy Vance told me that other day that the overall cost is likely to be on the order of $8 billion in the coming year and I can understand Bob's worry that in the nature of things, these projected costs will be sure to come out pretty quickly, especially if he looks as if he was trying to pull a fast one. *I have not told Bob that I am reporting his worry to you; don't give me away.*"[51] Bundy recalled that by this time "my own role has become that of the staff officer who knows the big decision is made and is working to help in its execution. Obviously I have had my own views on what ought to be done and how, but since on balance I am in favor of trying harder, not heading for the exit, I am ready to help the President do it his way; he's the boss. I am for more explanation, and more Congressional participation; I am in favor of more emphasis on the GVN contribution; I am in favor of a less open-ended commitment to [General Westmoreland]. The President knows all that and prefers his course. On negotiating when we can, on keeping out of war with China, we have at this point no difference. I help him. That's an indispensable part of what the White House staff is for."[52]

Between July 21 and July 26 President Johnson decided that he would not fight a major war at the troop levels recommended by either McNamara or the Joint Chiefs. Nor would he accept the consequences of what he perceived as George Ball's negotiated surrender. "In 1965," McGeorge Bundy later recalled, ". . . I thought that a decision to cut our losses and settle for the best we could get with the level of commitment we then had would have had very grave consequences in the world and the country, as well as in Vietnam, because *in fact* it was, and would be seen as, doing less than those who counted on us had been given all sorts of reasons to expect—not least in the series of public statements made by the President himself in preceding months. . . ."[53] Johnson would not lose Vietnam by running away. And so the decision was made to lose Vietnam slowly. The president and his advisors, of course, did not see it this way, but in retrospect it seems perfectly clear that the United States had little chance of achieving its limited goal against a country waging total war.

On July 27 the president convened a special meeting of the National Security Council to discuss McNamara's recommendation and the president's decision. Bromley Smith's "summary notes" provide a useful perspective to both the dialogue and the framing of issues.[54] The president first asked Secretary Rusk to review the political situation. Rusk reported that the Chinese remained opposed to any negotiations between North Vietnam and the US/GVN. The United States did not know what the North Vietnamese would do if Rolling Thunder attacks were stopped. Moscow and Hanoi were somewhat "cautious"—and the United States intended to keep contacts open in the event a new position evolved. Finally, the "actions we are taking should be presented publicly in a low key but in such a way as to convey accurately that we are determined to prevent South Vietnam from being taken over by Hanoi. At the same time, we seek to avoid a confrontation with either the Chinese Communists or the Soviet Union."

McNamara then followed with a summary of the military situation: (1) The number of Viet Cong forces has increased and the percentage of these forces committed to battle has increased; (2) The geographic area of South Vietnam controlled by the Viet Cong has increased; (3) The Viet Cong has isolated the cities and disrupted the economy of South Vietnam. The cities are separated from the countryside; (4) Increased desertions from the South Vietnamese army have prevented an increase in the total number of South Vietnamese troops available for combat; (5) About half of all army helicopters are now in South Vietnam in addition to over 500 U.S. planes. The secretary then focused on the military requirements: (a) More combat battalions from the United States are necessary. A total of thirteen additional battalions needed to be sent now. On June 15 a total of 75,000 men, or fifteen battalions, was announced; (b) A total of twenty-eight battalions was now necessary; (c) Over the next fifteen months, 350,-000 men would be added to regular U.S. forces; (d) In January, Congress would be asked for a supplementary appropriation to pay the costs of the Vietnam War. We would ask now for a billion, in addition to the existing budget.

The president then took control of the meeting: "The situation in Vietnam is deteriorating. Even though we now have 80 to 90,000 men there, the situation is not very safe. We have these choices:"

   a. Use our massive power, including SAC, to bring the enemy to his knees. Less than 10% of our people urge this course of action.

   b. We could get out on the ground that we don't belong there. Not very many people feel this way about Vietnam. Most feel that our national honor is at stake and that we must keep our commitments there.

   c. We could keep our forces at the present level, approximately 80,000 men, but suffer the consequences of losing additional territory and of accepting increased casualties. We could "hunker up." No one is recommending this course.

   d. We could ask for everything we might desire from Congress—money, authority to call up the reserves, acceptance of the deployment of more combat battalions. This dramatic course of action would involve declaring a state of emergency and a request for several billion dollars. Many favor this course. However, if we do go all out in this fashion, Hanoi would be able to ask the Chinese Communists and the Soviets to increase aid and add to their existing commitments.

   e. We have chosen to do what is necessary to meet the present situation, but not to be unnecessarily provocative to either the Russians or the Communist Chinese. We will give the commanders the men they say they need and, out of existing material in the U.S., we will give them the material they say they need. We will get the necessary money in the new budget and will use our transfer authority until January. We will neither brag about what we were doing or thunder at the Chinese Communists and the Russians.

Johnson explained that he favored the last option—doing what was necessary to meet the situation but avoiding a call-up of Reserves. In

The Vantage Point Johnson wrote that he had concluded that "the last course was the right one. I had listened to and weighed all the arguments and counterarguments for each of the possible lines of argument. . . . Did anyone object to this course of action? I questioned each man in turn. Did he agree? Each nodded his approval—said yes."[55] But Johnson failed to understand the nature of unanimity and its future costs. To wit, when the president had conducted a similar poll at the July 21 meeting (where only the first four options existed) unanimity also prevailed, *but in favor of a Reserve call-up.* Now, less than a week later, Johnson secured another unanimous decision but without the Reserves. The president had succeeded in forging consensus between his advisors on the decision to move ahead with the Americanization of the war. "The key moment," according to David Halberstam, "was when he came to General Wheeler and stood looking directly at him for a moment. 'Do you, General Wheeler, agree?' Wheeler nodded his agrement. It was said, by someone who was present, an extraordinary moment, like watching a lion-tamer dealing with some of the great lions. Everyone in the room knew Wheeler objected, that the Chiefs wanted more, that they wanted a wartime footing and a call-up of the reserves; the thing they feared most was a partial war and a partial commitment.[56] Wheeler later explained that "we felt that it would be desirable to have a reserve call-up in order to make sure that the people of the US knew that we were in a war and not engaged at some two-penny military adventure. Because we didn't think it was going to prove to be a two-penny military adventure by any manner or means." The military advocated closing the port of Haiphong and, according to Wheeler, "really undertaking an air and naval campaign against North Vietnam that would teach them what war was all about, [so] they wouldn't be so damned eager to indulge in one."[57] According to the BDM study, "throughout early 1965, planners within the Department of the Army and at CONARC Headquarters generally assumed that any augmentation of the Army's force structure would include at least a partial call-up of Reserve components for a maximum period of 12 months. Troop lists for these contingency plans were rendered useless on July 28, 1965, when President Johnson announced plans for the major infusion of US forces into South Vietnam, an immediate increase to 125,000 men, with additional forces to be deployed as necessary. This buildup would be accomplished by increased draft calls."[58]

For the moment, President Johnson's decision was a masterful one. He actually succeeded in presenting himself as a president exercising restraint in the commitment of U.S. troops. Moreover, most political elites and certainly the general public viewed the decision with a sigh of relief. The United States was not, after all, going to war—or so the soft sell looked. The president could pursue his guns and butter strategy without exposing the depth of U.S. invovlement. The decision, according to William Bundy, reflected President Johnson's "hope and gamble that by gradual rather than abrupt techniques of leadership the country and the Congress could be brought to support to the full both war and domestic reform—or that the war would develop in line with the more optimistic predictions given to him, and thus reduce the choice."[59]

What began on July 17 as "the day Vance told McNamara that the President had decided to go ahead with the plan to deploy 34 US battalions and that he was favorably disposed to the call-up of reserves and extension of tour of active duty personnel" ended with the July 28 press conference. During a backgrounding session Secretary McNamara reviewed the five alternatives considered by the president and his advisors: (a) intensification of military pressure on the Communist block; (b) completely withdrawing all U.S. forces from South Vietnam; (c) remaining in South Vietnam with essentially the present force structure; (d) providing additional forces to South Vietnam together with a call-up of Reserve components to replace these forces; and (e) providing additional forces to South Vietnam and activating additional units of the regular forces to replace these forces. McNamara, speaking rather candidly, noted that "little consideration was given to alternatives (a) and (b) above." Alternative (c) "would limit risks and expenses, but would result in a deteriorating situation. After considerable thought alternative (e) was determined to be the most desirable since components of the reserves are a perishable commodity, i.e., Congress would probably only authorize the call-up for a period of one year. It was considered the most acceptable course of action to continue to increase the readiness of the reserve components and use them only when they can be utilized more effectively than it was thought they might be at this time." Moreover, according to the secretary of defense, the rapidly deteriorating situation in Saigon left the United States with no legitimate question other than "what additional forces were required"—not whether these forces could accomplish their goals.

In retrospect, most advisors did *not* know of the president's decision on the forty-four battalions *because* Johnson still wanted debate on the issue. This offers a fascinating insight into how presidents can utilize an advisory system to legitimize the process of option selection to political elites while building an internal consensus. Prof. Alexander George has identified four reasons for such consultation between presidents and advisors. First, and most obvious, presidents meet with advisors for gathering information, thereby satisfying their cognitive needs. Second, presidents meet with advisors to seek emotional support in coping with the strains and uncertainties of critical decisions. Third, presidents seek from advisors their understanding and support for the politics of a decision. Advisors need to be brought on board; the president needs to shape a consensus within the administration. Finally, the president is *expected* to consult with advisors by both Congress and the general public. Decisions are often legitimized by seeking the opinions of experts and giving the appearance that various options are under consideration. "Of course," George warns, "a President's incentives for consulting may include more than one of these objectives, and his purposes in doing so may vary from one situation to another."[60] What better way to lead the nation into war than to let American citizens believe that the experts were carefully deliberating on all available policy options. Besides, the president was undoubtedly undergoing personal stress and the consultation provided emotional support during a period of great uncertainty. But the president had good political reasons for stalling on a decision of this magnitude, especially if a Reserve call-up would be involved. Lyndon Johnson had no intention of leading his country into war with both Medicare and civil rights legislation locked in crucial committee debate. Sending McNamara to Saigon, the NSC and cabinet meetings, established a timetable of their own. The formal announcement could not come until late July—and this suited the president's short-term political needs. The technique of leadership failed in the long run. President Johnson soon learned exactly what George Ball had meant when he wrote, "once on the tiger's back you cannot be sure of picking a place to dismount."[61] I am reminded of a cable from Graham Martin, U.S. ambassador to Thailand, to William Bundy on the eve of Bundy's "Middle Way" hearing: "As a student for a quarter century of the limited application of military force to achieve fulfillment of national policy, I still insist that achievement of our objectives in SEA is a perfectly feasible operation. But the application of military force must be kept limited, and tactical military advantages of increasing the force must always be weighed in view of the fact that military force here, while vital and essential, is nevertheless a small element in a much more complex political and psychological operation." Martin concluded his lengthy critique of those who favored military escalation with a prediction: "If we fail to achieve our objective in South Vietnam, I am rather certain that future historians will record that it was only because we refused to use intelligently the resources available to us."[62] In the next chapter we will weigh this failure in intelligence with the failure of political leadership, and we will see how the president and his advisors contributed to the planning of a tragedy—tragic because it need not have happened.

V

Components of the Decision Process

Thirty thousand American troops died in Vietnam between July 28, 1965, and the inaugeration of Richard Nixon in January 1969. "How," asked James C. Thomson, Jr., "did men of superior ability, sound training and high ideals—American policymakers of the 1960s—create such a costly and divisive policy?"[1] I believe that the primary source documents provide several answers to Thomson's legitimate query—each of these will be explored below.

How Valid Were the Assumptions?

The documents show that the principals accepted containment of communism and the domino theory as basic premises for formulating policy and not as hypotheses for anlysis. Moreover, the principals approached the problem definition stage with twenty years of intellectual baggage shaped by visions of Soviet-inspired and aggressive communism. There was an almost talmudic adherence to the containment strategy outlined by George Kennan which called for an "unalterable counterforce at every point where they [Communists] show signs of encroachment."[2] But in 1965 the principals expanded significantly on the definition of containment and, for that matter, of world communism. Containment of Soviet aggression was originally conceived as limited in both geographical scope and objective. As Vietnam *became* an increasingly important component in U.S. global interests, not losing Vietnam assumed an equally high stature. According to the BDM study, "Early on, American leadership mistakenly believed Vietnam to be vital not only for itself, but for what they thought its 'loss' would mean internationally and domestically. Once the commitment was made, each subsequent president reaffirmed the commitment rather than reassessing the basic rationale as to whether vital US interests were involved or not."[3]

The cognitive error was not Johnson's alone. Six postwar presidents and their advisors refused to think critically about the changing nature of Asian communism. As the BDM study put it:

> All of the presidents had lived through Manchuria, Munich, Poland, Yalta, the "loss" of China, the Korean War, and the McCarthy era. Each drew the lesson that the United States could not afford to be soft on communism, specifically that he could not be the president who permitted the "loss" of Vietnam to communism. *Their close advisers reinforced their own anticommunist orientation. There is no question that the presidents and their advisers were conditioned by such past experiences when considering how to deal with the conflict in Vietnam.*
>
> Like leaders in any organization, presidents are not immune to confusing dissent with disloyalty. The Vietnam experience should point to some of the dangers in such confusion. *Premises fail to receive the critical examination they require in formulating a sound policy that keeps pace with changes in a dynamic world.* There was a time when monolithic communism may have justified the anticommunist approach of the US in the 1950s. Equally, it seems possible that the US might have tailored its policy toward Vietnam more closely to observable changes in the Sino-Soviet relationship earlier than it did (during the Nixon presidency). Unfortunately, the problem arose that the investment of US political, economic and military prestige, not to mention US casualties, came to override the intrinsic importance of Vietnam to the US.[4]

Decision-makers constantly justified their views on the necessity of Communist containment with references to another "appeasement at Munich" or another "loss of China." These "simplistic adages were often used," according to the BDM study, "in lieu of developing more precise and perhaps more convincing explanations for making a particular policy decision. In addition, they often came to be voiced indiscriminately, leading to generalization, overuse, and misapplication."[5] The BDM study identified a direct cause-and-effect relationship: "The American experience in Vietnam points to the danger of having one fundamental principle—anticommunism—elevated to the status of doctrine for all regions of the world. By elevating a principle to the level of doctrine, further debate of the subject is minimized, thereby reducing the possibility that legitimate dissenting views will receive sufficient attention at the national policy-making level. What tended to happen in Vietnam was that consensus building on the premise of anticommunism was achieved to give coherence to Vietnam policy at the national level, at the sacrifice of a needed closer examination of the accuracy of that premise."[6]

The logical companion to containment was the domino theory. Clark Clifford, for example, referred to the "solid phalanx of advice from [LBJ's] main advisors . . . the unanimous sentiment among his senior advisors that the domino theory was unquestionably so."[7] "The 'domino' theory," according to the BDM study, "saw any conflict with the communists as a test of the US's national resolve and credibility. The communists had threatened to take over 'free world' territory in Berlin, Korea, Iran, Guatemala, Lebanon and the Dominican Republic and actions taken by the US to prevent the loss of these territories were viewed by many as American Cold War successes. Conversely, the communists gaining control over China and Cuba were viewed as Cold War defeats for the U.S. Each successive US president found himself bound, in large measure, by his predecessor's doctrine and thereafter often analyzed issues from the same perspectives, continuing policies long after they had outlived their usefulness."[8] As a result even support for the repressive and authoritarian Diem was justified as a regrettable means to a nobler end— saving the world from Soviet-inspired Communist aggression. Decision-makers eventually abandoned all of the original preconditions for policy—particularly a stable and meritorious GVN—to pursue the ultimate goal of halting communism in Southeast Asia. Acceptance of the containment legacy led decision-makers to become preoccupied with the question of "how" the government of South Vietnam could be saved, and never with "why" the government was worth saving. Moreover, the stakes were simply too great—freedom stood in the balance. Dean Rusk placed the stakes within the parameter of another world war: "My generation of students was led down the trail into the catastrophe of a World War II which could have been prevented. We came out of that war with a strong feeling that collective security was the key to the prevention of World War III. It was written into Article I of the United Nations Charter and reinforced by security treaties in this hemisphere, across the Atlantic, and across the Pacific. Vietnam involved to some of us the integrity of the system of collective security whose main purpose was to prevent World War III."[9]

One of the best examples of how these views of the world influenced the problem definition stage occurred *just prior to* Secretary McNamara's trip to Saigon, when the president met with his consultants on foreign affairs.* Writing under separate cover to his personal friend McGeorge Bundy, consultant and former State Department official Roswell Gilpatric summarized the consensus of these consultants: "The US *has a commitment* in South Vietnam, nonfulfillment of which would have extremely grave consequences not only in Asia but in Europe. (2) Of the courses of action open to the US in order to make good on that commitment, some are either inadequate or undesirable, viz., (a) the role up to now played by US forces, namely, training, supporting, advising, and otherwise assisting the South Vietnamese, is not enough to keep South Vietnam from losing out to the Viet Cong backed up by the North Vietnamese, (b) strikes against the Hanoi-Haiphong area would probably cause the USSR to react positively because it would otherwise be shown incapable of protecting North Vietnam. (3) Hence, in order to hold on in South Vietnam, *the US faces a new role: that is taking a major part in the combat itself.* This means large additional forces and probably much heavier casualties. To carry out this role with some prospect of success calls for the application of whatever amounts of military power may be needed, perhaps as much as brought to bear in Korea fifteen years ago."[10]

William Bundy's report on the meeting graphically depicts these shared views of the world:

---

*A group of distinguished foreign policy experts picked during the 1964 campaign to lend credibility to Johnson's foreign policy background: Robert Lovett, John McCloy, Arthur Dean, Gen. Omar Bradley, John Cowles, Dean Acheson.

1. Stakes and Objectives in South Vietnam

The group, with the possible exception of Mr. [Arthur] Larson, felt that *the stakes were very high indeed.* They concurred in the Administration judgment that Thailand could not be held if South Vietnam were taken over, and they thought that the effects on Japan and India could be most serious. They particularly felt that the effect in Europe might also be most serious, and that de Gaulle would find many takers for his argument that the US could not be counted on to defend Europe. They also felt that South Vietnam was a *crucial test* of the ability of the free world and of the US to counter the Communist tactic of "wars of national liberation," and that a US defeat would necessarily lead to worldwide questioning whether US commitments could be relied on. It was the feeling of the group that these consequences would be accentuated if the US by its own decision withdrew from South Vietnam, or if the US suffered a military defeat there. On the other hand, the group felt that the consequences would not be much reduced if a Communist takeover took place as a result of a change in government in Saigon, as a result of which the US was asked to leave. *Mr. Larson appeared to dissent from this assessment, in line with his over-all view that we should be seeking UN action or serious negotiations.*

2. Increase of Combat Forces in South Vietnam

In line with their view of the grave stakes, the group generally felt that there should be no question of making whatever combat force increases were required. Several members of the group thought that our actions to date had perhaps been too restrained, and had been misconstrued by Hanoi that we were less than wholly determined.

3. Prognosis of the Situation

Mr. McCloy spoke at some length—both in the Panel and in the later plenary session—on the degree to which he had been impressed during the discussion with the toughness of the situation. He thought that it was most unlikely that merely blunting the monsoon offensive would bring Hanoi to a negotiating mood, and that the situation would probably remain critical for a long time. He was particularly concerned that the Soviets might be brought increasingly to what he called an "annealing" of the Sino-Soviet relationship, i.e., the Soviets competing with the ChiComs and acting on parallel lines, although with no necessary resolution of the basic policy differences between them.

While others did not express themselves at length on this question, it seemed clear that Mr. McCloy's view had many takers both in the Panel and in the plenary session.

In the plenary session, Mr. Dean said that he thought there was a great deal of sentiment in the country for doing whatever it took, if we were going to go on at all. Mr. Lovett made the point that it was not useful to talk about "victory," that what was really involved was preventing the expansion of Communism by force; in a sense, avoiding defeat. This view seemed to be generally shared.[11]

The Third Phase

The assumption by McNamara, Westmoreland, and the Joint Chiefs that the Viet Cong were about to abandon their successful guerrilla tactics in favor of more conventional regiment-size confrontations was pivotal to the reasoning of the July 28 decision. According to McNamara, "the enemy clearly was moving into the third phase of revolutionary warfare, committing regiments and subsequently divisions to seize and retain territory and to destroy the government's troops and eliminate all vestiges of government control."[12] In his memoirs Admiral Sharp wrote, "in early June we had become very concerned that the communists might be about ready to increase the intensity of the conflict. Evidence indicated that the North Vietnamese were now capable of mounting regiment-size operations in many locations throughout the country and battalion-size operations almost anyplace."[13]

Secretary McNamara's forty-four–battalion request was predicated on the assumption that U.S. troops, for the most part, would be engaging main force and not guerrilla units. But the president's advisors were in bitter disagreement over the question of a Third Stage. The case provides an excellent example of how a determined president might have shifted the burden of proof to Westmoreland or McNamara and received answers which were totally incompatible with the preferred option. George Ball, the CIA, the State Department, McGeorge Bundy, and William Bundy all recorded their *rejection* of Westmoreland's claim that the so-called Third Stage was underway. Unfortunately, little of the correspondence between advisors ever reached the president's desk, especially since Johnson acknowledged its import ("he seemed to agree") when Ball raised the point during the July 21 meeting.[14]

The debate at the staff level is quite revealing. After reading McNamara's June 26 memorandum, William Bundy instructed the State Department Office of Intelligence and Research to examine whether or not the Communists were moving into the Third Stage phase of warfare as predicted by General Giap.[15] In a July 23, 1965, *Secret—Limited Distribution* report, State Department officials concluded "that their pattern of behavior in Vietnam to date and their probable expectations as to the future argue *against the hypothesis that the communists are preparing to enter the third stage. . . .* We do not believe that the criteria established by Giap for the third stage —size of unit, scale of operation, and nature of attack—have been or are about to be met in South Vietnam. Our examination of Viet Cong capabilities, the campaign against GVN lines of communication, the communist attack pattern, and the content of communist propaganda, persuades us rather that the VC will continue to employ guerrilla tactics with only intermittent recourse to spectacular, multi-battalion attacks against major ARVN reinforcement, and are not now capable of initiating a drastically different phase of warfare."[16] Moreover, it was unwise to equate increased numbers with a basic change in strategy: "The role of attacks in Communist strategy in South Vietnam has been a steadily diminishing one. In 1962 there were 5,509 attacks; in 1963 there were 4,494; in 1964 there were 1,833. At the same time the incidence of acts of terror has increased markedly with 8,875 in 1962; 9,375 in 1963; and 18,656 in 1964. This pattern was accelerated in the first six months with a total of 406 attacks as compared with 9,324 terror incidents, or roughly a better than 20 to 1 ratio of terror attacks in the first six months of 1965, as compared to a roughly 10 to 1 ratio in 1964."

The report concluded that to accept the assumption of a conventional phase was to be victimized by Communist propaganda: "While both Hanoi and NFLSV propaganda continue to claim 'bigger and bigger' victories for the 'Liberation Armed Forces and Guerrillas' *there are no indications that they have altered their traditional guerrilla strategy and tactics, despite occasional references to the development of conventional warfare in the South."* The State Department cited Ho Chi Minh's remarks that "we are determined to fight till final victory even if we have to go on fighting another 5 years, 10 years, 20 years or even longer" as *"hardly suggesting that the DRV is pushing for an early victory by shifting to conventional warfare."*

No doubt this was a period of greater intensification of the war effort by the DRV/VC. Taylor had cabled President Johnson on July 11, for example, that "the intensification of the war as reflected in recent major military encounters *has created a feeling* that the military aspect is approaching some climactic stage. The *aura* surrounding the success or failure of the VC monsoon offensive puts a premium on its outcome with the prospect that the apparent victor will gather the confidence—and concomitant support from the people— essential to successful resolution of the situation."[17] A CIA report of June 29 maintained, however, that VC capability to mount and sustain large-scale military engagements at reinforced regimental strength reflected "no marked change as yet in the essential guerrilla character of the VC military effort."[18] More intensive, yes. Larger scale, yes. Change in basic military tactics, no.

George Ball also rejected McNamara's "unproven" assumption of a Third Stage.[19] Writing to the president, Ball noted that "implicit in arguments for greatly augmented United States combat forces in South Vietnam is the assumption that the Viet Cong have entered— or are about to enter—their so-called 'third phase' of warfare, having progressed from relatively small-scale hit and run operations to large unit, fixed position conventional warfare. *Yet we have no basis for assuming that the Viet Cong will fight a war on our terms* (McGeorge Bundy's very point to McNamara)[20] when they can continue to fight the kind of war they fought so well against both the French and the GVN." Ball noted that "we can scarcely expect [General Giap] to accommodate us by adopting our preferred method of combat, regardless of how many troops we send. There is every reason to suppose that the Viet Cong will avoid providing good targets for our massive bombing and superior firepower."

In his July 1 memo to the president, William Bundy agreed with Ball's rejection of McNamara's thesis: "As for major additional ground deployments, the first argument is simply whether they would be militarily effective. As the Ball paper points out, Hanoi is by no means committed to a really conventional type of war and they could easily go on making significant gains while giving us precious few opportunities to hit them."[21]

Even after the July 21 NSC meeting, Chester Cooper tried to convince McGeorge Bundy to convince McNamara that "we and the

GVN will be faced with the problem of guerrilla rather than positional warfare."[22] But by now reasonable questions of the Third Stage were listened to but not heard. The momentum was simply too great, the reasons perceived as too just, the lessons of history too clear—for erroneous tactics to have thrown things off schedule.

Do We Still Lose Even If We Win?

A great deal of uncertainty pervaded the decision process. On July 2 Secretary McNamara asked General Wheeler to form a small group of experts to address the question "If we do everything we can, can we have assurance of winning in South Vietnam?"[23] General Wheeler asked General Goodpaster, assistant to the chairman, JCS, to chair the group, and John McNaughton, assistant secretary of defense, provided the staff support. McNaughton, McNamara's closest civilian associate, offered a fascinating perspective on the degree of uncertainty facing decision-makers in early July. He believed that the forty-four–battalion program would be sufficient only through 1965 and urged Goodpaster to "produce a clear articulation of what our strategy is for winning the war in South Vietnam, tough as that articulation will be in the nature of the problem." McNaughton raised several important points: "I think we might avoid some spinning of wheels if we simply assumed that the GVN will not be able to increase its forces in the relevant time period. Indeed, from what Westy has reported about the battalions being chewed up and about their showing some signs of reluctance to engage in offensive operations, we might even have to ask the question whether we can expect them to maintain present levels of men—or more accurately, present levels of effectiveness." McNaughton offered a particularly astute assessment of the political situation in Saigon:

> Is it necessary for us to make some assumption with respect to the nature of the Saigon government? History does not encourage us to believe that Ky's government will endure throughout the time period relevant to the study. Ky's behavior is such that it is hard to predict his impact—he could, by his "revolutionary" talk and by his repressive measures generate either a genuine nationalist spirit or a violent reaction of some sort. I would think that the study must make some observa-

tion, one way or the other, as to things which might happen to the government which would have a significant effect on the conclusions of the study. My own thought is that almost anything within the realm of likelihood can happen in the Saigon government, short of the formation of a government which goes neutral or asks us out, without appreciably affecting the conduct of the war. *The key point may be whether the Army rather than the government holds together.*

With regard to the question "If we do everything we can, can we have assurance of winning in South Vietnam?":

One key question, of course, is what we mean by the words "assurance" and "win." My view is that the degree of "assurance" should be fairly high—better than 75% (whatever that means). With respect to the word "win," this I think means that we succeed in demonstrating to the VC that they cannot win; this, of course, is victory for us only if it is, with a high degree of probability, a way station toward a favorable settlement in South Vietnam. I see such a favorable settlement as one in which the VC terrorism is substantially eliminated and, obviously, there are no longer large-scale VC attacks; the central South Vietnamese government (without having taken in the Communists) should be exercising fairly complete sovereignty over most of South Vietnam. I presume that we would rule out the ceding to the VC (either tacitly or explicitly) of large areas of the country. More specifically, the Brigadier Thompson suggestion that we withdraw to enclaves and sit it out for a couple of years is not what we have in mind for purposes of this study.

At the moment, I do not see how the study can avoid addressing the question as to how long our forces will have to remain in order to achieve a "win" and the extent to which the presence of those forces over a long period of time might, by itself, nullify the "win." . . . *I think we should find a way to indicate how badly the conclusions might be thrown off if we are wrong with respect to key assumptions or judgments.*

On July 14 Wheeler informed McNamara that "there appears to be no reason we cannot win *if such is our will*—and if that will is manifest in strategy and tactical operations." This was, of course, the unlimited options/no upper limit strategy—which Johnson refused to accept.[24]

Challenges to the logic of U.S. involvement continued when McNaughton sent McNamara a "numbers game" scenario of possible options—illustrating that the probability for success and failure increased with each increment and each year. U.S. aims were identified as "70%—to preserve our national honor as a guarantor (and the reciprocal: to avoid a show-case success for Communist 'wars of liberation'); 20%—to keep SVN (and then adjacent) territory from hostile expansive hands; 10%—'answer the call of a friend,' to help him enjoy a better life. Also—to emerge from crisis without unacceptable taint from the methods used." The memo is reproduced below:

The issue: What is the optimum balance between various outcomes and efforts to get them?

1. Outcomes: (A) Win, defeating the VC (à la Malaya/Philippines).
            (B) Compromise with the VC (à la Laos 1962/Vietnam 1954).
            (C) Capitulate to the VC (à la Algeria).

2. Efforts: (1) More than 75,000 (probably 200–400,000+) US personnel.
            (2) 75,000 US personnel (the "reserve–call-up breakpoint").
            (3) 0 US personnel.

The options: Assuming maximum ingenuity on the all-important political side, the estimated probabilities of the 5 combinations of outcomes/efforts are as indicated below. (Notice that, of the "tolerable options," only B1 looks promising.)

Outcome/Effort Combinations	Probabilities of Success/Inconclusiveness/Collapse		
	By 1966	*By 1967*	*By 1968*
A1 ("win" with 200–400,000+ US)	20/70/10	40/45/15	50/30/20
A2 ("win" with 75,000 US)	10/70/20	20/50/30	30/30/40
B1 ("compromise" with 200–400,000+ US)	40/50/10	60/25/15	70/10/20
B2 ("compromise" with 75,000 US)	20/60/20	30/40/30	40/20/40
C3 (capitulate and withdraw)	0/0/100	0/0/100	0/0/100

Outcomes/efforts/collapse costs. There has been no decision taken putting on the same value scale (a) desirability of various outcomes, (b) undesirability of various efforts, and (c) undesirability of having tried and failed. For example:

—Is a collapse at a 75,000 level worse than an inconclusive situation at a 200–400,000+ level? Probably yes.
—Is a 60% chance of a "compromise" better than a 40% chance of "winning"? Probably yes if the compromise is tolerable.
—Is a 40% chance of "compromise" in 1966 better than a 40% chance of "winning" in 1967? Query.[25]

In his concluding prognosis, McNaughton wrote: "even if 'success,' it is not obvious how we will be able to disengage our forces from South Vietnam. It is unlikely that a formal agreement good enough for the purpose could possibly be negotiated—because the arrangement can reflect little more than the power situation. Most likely, in the case of success, is a settling down into a 'compromise'-like situation with a large number—perhaps 2 divisions—of US forces required to stay for a period of years. During that period of time, any number of things can change the picture beyond prediction."

According to the *Pentagon Papers*, "the McNaughton memorandum is of interest because it demonstrates several important items. First, the fact that the question about assurance of winning was asked indicates that *at the Secretary of Defense level there was real awareness that the decision to be made in the next few weeks would commit the US to the possibility of an expanded conflict.* The key question then was whether or not we would become involved more deeply in a war which could not be brought to a satisfactory conclusion. Secondly, the definition of 'win,' i.e., 'succeed in demonstrating to the VC that they cannot win,' indicates the assumption upon which the conduct of the war was to rest—that the VC could be convinced in some meaningful sense that they were not going to win and that they would then rationally choose less violent methods of seeking their goals. But the extent to which this definition would set limits of involvement or affect strategy was not clear. Thirdly, the assumptions on the key variables (the infiltration rates, the strength of GVN forces, the probable usefulness of Third Country forces, the political situation in South Vietnam) were rightfully pessimistic and cautious."[26]

But the expressions of doubt were never to be publicly aired. When Sen. Mike Mansfield wrote with the question "The main perplexity in the Vietnam situation is that even if you win, totally, you still do not come out well. What have you achieved?"[27] McNamara's response reflected just how committed he was to a definition which greatly raised the stakes of losing: "South Vietnam *is vital* to the United States in the significance that a demonstrable defeat would have on the future effectiveness of the United States on the world scene—especially in areas where people are depending upon our guarantee of their independence. It is a *vital US concern* to maintain *our honor* as an ally and our formidability as an opponent. As for how the situation in Vietnam will ultimately come out, we cannot now know. *But there is a range of outcomes—many less than perfect ones —that would satisfy American vital interests.* Our objectives, after all, are quite limited in Vietnam. They are, first, to permit the South Vietnamese to be independent and make a free choice of government and second, to establish for the world that Communist externally inspired and supported wars of liberation will not work."[28] No logic to the contrary would be allowed to disrupt that line of reasoning.

In his memoirs Ambassador Taylor asked, "how were we trapped into such a costly venture? Who or what was responsible for this miscalculation?" Taylor then excused decision-makers by noting that "the requirement for a decision always preceded the availability of most of the needed information."[29] But Taylor's judgment needs some qualification. The evidence in this book shows that the problem was not necessarily one of information scarcity, but an insensitivity to how expert knowledge should be utilized.

It is not infrequent that one hears the question: If Southeast Asia in general and Vietnam in specific were all that important to U.S. security interests, why didn't the United States (once the Ball scenerio had been rejected) just use its power to win and then defend South Vietnam? The primary constraint on U.S. policy was the belief that provocative military measures against the North would bring Chinese troops into the war. President Johnson maintained that it would take only one stray bomb for the cloning of Korea. For that reason he would not risk bombing the dikes or mining Haiphong harbor. According to Doris Kearns, Johnson "lived in constant fear of triggering some imaginary provision of some imaginary treaty" between the Chinese and Hanoi.[30]

There are several different opinions on this important issue. According to Clark Clifford, "the military would have liked to have invaded North Vietnam. President Johnson knew this was wrong because North Vietnam has a mutual assistance pact with Red China and just as soon as we invaded North Vietnam, the North Vietnamese would have triggered that pact and just hordes of Chinese troops would have come over. Every expert that I know in that part of the world agrees to that statement so there he turned the military down."[31] Ambassador Taylor disagreed with this view, arguing that Washington was unduly apprehensive about possible Chinese reinforcements. In Saigon, "we doubted that either Hanoi or the Vietcong would ever request or accept Chinese combat forces in their country. For centuries the Chinese had been regarded as hated, foreign oppressors by all Vietnamese, North and South, and that historical attitude was not likely to change."[32] In his memoirs Admiral Sharp lamented that the military was never allowed to fight the war "to win" because "political and diplomatic circles in Washington were disproportionately concerned with the possibility of communist and Soviet intervention"—characterized by frequent reference to "mythical hordes" of Chinese streaming into Vietnam should the United States pose a threatening glance.[33] The important point is, however, that President Johnson defined the situation in a way which severely constrained his military options and ultimately undid his political base. In doing so he revealed a fundamental misunderstanding of his adversary's goals and purposes. According to Ambassador Taylor, "in 1965 we knew very little about the Hanoi leaders other than Ho Chi Minh and General Giap and virtually nothing about their individual or collective intentions. We were inclined to assume, however, that they would behave about like the North Koreans and the Red Chinese a decade before; that is, they would seek an accommodation with us when the cost of pursuing a losing course became excessive. Instead, the North Vietnamese proved to be incredibly tough in accepting losses which, by Western calculation, greatly exceeded the value of the stake involved."[34] McGeorge Bundy offered a particularly revealing retrospective evaluation of these constraints: "Obviously the President is the chief actor, but I think everyone else has his share of responsibility, including those who differed over this or that part of the problem—or on the basic go-in or get-out question itself. I know I never found out how to connect LBJ's extraordinary abilities and energies to the questions of operational judgment and tactical and political detail that were so crucial. Perhaps there was no way—but then there should have been ways to help McNamara —or to choose more imaginative field leaders—military or political or both—and to deal with some of the constraints that may have been excessive."[35]

Since the U.S. goal was only to deny the Communists a victory and not to gain a military victory for itself, the principals proceeded from the premise that the greatest military power on the planet would eventually destroy the VC in South Vietnam and hit the DRV hard enough in North Vietnam to force a negotiated settlement on Hanoi. This strategy ignored the basic fact that Hanoi's *national* strategy was based on protracted struggle: "The leaders of the DRV had no rigid timetable for the struggle in the South. Rather the regime was confident that *the longer the war lasted, the more serious the 'inherent contradictions' in the US and US-GVN relationship would become.* Thus, while the North Vietnamese communists spoke of winning the decisive victory, *their definition of victory* did not imply the final seizure of power from the Saigon government. Instead, it meant either decisive victory on the battlefield, causing a turning point in the war, or partial annihilation of US and ARVN forces, forcing an American withdrawal. Decisive victory was, therefore, to take place within the context of protracted armed and political struggle."[36]

North Vietnam was involved in a total, not limited war. George Ball recalled that "On his first visit to Vietnam, in 1962, Secretary McNamara reported to the President that 'every quantitative measurement we have shows we are winning the war'—a comment that, as I came to understand, illustrated the Secretary's habitual practice of considering problems in quantitative terms. He was a superb Secretary of Defense—brilliantly skilled in planning, budgeting, devising, and administering efficient procurement policies and controlling all aspects of a great, sprawling part-military, part-civilian Department. But the very quantitative discipline that served him so splendidly as Secretary of Defense tended to interfere with his being a thoroughly successful Secretary of War. . . . What the McNamara approach lacked, of course, was any method of quantifying the quintessential advantage of the North Vietnamese and Viet Cong— the incomparable benefit of superior *élan,* of an intense spirit compounded by the elemental revolutionary drives of nationalism and anti-colonialism. Since anything that could not be quantified tended to be left out of the McNamara equation, the answer never came out right."[37]

The Missing Piece of the Puzzle

We conclude where we started—with questions about the personality of the real principal, Lyndon Johnson. What force did this powerful personality cast over the decision process? Was this the terrifying Caligula whom no one dared challenge? Or was the July 28 decision locked in by events, politics, and human beings unwilling, like most of us, to reject the basis for our political cognitions? Or in a perverse sort of way, was perhaps making a bad military decision in 1965 the best of all available political decisions for a president who still dreamed of increasing his legislative scorecard?

The documents show that the president and his advisors were remarkably consistent in their belief that they had correctly defined the problem and the stakes in Vietnam. Lyndon Johnson was indeed exposed to dissenting views—Ball and Clifford in particular. Ball never held back and neither he nor Clifford was "beaten" into submission—just outnumbered. To wit, McGeorge Bundy's critique of McNamara's June 26 memo contained all the ingredients of a devil's advocacy process—but Bundy was either brought into line by the president or counted heads and realized that he was a loser in this battle. Ball was also outranked by the major principals. It made a great deal of difference that the paper trail on the president's desk included recommendations for escalation from the secretary of defense, the chairman of the Joint Chiefs of Staff, General Westmoreland, and, most important, Ball's boss, the secretary of state.

In the final analysis the president and not his advisors must accept most of the blame. Johnson was the cause of his ultimate undoing. The president was involved in a delicate exercise of political juggling. He "had known when he sent McNamara to Saigon that the purpose was to build a consensus on what needed to be done to turn the tide —not to cover a retreat. Within that purpose he was glad to have all sorts of options . . . [discussed], but his own priority was to get agreement, at the lowest level of intensity he could, on a course that would meet the present need in Vietnam and not derail his legislative calendar."[38] Above all else, Johnson wanted to buy time and

McNamara's plan allowed the president to hold on in Vietnam and to continue to build a Great Society at home. Johnson believed that to accept Ball's advice would be political suicide and result in political paralysis for the next three years. The domestic repercussion if the United States abandoned its commitment would be too great for a four-year president ever to recoup. Congress, Johnson believed, would turn on the president and the right-wing backlash would be devastating.* Television screens would relay the "Communist carnage" into living rooms across the country. The rights of people to live in freedom would be trampled on. Hanoi's propaganda would focus on the United States as a paper tiger; China and the Soviet Union would laugh in the face of U.S. integrity, and there was always the spectre of China's "picking up the pieces at the fringe." Allies would never again trust the seal on the treaty with the United States. Johnson believed that Ball was wrong. There was no way to lose with honor. On the other hand, the Joint Chiefs' option raised the possibility of nuclear confrontation. Besides, how could the most powerful military apparatus in the world not achieve the relatively simple goal of denying Hanoi a victory? The United States sought no military victory of its own, no territory, nothing except the goal of convincing Hanoi it could not unify Vietnam by force. In 1965 Lyndon Johnson believed that with one or two lucky breaks this relatively simple goal could be achieved.

Thus did Lyndon Johnson commit slow political suicide. Once he decided to fight the war, his greatest tactical error as a *political* leader came when he rejected the advice of civilian and military advisors on the question of mobilizing the nation's resources. In deciding *not* to mobilize the Reserves, *not* to seek a congressional resolution or declaration of national emergency, *not* to present the program in a prime-time address to Congress or the nation (rather than an afternoon press conference), and *not* to disclose publicly the full extent of the anticipated military call-up, the president's credibil-

---

*When Vice-President Humphrey suggested otherwise, his counsel was no longer sought. On February 15, 1965, Humphrey wrote to Johnson that "it is always hard to cut losses. But the Johnson administration is in a stronger position to do so now than any Administration in this century. 1965 is the year of minimum political risk for the Johnson administration. Indeed, it is the first year when we can face the Vietnam problem without being preoccupied with the political repercussions from the Republican right."[39]

ity soon came unraveled. This was not the infamous "Caligula," but rather the soft-selling *Homo politicus*—who believed that losing Vietnam in the summer of 1965 would wreck his plans for a truly Great Society. In doing so he apparently gave very little attention to where he would be six months or one year down the road. But for the moment he pulled it off. On July 28 the country gave a sigh of relief. Lyndon Johnson was acting with restraint. The Reserves were not going to war, the nation was not mobilizing—the soft sell brought Johnson time and support.

Time and support for what? Vietnam was *not* the only important item on the president's agenda the week of July 21. As Johnson explained in *The Vantage Point,* Medicare and the Civil Rights Bill were at crucial stages in conference committee. But even more important, the curtain was closing on a historic era: "In all, thirty six major pieces of legislation had been signed into law, twenty six others were moving through the House and Senate, and eleven more awaiting scheduling."[40] A divisive debate would, in the president's opinion, have ruined his vision of a great America. On July 27 Johnson told his Cabinet that the past week had been "the most productive and most historic legislative week in Washington during this century. . . . Thus the books were closing on our campaign to take action against the most pressing problems inherited from the past—the 'old agenda.' "[41] But Johnson now recognized "the urgent and unavoidable need to begin work on a new agenda."[42] The following two memos from McGeorge Bundy illustrate Johnson's intent as well as his understanding that so much of this had to be kept secret:

THE WHITE HOUSE
WASHINGTON

Monday, July 19, 1965
8:15 P.M.

MEMORANDUM FOR THE PRESIDENT

SUBJECT: The Reasons for Avoiding a Billion Dollar Appropriation
in Vietnam*

1. It would be a belligerent challenge to the Soviets at a time when it is important to do only the things which we have to do (like calling reserves).

2. It would stir talk about controls over the economy and inflation—at a time when controls are not needed and inflation is not that kind of a problem.

3. It would create the false impression that we have to have guns, not butter—and would help the enemies of the President's domestic legislative program.

4. It would play into the hands of the Soviets at Geneva, because they could argue that it was a flagrant breach of the policy of "mutual example" on defense budgets.

5. It is not needed—because there are other ways of financing our full effort in Vietnam for the rest of the calendar year, at least.

THE WHITE HOUSE
WASHINGTON

Friday, July 23, 1965

MEMORANDUM FOR THE PRESIDENT*

SUBJECT: Reasons for Avoiding a big Military Appropriation in
          Vietnam

1. It would be a belligerent challenge to the Soviets at a time when it is important to do only the things which we have to do.

2. It would stir talk about controls over the economy and inflation—at a time when controls are not needed and inflation is not that kind of a problem.

3. It would play into the hands of the Soviets at Geneva and elsewhere, because they could argue that it was a flagrant breach of the policy of "mutual example" on defense budgets.

4. It is not needed—because there are other ways of financing our full effort in Vietnam for the present.

And in the short run Johnson succeeded—only to prove the bankruptcy of his leadership. Six months following the July 28 decision

*This memo had a line drawn through it, paragraph 3 was lined out, and Johnson had handwritten on the bottom "Rewrite eliminating 3 — L." Bundy also removed the reference to the Reserves in paragraph 1.

Johnson went to Congress and declared, "I believe we can continue the Great Society while we fight in Vietnam." Johnson wrote in *The Vantage Point*, "in that sentence, to which the Congress responded with heartening applause, the turmoil of months was resolved, and the Great Society moved through midpassage into its final years of creative activity and accomplishment."[43]

In the end Lyndon Johnson was not misled by advisors. He had no reason, no incentive to lead a searching reevaluation of U.S. policy. In the Preface I asked if Johnson could have led America away from war in 1965. The documents show that at no stage was this option ever fully staffed out by the president's assistants. No one was planning the politics of getting out by December if the July decision was ineffective. It could and should have been done—it was certainly less a threat than Johnson believed. He sought only to hide in the middle of two extremes. He had weighed all the costs and then used his great talents to forge a marginal consensus—enough to get the United States into war, but insufficient for war termination. Moreover, Johnson did not act indecisively. He chose between short- and long-run risks, and his fatal mistake occurred in that choice. In holding back from total commitment Johnson was juggling the Great Society, the war in Vietnam, and his hopes for the future. He *chose* to avoid a national debate on the war, to keep the Reserves home, and to buy time for a domestic record meriting nothing less than Mount Rushmore (he would later settle for the Johnson Library).

On June 30, 1965, McGeorge Bundy wrote to the president with a comparative analysis of the "French, 1954–United States, 1965 situation."[44] Bundy concluded his memorandum with the following analogy: "The US in 1965 is responding to the call of a people under Communist assault, a people undergoing a non-Communist national revolution; neither our power nor that of our adversaries has been fully engaged as yet. At home we remain *politically strong* and, in general, *politically united.* Options, both military and political, remain to us that were no longer available to the French." How long, however, would a democracy support a limited and hidden war? Yet it need not have been that way. To George Ball, "a determined President might at any point have overruled those advisers, accepted the costs of withdrawal, and broken the momentum, but only a leader supremely sure of himself could make that decision, and Lyndon Johnson, out of his element in the Vietnam War, felt no such certainty."[45] The NSC meeting of July 21 illustrates the point. Ball had just presented his case for cutting our losses. Ambassador Lodge challenged the undersecretary, primarily on the grounds that the central lesson of history was "indolence at Munich," not Korea or the French experience at Dien Bien Phu. Ball argued back—the United States would never win this war. Nobody had yet produced a convincing case that the United States could achieve its military goals and remain politically united at home. Ball was *not blaming Johnson* —*previous* administrations had underestimated the situation. It would take a long and protracted war, however, to reveal just how bad the strategic errors had been. Ball seemed to grasp the implication for long-term political leadership even better than Johnson, warning the president that should he proceed as recommended by McNamara, public opinion would soon turn against the president. The Great Society would crumble, and bring Johnson down as well.

In *The Vantage Point* President Johnson reflected on the critical choices of July 1965: "The demanding decisions of those trying days relating to Vietnam were decisions involving our nation's integrity and its security. But they also involved what I considered to be the promise of the American future. In a wondrous time of hope and optimism we had begun the building of a better society for our people. The danger that we might have to slow that building in order to take care of our obligations abroad, brought added anguish. *So on that July 27, 1965, two great streams in our national life converged —the dream of a Great Society at home and the inescapable demands of our obligations halfway around the world. They were to run in confluence until the end of my administration.*"[46] They were, in fact, to bring an end to his administration. Lyndon Johnson's greatest fault as a political leader was that *he chose* not to choose between the Great Society and the war in Vietnam. Instead, he sought a pragmatic guns-and-butter solution for avoiding what he believed would have surely been a divisive national debate in order temporarily to protect his Great Society. Columnist Joseph Alsop caught this private agony of a public man while watching the president's July 28 press conference. Writing as a self-confessed "practitioner of Johnsonology—the increasing band of those who spend a good deal of time trying, with mingled admiration and exasperation, to figure out what makes Lyndon B. Johnson tick," Alsop observed:

As the President talked on in his sincere, almost ostentatiously fatherly way, he painted a self-portrait of a man forced by an unkind fate to face in two directions at once. The harsh necessities of the Vietnamese War have driven him to give most of his attention to thorny questions about America's vital interests overseas—with which he is not at home.

But all the while, he keeps one eager eye over his shoulder, on the arena of domestic affairs—where he is very much at home. His press conference came alive, it carried absolute conviction, when he began to talk of all his hopes of making America a better place to live in during his Presidency. This was deeply meant, and therefore genuinely stirring.

But, by implication at least, this also revealed the nature of the double handicap under which President Johnson labors when he wearily returns to the questions about Viet-Nam, which are always there on his desk, crying out for answers.

He not only resents having to answer such questions, because he thinks he would be better employed doing what comes naturally. As an unparalleled master of domestic politics, he also thinks first about internal political repercussions. What will be said, and thought if he does this or that, is his immediate, instinctive calculation. The crucial calculations about what needs to be done are unavoidably subordinated.

Here is one essential difference between Lyndon Johnson and his hero, Franklin D. Roosevelt. When Mr. Roosevelt finally had to turn his main attention to foreign affairs, he always decided, first of all, what ideally needed to be done. And only after that decision, did he begin to figure out how he could get away with doing it, or how close he could come to doing it.

Hence a majority of one vote in the House was quite enough for Mr. Roosevelt, whereas a nine-to-one majority is not enough for Mr. Johnson. By the same token—and this is his second handicap—Mr. Johnson so far has gone on vainly trying to deal with overseas problems as though they resembled domestic problems.

When tackling domestic problems with his computer-like mind, he has always been able to figure out a solution that promised real progress, yet minimized or altogether avoided controversy. Unfortunately, no one on earth can figure out this kind of promising yet relatively painless solution in a bitter war against a ruthless enemy.

Yet the President, thus far, has obviously been reluctant to believe that such solutions are impossible in Viet-Nam. In the face of all the contrary evidence, he tried for a year to put political arrangements ahead of military action.

One must still wait and see, in short. Meanwhile, *it must be said there is a genuine element of pathos (and pray God, the pathos does not turn into tragedy) in the spectacle of this extraordinary man in the White House wrestling with the Vietnamese problem,* which is so distasteful to him, and all the while visibly longing to go back to the domestic miracle-working he so much enjoys.[47]

The pathos did indeed turn to tragedy. Johnson used the advisory process to legitimize the decision to political elites and the general public. On July 28, 1965, Lyndon Johnson chose a path which turned Vietnam into America's nightmare. But elements of pathos soon manifested themselves. In June 1966 John Kenneth Galbraith wrote to the president, "As you know, I am completely convinced, and now with the Buddhists more than ever, that we have no future in Viet Nam. But I am not writing to argue on this. I am writing to say that, as a matter of political craftsmanship, I fully believe that, should it be your decision, a script could be written—speeches, involvement of Congress and the U.N., discussion and approval of other Asian countries, concern for self-determination and religious freedom, etc., etc.—that would enable your Administration to accept, with dignity and even credit and applause, any bargain we might get down to orderly withdrawal. It would take brains and skill but it could be done.

"Should the time ever come when you want such a hand, I am yours to command. This is the purpose of this letter which involves no false modesty, although you have some idea of my talents in these matters. *I don't for a moment believe that your presidency need be ruined by this misadventure.*"[48]

Johnson responded with a personal letter to Galbraith (written almost one year to the day after the 1965 decision). The letter shows a president heading for personal defeat: "I have never doubted your talent for political craftsmanship, and I am sure you could devise a script that would appear to justify our taking an unjustifiable course in South Vietnam. But I hope that I never have to take you up on it. To get out of Vietnam before the North gives up its support of the war there, in my opinion, would be unfortunate and wrong. I'm not even sure you and I together could convince the other nations of Asia that it would be to their benefit for us to turn around now. I know it wouldn't, so I would be at best a half-hearted persuader.

"I do want to get out—and will, as I said yesterday, when North

Vietnam wants to talk about a peaceful settlement or end the fighting. One of these days you are going to see what we are doing and what it means for the rest of Asia, and then, I hope, you will quietly be grateful that I summoned the extraordinary restraint not to accept for the time being your good offer."[49]

By 1968 the president would run *from* office—his dream of a Great Society ruined by the war. In the end Johnson would fail to make the transition described to him by Vice-President Humphrey: *"President Johnson is personally identified with, and greatly admired for, political ingenuity. He will be expected to put all his great political sense to work now for international political solutions. People will be counting on him to use on the world scene his unrivaled talents as a politician. They will be watching to see how he makes this transition from the domestic to the world stage."*[50]

The personal tragedy was obvious to former President Eisenhower, who on March 31, 1968, following Johnson's announcement that he would not seek reelection, recorded in his diary: "to me it seems obvious that the President is at war with himself and while trying vigorously to defend the actions and decisions he has made in the past, and urging the nation to pursue those purposes regardless of costs, he wants to be excused from the burden of office to which he was elected."[51] Therein rested the legacy of July 1965—a personal and national tragedy.

Notes

Unless otherwise noted all references apply to the Presidential Papers of Lyndon Baines Johnson, 1963–1969, located in the Lyndon Baines Johnson Library, Austin, Texas. Because I have made extensive use of the National Security File, National Security Council History, "Deployment of Major U.S. Forces to Vietnam, July 1965," it is cited separately as *NSC History—Troop Deployment*. This National Security File served as the working file of President Johnson's assistant for national security affairs, McGeorge Bundy. The NSC History contains declassified White House and NSC staff memos, State and Defense Department cables, and CIA reports. The eight-volume BDM Corporation study "The Strategic Lessons Learned in Vietnam" is cited by volume number. The eight volumes are: 1. "The Enemy"; 2. "South Vietnam"; 3. "U.S. Foreign Policy and Vietnam, 1945–1975"; 4. "U.S. Domestic Factors Influencing Vietnam War Policy Making"; 5. "Planning the War"; 6. "Conduct of the War"; 7. "The Soldier"; 8. "The Results of the War."

Preface

1. Lyndon Baines Johnson, *The Vantage Point* (New York: Holt, Rinehart and Winston, 1971), pp. 322–23.

2. *New York Times,* July 23, 1965, p. 1.

3. "The President's News Conference of July 28, 1965," *Public Papers of the Presidents of the United States, 1965,* Book 2, June 1 to December 31, 1965 (Washington, D.C.: U.S. Government Printing Office, 1966), pp. 794–805. [Hereafter cited as *Public Papers.*]

4. Transcribed notes from Press Backgrounding, July 28, 1965, *NSC History—Troop Deployment.*

5. Declassified on March 9, 1981, the study identifies lessons which U.S. military leaders and U.S. civilian policy-makers should have learned or should now be learning from the U.S. experience in Vietnam. Membership on the BDM senior review panel included: Peter Braestrup, editor, *Wilson Quarterly,* former Saigon bureau chief for the *Washington Post* and author of *Big Story;* William E. Colby, LL.B., former ambassador and deputy to COMUSMACV for CORDS, and former director of the Central Intelligence Agency; Vincent Davis, professor and director of the Patterson School of Diplomacy and International Commerce, University of Kentucky; Fred Greene, professor, Williams College, and former director, Office of Research for East Asian Affairs, Department of State; John H. Hallowell and James B. Duke, professors of Political Science, Duke University; Thomas L. Hughes, LL.D., president of the Carnegie Endowment for International Peace, former director for intelligence and research, U.S. Department of State with rank of assistant secretary of state; U. Alexis Johnson, chairman of the senior review panel, career ambassador, former undersecretary of state and former ambassador to Czechoslovakia, Thailand, and Japan, and (1964–1965) deputy ambassador to Maxwell Taylor in the Republic of Vietnam; Burton M. Sapin, dean, School of Public and International Affairs, The George Washington University, former foreign service officer; Kenneth W. Thompson, director, White Burkett Miller Center of Public Affairs, University of Virginia; Gaston Sigur, director, Institute of Sino-Soviet Studies, The George Washington University; John W. Vogt, General, USAF (Ret.), formerly J-3 and director, Joint Staff and DEPCOMUSMACV and commander, 7th Air Force.

6. Jack Valenti, *A Very Human President* (New York: W. W. Norton, 1975), pp. 317–19.

7. See Lady Bird Johnson, *A White House Diary* (New York: Holt, Rinehart and Winston, 1970), p. 248.

I. Introduction

1. Chester Cooper, *The Lost Crusade* (New York: Dodd, Mead, 1970), p. 223.

2. Johnson, *The Vantage Point,* p. 149.

3. David Halberstam, *The Best and the Brightest* (New York: Random House, 1972), p. 432.

4. George Reedy, "Lyndon B. Johnson: A Retrospective on His Life," paper delivered at the National Portrait Gallery, The Smithsonian Institution, Washington, D.C., October 30, 1980.

5. See Larry Berman, "Johnson and the White House Staff," in *Exploring the Johnson Years*, edited by Robert A. Divine (Austin: University of Texas Press, 1981), pp. 187–213.

6. Memo, Harry McPherson to the President, July 13, 1965 (emphasis added).

7. Alan Otten, "The Consenting Advisors," *Wall Street Journal*, February 27, 1967. Otten was viewed as a real problem by the staff. On May 27, 1966, Joseph Califano wrote to Bill Moyers that "Al Otten talked to me today. ... He clearly subscribes to the theory that the Administration is 'tired' and that an influx of new blood is needed. ... He thought the White House staff was feuding and tired. I told him that I thought the White House staff worked better together than any staff I had ever seen. ... Otten volunteered that he is preparing a piece on the White House staff and that he thought the staff was tired, just as the Administration was tired. I think we can anticipate a fairly rough piece from Otten on this subject" (Memo, Califano to Bill Moyers, May 27, 1966). By January 9, 1967, McPherson wrote to the president, "Al Otten came to see me today—the first time since two months ago, when I told him he ought to quit the White House because his deep antipathy to your Administration was destroying his objectivity and balance as a reporter" (Memo, Harry McPherson for the President, January 9, 1967).

8. Memo, Harry McPherson to George Christian, February 28, 1967.

9. John Stoessinger, *Crusaders and Pragmatists* (New York: W. W. Norton, 1979), pp. 183–196.

10. Halberstam, *The Best and the Brightest*, p. 434; Stoessinger, *Crusaders and Pragmatists*, p. 185.

11. Stoessinger, *Crusaders and Pragmatists*, p. 186.

12. Ibid., p. 190.

13. C. V. Wedgewood, *William the Silent* (New York: W. W. Norton, 1967), p. 35.

II. The Road to July 1965

1. "Peace Without Conquest," address at Johns Hopkins University, April 7, 1965, *Public Papers 1965*, Book 1, January 1 to May 31, 1965, pp. 394–98.

2. George F. Kennan ["X"], "The Sources of Soviet Conduct," *Foreign Affairs* 25 (July 1947): 575.

3. See Briefing Book on Vietnam, February 1968. Also see BDM Study, vol. 3, sect. 3, p. 11.

4. *Public Papers*, Pres. Dwight D. Eisenhower, April 1954. See also *Public Papers*, President Eisenhower's Remarks, August 4, 1955, p. 540; *Public Papers*, State of the Union Message, February 3, 1953, p. 89.

5. *Public Papers*, "Address at the Gettysburg College Convocation: The Importance of Understanding," April 4, 1959, p. 76.

6. Briefing Book on Vietnam, February 1968, p. I–86.

7. Ibid. See also U.S., Congress, House, Committee on Armed Services,

United States–Vietnam Relations, 1945–1967: A Study Prepared by the Department of Defense (Washington, D.C.: U.S. Government Printing Office, 1971), Book 7, sect. B-12. [Hereafter cited as *USVN*.]

8. NSC, "Review of U.S. Policy in the Far East," August 1954, *USVN*, Book 10, pp. 731–41.

9. The BDM Study offered the following insights based on their analysis of NSC 5429/2: (1) no policy had yet been formulated by the United States for dealing effectively with countries of the Third World; (2) the assumption had been made that formal alliances such as SEATO, using NATO as the model, would be useful in dealing with Asian communism; (3) the United States still did not understand the importance of nationalism in Indochina and the need to address problems that had arisen from years of colonialism in SEA before trying to marshal support against communism; (4) the United States had a condescending attitude toward the Asian peoples and their ability to deal with their own problems (BDM Study, vol. 3, p. A-28).

10. National Intelligence Estimate 63-5-54, "Post-Geneva Outlook in Indochina," August 3, 1954, *USVN*, Book 10, p. 692.

11. BDM Study, vol. 3, sect. 1, p. 28

12. Eisenhower to Diem, October 1, 1954, in George M. Kahin and John W. Lewis, *The United States in Vietnam* (New York: Dell, 1969), pp. 456–57; *Public Papers*, Dwight D. Eisenhower, 1954 (1960), p. 383.

13. BDM Study, vol. 25, sect. 1. See also vol. 5, sect. 2.

14. Ibid., vol. 2, sect. 1.

15. Hans J. Morgenthau, "The 1954 Geneva Conference: An Assessment," in American Friends of Vietnam, *America's Stake in Vietnam* (Washington, D.C.: Washington Business Service, Inc., 1956), p. 69.

16. See John F. Kennedy, *The Strategy of Peace*, edited by Allan Nevins (New York: Harper and Row, 1960). See also, W. W. Rostow, "JFK and Southeast Asia," paper presented at the Conference on the Presidency of John Fitzgerald Kennedy, Los Angeles, November 14, 1980.

17. NSC 5519, "Draft Statement and NSC Staff Study on US Policy on All-Vietnam Elections," May 17, 1955 (BDM Study, vol. 3, sect. 2, p. 15).

18. See *America's Stake in Vietnam*, pp. 10–11; Wesley R. Fishel (ed.), *Vietnam: Anatomy of a Conflict* (Itasca, Ill.: F. E. Peacock, 1968), pp. 142–47; Briefing Book on Vietnam, 1:50.

19. Richard Stavins et al., *Washington Plans an Aggressive War* (New York: Vintage Books, 1971), p. 20.

20. Joseph Buttinger, *Vietnam: A Dragon Embattled* (New York: Praeger, 1967), 1:251.

21. "Message to President Diem on the Fifth Anniversary of the Independence of Vietnam, October 26, 1960," *Public Papers*, Dwight D. Eisenhower, 1960 (1961), p. 808.

22. BDM Study, vol. 3, sect. 2, p. 7.

23. The Clifford memo is reproduced in Rostow, "JFK and Southeast Asia."

24. BDM Study, vol. 3, sect. 2, p. 23.

25. Ibid., p. 24. See *Public Papers,* March 23, 1961.

26. Ibid.

27. Ibid.

28. W. W. Rostow, *The Diffusion of Power* (New York: Macmillan, 1972), p. 265. See also, *The Pentagon Papers: The Defense Department History of the United States Decisionmaking on Vietnam,* edited by Senator Gravel (Boston: Beacon Press, 1971), 2:6, 27. See also memorandum, W. W. Rostow to McGeorge Bundy, "Meeting Saturday Morning, January 28 in the President's Office, on Viet-Nam," January 30, 1961, JFK Library, National Security File, Vietnam Country File, 1/61–3/61, cited in Leslie Gelb and Richard Betts, *Irony of Vietnam: The System Worked* (Washington, D.C.: Brookings Institution, 1979), p. 70. See also Rostow, "JFK and Southeast Asia."

29. Rostow, "JFK and Southeast Asia," p. 20.

30. Ibid., p. 22.

31. Ibid.

32. Ibid., p. 25.

33. See *Pentagon Papers,* 2:35–47, 637–42. Brig.-Gen. Edward Lansdale served as operations officer to the task force.

34. Ibid., p. 51.

35. *Public Papers,* John F. Kennedy, May 13, 1961. See State Department Briefing Book, 1:50.

36. *Pentagon Papers,* 2:59. Compare this with the terminology in Ball's memoranda of June 28 and July 1.

37. *Pentagon Papers,* 2 (sect. B.4): 84–96, 245–46, 258–59, 291–96. See also Maxwell Taylor, *Swords and Plowshares* (New York: W. W. Norton, 1972), pp. 242–44; Rostow, *Diffusion of Power,* p. 275.

38. *Pentagon Papers,* 2 (sect. 4-B.1): 118.

39. Ibid., pp. 125–33.

40. Warren Cohen, *Dean Rusk* (New York: Cooper Square Publishers, 1980), pp. 181–82.

41. George Ball prepublication manuscript. For more detailed discussion, see George Ball, *The Past Has Another Pattern* (New York: W. W. Norton, 1982.)

42. See BDM Study, vol. 4, sect. 2, pp. 26–28.

43. John Kenneth Galbraith, quoted in National Broadcasting Company, "Vietnam Hindsight," part 1, act 3, pp. 11–12 (broadcast December 21, 1971).

44. Quoted in Henry Fairlie, *The Kennedy Promise* (Garden City, N.Y.: Doubleday, 1973), pp. 180–81.

45. *Pentagon Papers,* 2:126–27.

46. Ibid. See BDM Study, vol. 3, sect. 2.

47. Bruce Miroff, *Pragmatic Illusions* (New York: David McKay, 1976), p. 162. See *DOD US/VN Relations,* Book 3, sect. 4-B.5, pp. 1–5, "Overthrow of Ngo Dinh Diem." See also BDM Study, vol. 3, sect. 2, pp. 3–27.

48. *DOD US/VN Relations,* Book 12, p. 535.

49. See William Colby, *Honorable Men* (New York: Simon and Schuster, 1978), p. 120. Ambassador Nolting reported later that the announcement of

his replacement by Ambassador Lodge had come as a surprise to him. "I heard that I had been replaced by Ambassador Lodge in a radio broadcast while I was on vacation. It seems obvious to me that those who wanted to let Diem hang himself didn't want me back in Saigon" (*U.S. News and World Report*, July 26, 1971, p. 68). Ambassador Nolting provided BDM with a copy of this article. He still considers the U.S. role in that coup to have been our "cardinal mistake." See BDM Study, vol. 3.

50. *DOD US/VN Relations*, Book 3, sect. 4-B.5, p. 15, "Lodge vs. Diem, August 20–October 2."

51. State Department to Lodge and Harkins, *DOD US/VN Relations*, Book 12, sect. 5-B.4, p. 538.

52. Cablegram, Ambassador Henry Cabot Lodge to Secretary of State Dean Rusk, August 29, 1963, Subject: U.S. Policy Toward a Coup, in *Pentagon Papers*, Book 12, pp. 738–39. Later, General Harkins described Ambassador Lodge as pulling the rug "right out from under Diem." Although Harkins had been instructed from Washington to confer with General "Big" Minh, he was unable to comply with the instruction because the Vietnamese general refused to see him (U.S. Army Military History Research Collection, Senior Officers Debriefing Program, Report of an interview of Gen. Paul D. Harkins, April 28, 1974, by Maj. Jacob B. Couch, Jr., p. 54; see BDM Study, vol. 3).

53. *Pentagon Papers*, Book 12, pp. 738–39.

54. Colby, *Honorable Men*, p. 211.

55. *DOD US/VN Relations*, Book 12, sect. 5-B.4, p. 538.

56. Paul Kattenburg, *The Vietnam Trauma in American Foreign Policy, 1945-75* (New Brunswick, N.J.: Transaction Books, 1980), p. 120. David Halberstam wrote that "It was an important moment—the first time at a high-level meeting anyone had really said the unthinkable, coming significantly from the man who knew the most about the fabric of the society and the limits of it" (Halberstam, *The Best and the Brightest*, pp. 266–68).

57. *DOD US/VN Relations*, Book 12, sect. 5-B.4, p. 26.

58. They also predicted, "we believe the US part of the task can be completed by the end of 1965. . . ."

59. Interview with Lucien Conein, "Vietnam: The Ten Thousand Day War—Documentary," September 28, 1981. See "The Coup D'Etat of November 1, 1963" (original title: "From the Day of the First Republic's Overthrow to the Day the Second Republic of Vietnam was Founded"), from the private files of Lucien Conein (a copy was provided to BDM on August 25, 1979, p. 43; see BDM Study, vol. 3).

60. Taylor, *Swords and Plowshares*, pp. 301–2 (emphasis added).

61. BDM Study, 3:3–32, 5:2–28.

62. Gen. William C. Westmoreland, "Vietnam in Perspective," *The Retired Officer*, October 1978, pp. 21–24.

63. Quoted in State Department Briefing Book on Vietnam, 1:59.

64. Arthur M. Schlesinger, Jr., *Robert Kennedy and His Times* (New York: Ballantine Books, 1981), p. 781.

65. George C. Herring, *America's Longest War* (New York: John Wiley and Sons, 1979), p. 107.

66. Eric Goldman, *The Tragedy of Lyndon Johnson* (New York: Dell, 1968), p. 29.

III. The Decisions of Early 1965

1. McNamara to President Johnson, December 21, 1963. Also see *Vietnam: A History in Documents,* edited by Gareth Porter (New York: New American Library, 1981), #166.

2. Joint Chiefs of Staff Memo, JCSM–46–64, January 22, 1964.

3. Draft memorandum for the President by Assistant Secretary of Defense William Bundy, March 1, 1964, It is unclear whether or not the president read this memo.

4. Ibid.

5. BDM Study, vol. 3, sect. 3, p. 37.

6. See Stavins et al., *Washington Plans an Aggressive War,* pp. 94–103. Also see *DOD US/VN Relations,* "Military Pressures Against NVN," Book 3, sect. 4-C.2A, p. 9.

7. Joseph Goulden, *Truth Is the First Casualty: The Gulf of Tonkin Affair* (Chicago: Rand McNally, 1969), p. 160; See "Chronology of Events, Tuesday, August 4, and Wednesday, August 5, 1964, Tonkin Gulf Strike," National Security File, Country File: Vietnam. See also Eugene Windchy, *Tonkin Gulf* (Garden City, N.Y.: Doubleday, 1971); *Pentagon Papers,* 3:150; "The Gulf of Tonkin: The 1964 Incidents," hearings before the Senate Committee on Foreign Relations, 90th Cong., 2d sess. (Washington, D.C.: U.S. Government Printing Office, 1968).

8. Public Law 88–408.

9. Herring, *America's Longest War,* p. 123.

10. Stavins et al., *Washington Plans an Aggressive War,* Chap. 4.

11. Cable, President Johnson to Ambassador Taylor, December 1964, *Top Secret—NoDis, NSC History—Troop Deployment* (emphasis added).

12. Cables, Taylor to the President, January 6, 1965 (includes cables 2052, 2055, 2056, 2057, 2058), *NSC History—Troop Deployment.*

13. Ibid.

14. Taylor, *Swords and Plowshares,* p. 327.

15. Cable, Taylor to the President, January 6, 1965.

16. Cable, President Johnson to Ambassador Taylor, January 7, 1965, *Top Secret, NSC History—Troop Deployment* (emphasis added). See Embtel 2116, *NSC History—Troop Deployment.*

17. Draft Cable, President Johnson to Ambassador Taylor, January 7, 1965, *NSC History—Troop Deployment* (emphasis added).

18. Telegram, President Johnson to Ambassador Taylor, January 13, 1965, *Secret,* NSC History—Troop Deployment. On January 14 the secretary of state's name replaced the president's and the telegram was sent to Taylor

(see telegram, Rusk to Taylor, priority 1477, *NSC History—Troop Deployment*).

19. Cable, Ambassador Taylor to the President, January 27, 1965, *Secret, NSC History—Troop Deployment*. Taylor added, "until we see more clearly the form of the new government to emerge, I am of the opinion that we not commit ourselves publicly with regard to the action of the Armed Forces Council." The events between January 1964 and February 1965 almost defy believability: In January 1964, Maj.-Gen. Nguyen Khanh led a bloodless coup and seized power from the ruling military junta which had replaced Diem. On August 24, 1964, Khanh was elected president; on August 25, Khanh was forced to resign; on August 27 a military triumvirate assumed ruling responsibility; by September 3 Khanh was restored as premier; on September 13 Khanh squashed a coup attempt and was later replaced by Tran Van Huong; and in December, following Buddhist riots, the civilian High National Council, headed by Huong, was overthrown by rebel forces. On January 9, 1965, South Vietnam's civilian régime headed by Premier Tran Van Huong was restored to power in a compromise solution with the military; on January 27 Huong was deposed by a bloodless coup and Lt.-Gen. Nguyen Khanh was again given all powers to establish a stable government; by February 16 Dr. Phan Huy Quat was appointed by the South Vietnamese Armed Forces Council as premier; three days later Khanh stopped a coup attempt by dissident generals against Quat; on February 21 Khanh was ousted as chairman and armed forces commander of the South Vietnamese Forces Council, appointed "roving Ambassador," and sent to New York. By June Quat would resign and be replaced by a military triumvirate which would eventually settle on Air Vice Marshall Ky and Maj.-Gen. Nguyen Van Thieu.

20. Memo, McGeorge Bundy to the President, January 27, 1965, "Basic Policy in Vietnam," *Secret, NSC History—Troop Deployment*.

21. Memo, McGeorge Bundy to the President, January 27, 1965, "Draft Message to Max Taylor," *Top Secret, NSC History—Troop Deployment*.

22. Cable, President Johnson to Ambassador Taylor, January 27, 1965, #1549, *NSC History—Troop Deployment* (emphasis added). The president added that "it appears from your reports that, for better or worse, we may be increasingly dependent upon unreliable and unpredictable Buddhist leaders. It occurs to me that there is one man who has some unexpended personal capital with the Buddhists, and that man is Cabot Lodge. Unless you find it objectionable, I am thinking of asking him to come in Bundy's plane for a visit which might later be extended to other points. . . ." Lodge did not accompany Bundy.

23. Cable, McGeorge Bundy to General Taylor, January 28, 1965, *NoDis —Top Secret*, #1557, *NSC History—Troop Deployment*.

24. Ibid. (emphasis added).

25. Memo, McGeorge Bundy to the President, February 7, 1965, "The Situation in Vietnam," *Top Secret, NSC History—Troop Deployment* (emphasis added).

26. Memo, Nolting to Ken O'Donnell, January 31, 1964, *Confidential*.

27. Cable, Taylor to McGeorge Bundy, February 1, 1965, *Secret, NSC History—Troop Deployment*. Bundy later cabled Taylor regarding the future prospect of stable government in SVN: "Present directives make such a government an essential prerequisite for important additional US major action, but we now wonder whether this requirement is either realistic or necessary" *(NSC History—Troop Deployment)*.

28. Memo, Taylor to the President, February 23, 1965, *NSC History—Troop Deployment*.

29. Quoted in Anthony Lake (ed.), *The Vietnam Legacy* (New York: New York University Press, 1976), p. 183. See also Townsend Hoopes, *The Limits of Intervention* (New York: David McKay, 1969), p. 30.

30. Memo, McGeorge Bundy to the President, February 16, 1965, "Telegram to Ambassador Taylor," *Top Secret, NSC History—Troop Deployment*.

31. Memo, Bundy to the President, February 7, 1965, "The Situation in Vietnam" (emphasis added).

32. Memo, James C. Thomson, Jr., to McGeorge Bundy, "The Vietnam Crisis—One Dove's Lament," *Top Secret—Sensitive, NSC History—Troop Deployment*.

33. Ball ms. For more details, see Ball, *The Past Has Another Pattern*.

34. Hubert H. Humphrey, *The Education of a Public Man* (Garden City, N.Y.: Doubleday, 1976), pp. 320–24. Parts of the memorandum are reproduced in Chapter 5.

35. Ball ms. For more details, see Ball, *The Past Has Another Pattern*.

36. Ibid.

37. Memo, George Ball to the President, February 1965, Subject: Viet-Nam, *Top Secret*, personal papers of George Ball, Princeton, N.J.

38. Ball, *The Past Has Another Pattern*, in press.

39. Memo, Ball to the President, February 1965, Subject: Viet-Nam.

40. Ball ms. For more details, see Ball, *The Past Has Another Pattern*.

41. Memo, George Ball to Dean Rusk, Robert McNamara, and McGeorge Bundy, "How Valid Are the Assumptions Underlying Our Viet-Nam Policies?" October 5, 1964, *Top Secret, NSC History—Troop Deployment*.

42. Ball ms. For more details, see Ball, *The Past Has Another Pattern*. In his covering letters to "Dean, Bob and Mac," Ball wrote: "I am enclosing my skeptical thoughts on the assumptions of our Viet-Nam policy. This amplifies our conversation a week ago as I promised to do. The paper has the obvious limitations of a personal effort drafted mostly late at night and without benefit of staffing. I offer it as a focus for discussion and as an incitement to a broad study of the problem. Only five copies of this document have been prepared. I am sending one each to the three of you and am retaining two in my safe. I think you will agree that it should not be discussed outside the four of us until we have had a chance to talk about it."

43. Ball ms. For more details see Ball, *The Past Has Another Pattern*.

44. Memo, Ball to Rusk, McNamara, and Bundy, "How Valid Are the Assumptions Underlying Our Viet-Nam Policies?"

45. U.S., Department of State, Director of Intelligence and Research,

Intelligence Note, "The Effects of the Bombing of North Vietnam," June 29, 1965, *NSC History—Troop Deployment.*

46. Kattenburg, *The Vietnam Trauma in American Foreign Policy, 1945–75*, pp. 130–31.

47. Memo, Gen. Earle Wheeler to Secretary of Defense, April 6, 1965, "Overall Approval of Air Strikes Against North Vietnam, 7 February to 4 April 1965," CM–534–6J, *NSC History—Troop Deployment.*

48. See JCS/CINCPAC, February 12, 1965, *LimDis*, "Courses of Action: SE Asia—1st 8 weeks," REF JCS 2339/169 (JCSM 100–65), *NSC History—Troop Deployment.*

49. Gen. William C. Westmoreland, *A Soldier Reports* (Garden City, N.Y.: Doubleday, 1976), p. 123.

50. *Pentagon Papers*, 3:429.

51. Ibid.

52. Personal letter to the author, December 4, 1981.

53. Cable, Taylor to the President, February 22, 1965, *Top Secret—Limited Distribution*, #2699, *NSC History—Troop Deployment* (emphasis added).

54. Westmoreland, *A Soldier Reports*, p. 124.

55. Taylor, *Swords and Plowshares*, p. 338.

56. BDM Study, vol. 5.

57. Westmoreland, *A Soldier Reports*, p. 124.

58. Ibid.

59. Ibid., p. 127.

60. Ibid., p. 128.

61. Memo, McGeorge Bundy to the President, "Memorandum for Discussion, Tuesday, March 16, Policy on Vietnam," *Top Secret—Sensitive, NSC History—Troop Deployment.*

62. Westmoreland, *A Soldier Reports*, p. 129.

63. Ibid., pp. 129–30.

64. Cable, Ambassador Taylor to the President, March 17, 1965, *Re: MACV's 8250, NSC History—Troop Deployment.*

65. Taylor, *Swords and Plowshares*, pp. 339–41.

66. Memo, McGeorge Bundy to the President, March 31, 1965, "Your Meeting with Max Taylor at 5:15 This Afternoon," *Confidential, NSC History—Troop Deployment* (emphasis added). Three years later to the day, President Johnson would announce his withdrawal from the 1968 campaign.

67. Memo, McGeorge Bundy to the President, April 1, 1965, "Key Elements for Discussion, Thursday, April 1, at 5:30 P.M.," *Top Secret, NSC History—Troop Deployment.*

68. See transcript of White House news conference with George Reedy, 4:35 P.M., EDT, June 9, 1965, *NSC History—Troop Deployment.* See also NSAM 328, April 6, 1965, *Top Secret, NSC History—Troop Deployment.*

69. Westmoreland, *A Soldier Reports*, p. 135.

70. Cited in BDM Study, 3:119.

71. Memo, John McCone to Secretary of State, Secretary of Defense,

Special Assistant to the President for National Security Affairs, Ambassador
Maxwell Taylor, April 2, 1965, *Top Secret, NSC History—Troop Deployment.*

72. Letter, John McCone to the President, April 1, 1965, *Top Secret, NSC
History—Troop Deployment.*

73. Taylor, *Swords and Plowshares,* p. 341. See *Pentagon Papers,* 3: 103,
406, 408, 427–28.

74. Cable, Ambassador Taylor to Secretary Rusk, April 14, 1965, *Secret,*
#3384, *NSC History—Troop Deployment.* See State-Defense Message, *Lim-
Dis,* April 15, 1965, *Top Secret, NSC History—Troop Deployment.*

75. U.S. Grant Sharp, *Strategy for Defeat* (San Rafael, Calif.: Presidio
Press, 1978), p. 77.

76. Taylor, *Swords and Plowshares,* p. 342. See also cable, Taylor to
McGeorge Bundy and Secretary Rusk, April 17, 1965, Deptel 232, *Eyes Only,
NSC History—Troop Deployment.* Taylor demanded to know whether his
Embtel 3384 was even shown to the president.

77. Cable, Taylor to Bundy and Rusk, Deptel 232, April 17, 1965.

78. Taylor, *Swords and Plowshares,* pp. 341–42. Bundy immediately cabled back that "Secretary Rusk and I have reported your concerns to the
President in Texas and he has directed that all actions and visits be sus-
pended until after McNamara's meetings with Westmoreland in November.
. . . My own belief is your views and ours can be brought very close together
if we work at it. You can be sure that we will try to respect your heavy
responsibilities . . ." *(NSC History—Troop Deployment).*

79. Memo, McGeorge Bundy to the President, April 16, 1965, *Top Secret.*

80. Ibid.

81. Memo, Secretary McNamara to the President, April 21, 1965, *Top
Secret, NSC History—Troop Deployment.*

82. Sharp, *Strategy for Defeat,* p. 80. Taylor wrote to McNamara with
two amendments, which were *not* incorporated into McNamara's final report to the president: "I would like to amend the statement of my views
expressed in the memo for the President dated April 21 in two respects. A.
II, paragraph 1. 'This is because they believe that a settlement will come as
much or more from Viet Cong failure in the South as from DRV pain in the
North and that it will take more than six months, perhaps a year or two, to
demonstrate Viet Cong failure in the South.' Comment: This statement
suggests that it may take a year or two to break the will of Hanoi to continue
their present course even if we continue our bombing and introduce substantial U.S. forces. My view is that a favorable settlement should be possible
from a combination of continued air attacks and by the introduction of
sufficient U.S. and third country forces to demonstrate to Hanoi that the Viet
Cong have no ultimate chance of success. This process will probably take
months; how many is impossible to estimate. B. II, paragraph 2. 'All of them
envisioned a strike program continuing at least six months, perhaps a year
or two, avoiding the Hanoi–Haiphong–Phuc Yen areas during that period.'
Comment: I subscribe to this statement less the phrase 'perhaps a year or
two' " *(NSC History—Troop Deployment).*

83. Memo, McGeorge Bundy to the President, April 26, 1965, "Cable from Max Taylor," *(NSC History—Troop Deployment.*

84. Memo, George Ball to the President, April 21, 1965, "Should We Try to Move Toward a Vietnamese Settlement Now?" *Top Secret,* personal papers of George Ball, Princeton, N.J.

85. U.S., Central Intelligence Agency, Office of National Estimates, April 30, 1965, Special Memorandum No. 12–65, "Current Trends in Vietnam," *Secret, NSC History—Troop Deployment.*

86. Telegram, Taylor to Rusk, May 3, 1965, *Top Secret,* #3652, *NSC History—Troop Deployment.*

87. Cable, Taylor to Rusk, June 3, 1965, *Top Secret,* #4035, *NSC History—Troop Deployment.*

88. Taylor, *Swords and Plowshares,* pp. 403–5.

89. Cable, Taylor to Rusk, June 3, 1965 (emphasis added).

90. Bundy's views are interesting because on April 27 he informed the president, "Max [Taylor] now recommends a 9-battalion decision. My own view is that we ought to decide something more limited . . . the more gradual that we can keep this process of decision and action, the better" (Memo, Bundy to the President, April 27, 1965, *NSC History—Troop Deployment* [emphasis added]).

91. Embtel 4074, June 5, 1965, *NoDis, Top Secret, NSC History—Troop Deployment.*

92. See Department of State summary of INR Intelligence Note, May 25, *Secret/No Foreign Dissem.,* May 26, 1965, *NSC History—Troop Deployment.*

93. Ibid.

94. This information was supplied by a participant in the meeting.

95. Cable, General Westmoreland, June 7, 1965, "US Troop Deployment to SVN," *Top Secret—LimDis,* #19118, *NSC History—Troop Deployment* (emphasis added). "A broad review of force requirements has been conducted in light of changing situation in Southeast Asia and within RVN."

96. Ibid.

97. Westmoreland, *A Soldier Reports,* p. 139.

98. Cable, Secretary of State Rusk to Ambassador Taylor, State Department Message 2873, June 11, 1965, *Re:* MACV 19118, *NSC History—Troop Deployment.*

99. General Wheeler, Chairman JCS, to Secretary of Defense, June 11, 1965, "US/Allied Troop Deployments to South Vietnam (SVN)," JCSM–457–65, *Top Secret, NSC History—Troop Deployment.*

100. Earle Wheeler oral history interview, Johnson Library.

101. Cable, Taylor to the President, June 17, 1965, *Secret—NoDis,* #4220, *NSC History—Troop Deployment.*

102. Ibid.

103. COMUSMACV 20055, June 14, 1965, "Concept of Operations—Force Requirements and Deployments—South Vietnam," *Top Secret, NSC History—Troop Deployment* (emphasis added).

104. Memorandum for General Goodpaster, "Forces Required to Win in

South Vietnam," *Pentagon Papers,* 4:291.

105. Memo, W. F. Raborn to McGeorge Bundy, June 12, 1965, *NSC History—Troop Deployment.*

106. Memo, George Ball to the President, June 18, 1965, "Keeping the Power of Decision in the South Vietnam Crisis" *NSC History—Troop Deployment* (emphasis added).

107. Cable, Taylor to Rusk, June 28, 1965, *NSC History—Troop Deployment.*

108. Embassy Saigon No. 4402, U.S. Mission Message, *Top Secret,* attached to Bundy to the President, CAP 65363, *NSC History—Troop Deployment* (emphasis added).

109. Telegram, McGeorge Bundy to the President (at LBJ Ranch), June 26, 1965, *Secret, NSC History—Troop Deployment.*

110. Letter, Mike Mansfield to the President, June 22, 1965 (and enclosures of June 14, 1965, "Suggestions on the Vietnamese Situation," and June 9, 1965, "Vietnam"), *NSC History—Troop Deployment.*

111. Memo, George Ball to the President, June 28, 1965, "A Plan for Cutting Our Losses in South Viet-Nam," *Top Secret, NSC History—Troop Deployment.*

112. Cable, Taylor to the President, June 30, 1965, *NoDis,* #4434, *NSC History—Troop Deployment.*

113. See Embassy Saigon No. 4402.

IV. The Advisory Process at Work

1. Memo, McNamara to the President, June 26, 1965 (revised July 1, 1965), "Program of Expanded Military and Political Moves with Respect to Vietnam," *Top Secret, NSC History—Troop Deployment.* (Reprinted here as Appendix A.)

2. See Chapter Five for a discussion of the Third Stage.

3. *Public Papers,* April 25, 1965, press conference. See *New York Times,* April 26, 1965.

4. Memo, McNamara to the President, June 26, 1965 (July 1, 1965). On June 24, McGeorge Bundy informed the president that Rusk was "least negative," William Bundy "most negative," and McGeorge Bundy now favored "backing away" from going to the Security Council.

5. Ibid.

6. Memo, McGeorge Bundy to the Secretary of Defense, June 30, 1965, *Top Secret, NSC History—Troop Deployment* (emphasis added). (Reprinted here as Appendix B.)

7. Memo, Admiral Raborn to Secretary McNamara, June 30, 1965, "Comments on the Secretary of Defense's 26 June 1965 Memorandum, 'Program of Expanded Military and Political Moves with Respect to Vietnam,' " *Top Secret—Sensitive, NSC History—Troop Deployment* (emphasis added).

8. Ibid.

9. Memo, George Ball to the President, June 28, 1965, "A Plan for

Cutting Our Losses in South Viet-Nam" (emphasis added). This was only a seven-page summary of the proposed plan.

10. On June 29 Ball provided the complete nineteen-page memorandum.

11. Memo, Chester Cooper to Mr. Bundy, "Comments on Ball Paper, June 30, 1965," *Top Secret—Sensitive, NSC History—Troop Deployment* (emphasis added).

12. Memo, George Ball to the President, July 1, 1965, "A Compromise Solution for South Vietnam," *Top Secret,* personal papers of George Ball, Princeton, N.J. (Reproduced here as Appendix D.)

13. William Bundy, June 30, 1965, "Holding on in South Vietnam," *NSC History—Troop Deployment.*

14. Bundy received this assessment from Graham Martin, ambassador to Thailand. Cabling Bundy on June 30, Martin noted, "I must confess that I am rather startled by its [your memo] extreme pessimism, which I personally believe to be unwarranted. But having only recently returned from Washington, I am all too familiar with the enormous pressures with which you are contending." Martin hinted that civilian advisors were being misled by the military: "It was also axiomatic that any, repeat any, military commander would do his utmost to persuade his superiors to make available more than sufficient force to insure that he could handle the maximum—repeat, maximum—capability the enemy could bring to bear against him. As it looks from here, it does not seem that the situation in SVN is going all that badly" (Cable 2158, Martin [Bangkok] to Bundy, June 30, 1965, *Top Secret, NSC History—Troop Deployment*).

15. Memo, Dean Rusk to the President, July 1, 1965, "Vietnam," *Top Secret, NSC History—Troop Deployment* (emphasis added). See *Pentagon Papers,* Book 6, 4-C.7(a), p. 8; Warren Cohen, *Dean Rusk* (New York: Cooper Square Publishers, 1980), pp. 257–58.

16. Memo, George Ball to the President, June 23, 1965, "United States Commitments Regarding the Defense of South Vietnam," and cover memo, McGeorge Bundy to the President, June 27, 1965, *NSC History—Troop Deployment.*

17. Memo, McGeorge Bundy to the President, July 1, 1965, *Top Secret, NSC History—Troop Deployment* (emphasis added). (Reprinted here as Appendix C.)

18. Johnson, *The Vantage Point,* p. 144.

19. Taylor, *Swords and Plowshares,* pp. 348–49.

20. Cable, McNamara to Taylor, July 7, 1965, *Top Secret,* DEF 5319, *NSC History—Troop Deployment.*

21. Cable, Taylor to Secretary of State (to President), July 11, 1965, *NoDis, NSC History—Troop Deployment* (emphasis added).

22. Memo, McGeorge Bundy to the President, June 30, 1965, *Top Secret, NSC History—Troop Deployment.* On July 4, Bundy wrote Johnson, "we are over the hump on the Lodge transition except for details" *(NSC History—Troop Deployment).*

23. Cooper, *The Lost Crusade,* p. 281.

24. Notes of meeting in file, *NSC History—Troop Deployment.*

25. Johnson, *The Vantage Point,* pp. 143–44.

26. *Pentagon Papers,* 3:475. See Westmoreland, *A Soldier Reports,* p. 143.

27. Taylor, *Swords and Plowshares,* p. 348.

28. Ibid., p. 349.

29. Westmoreland, *A Soldier Reports,* p. 142.

30. Embtel 205, June 20, 1965, *NSC History—Troop Deployment.* From Saigon, Lodge cabled the president: "No one can establish schedules or make predictions. As President Johnson has often said of the American pioneers —from Plymouth Rock to the Far West—we must endure, we will learn and opportunities will come. But our grandchildren will not live to see the day that a united China does not probe in Southeast Asia" (cable, Lodge to the President, June 29, 1965, *NSC History—Troop Deployment*).

31. McGeorge Bundy to the President, July 18, 1965, 8:25 P.M., "Vietnam Planning at the Close of Business, July 18 (Sunday)," *NSC History—Troop Deployment* (emphasis added).

32. Memo, Secretary McNamara to the President, July 20, 1965, "Recommendations of Additional Deployments to Vietnam," *NSC History—Troop Deployment.*

33. Ibid. (emphasis added).

34. Westmoreland, *A Soldier Reports,* p. 142.

35. Memo, McNamara to the President, July 20, 1965, "Recommendations of Additional Deployments to Vietnam."

36. Memo, Chester Cooper to Secretary McNamara, July 20, 1965, *NSC History—Troop Deployment* (emphasis added).

37. Johnson, *The Vantage Point,* p. 146.

38. Valenti, *A Very Human President,* pp. 317–19.

39. Cooper, *The Lost Crusade,* pp. 281–82.

40. I have used Valenti's verbatim account of the meetings and checked them with at least two independent sources. See Valenti, *A Very Human President,* pp. 318–63 (emphases added).

41. Personal letter to the author.

42. Ball ms. For more details, see Ball, *The Past Has Another Pattern.*

43. William Bundy oral history, Johnson Library (emphasis added).

44. Memo, Chester Cooper to McGeorge Bundy, July 21, 1965, *NSC History—Troop Deployment.*

45. Memo, McGeorge Bundy to the President, July 21, 1965, "Timing of Decisions and Actions in Vietnam," *NSC History—Troop Deployment.*

46. See Irving Janis, *Victims of Groupthink* (Boston: Houghton Mifflin, 1972), pp. 120–21.

47. See letter, Clark Clifford to the President, May 17, 1965, *NSC History —Troop Deployment* (emphasis added). Also see Valenti, *A Very Human President.*

48. *Public Papers,* July 9, 1965, press conference.

49. Ibid., July 13, 1965.

50. William Bundy oral history, Johnson Library.

51. Memo, McGeorge Bundy to President Johnson, July 21, 1965, "Timing of Decisions and Actions in Vietnam" (emphasis added).

52. Personal letter to the author.

53. Ibid.

54. Summary notes of 553rd NSC meeting, *For the President Only. Top Secret—Sensitive*, July 27, 1965, Subject: "Deployment of Additional US Troops to Vietnam" *NSC History—Troop Deployment.*

55. Johnson, *The Vantage Point*, p. 149.

56. Halberstam, *The Best and the Brightest*, pp. 599–600.

57. Earle Wheeler oral history, Johnson Library.

58. BDM Study, vol. 5, sects. 2 and 3.

59. William Bundy, unpublished manuscript, personal papers of William Bundy, New York, N.Y.

60. Alexander George, *Presidential Decisionmaking in Foreign Policy: The Effective Use of Information and Advice* (Boulder, Colo.: Westview Press, 1980), p. 81.

61. George Ball, "Top Secret: The Prophecy the President Rejected," *Atlantic Monthly*, July 1972, pp. 35–49. See also memo, George Ball to Dean Rusk, Robert McNamara, and McGeorge Bundy, October 5, 1964, "How Valid Are the Assumptions Underlying Our Viet-Nam Policies?"

62. Cable 2158, Martin [Bangkok] to Bundy, June 30, 1965, *Top Secret, NSC History—Troop Deployment.*

V. Components of the Decision Process

1. James C. Thomson, Jr., "How Could Vietnam Happen? An Autopsy," *Atlantic Monthly*, April 1968, p. 47. George Reedy recalled, "How we got into Viet Nam will always be a mystery to me. It was a venture which ran counter to his basic instincts. As the Senate Democratic Leader, he had played an important role in damping down hotheads who wanted to go to the aid of the French at Dien Bien Phu. He was sufficiently steeped in military doctrine to know of the traditional US Army disinclination to fight a war on the mainland of Asia. During his service as Vice President, he had hinted to me and to others close to him of his repugnance over what he regarded as US machinations in Southeast Asia. And in the early days of his Presidency, when South Viet Nam was not even a public issue, he told me of his fears that it would bring him down in ruins" (Reedy, "Lyndon B. Johnson: A Retrospective on His Life," October 30, 1980).

2. Kennan ["X"], "The Sources of Soviet Conduct."

3. BDM Study, vol. 3.

4. Ibid. (emphasis added).

5. Ibid.

6. Ibid.

7. Clark Clifford oral history, Johnson Library.

8. BDM Study, vol. 3.

9. Personal letter to the author.

10. Letter, Gilpatric to McGeorge Bundy, July 9, 1965, *NSC History—*

Troop Deployment. On July 1 Jack Valenti wrote to Johnson, "Bundy suggests that you might choose to meet with your consultants on foreign affairs —all of whom are secure and all of whom can be trusted" (memo, Valenti to the President, July 1, 1965) The president approved a July 8 meeting.

11. William Bundy, "Report on Meeting with Foreign Affairs Consultants," July 22, 1965, *NSC History—Troop Deployment.* Recently released minutes from Cabinet meetings show how little these basic convictions changed between 1965 and 1967. During an August 23, 1967, Vietnam briefing, Secretary Rusk offered the following perspective: "Vietnam itself is only part of any answer. . . . The issue is whether a militant Communist faith in violence and subversion can succeed in Asia. Just ahead we face the prospect of a billion Chinese. . . . Asia has about a decade to pull up its socks and get ready to face these one billion Chinese with one billion Asians united in resistance and freedom. We can't duck it. . . . This is a desperate threat to the American people. Beyond the present and ten-year danger, the immediate and future validity of the American word is equally at stake in Vietnam. It is our promise that is at stake in Vietnam. We made a commitment to meet a common danger. If we break our word, will the Communist chieftains ever believe an American President when he says 'This won't go.'? President Kennedy had to put his word on the line in Vienna with Khruschev. The Soviets believed it when an American President promised 'to go to war' rather than yield to threats. The Cuban Missile Crisis is another case of a President's word being vital to the avoidance of war. . . . The President's credibility is the principal element supporting peace in the world" (Cabinet Meeting Minutes, August 23, 1967).

12. See memo, Secretary McNamara to the President, June 26, 1965, "Program of Expanded Military and Political Moves with Respect to Vietnam," and memo, Secretary McNamara to the President, July 20, 1965, "Recommendations of Additional Deployments to Vietnam."

13. Sharp, *Strategy for Defeat,* pp. 89, 91.

14. See Valenti, *A Very Human President,* pp. 327–28.

15. See memo, George Ball to the President, June 28, 1965, "A Plan for Cutting Our Losses in South Viet-Nam." See also Department of State, *Secret —Limited Distribution,* Office of Intelligence and Research, July 23, 1965, *NSC History—Troop Deployment.*

16. Ibid.

17. Cable, Taylor to Secretary of State (to President), July 11, 1965.

18. Central Intelligence Agency, Office of Current Intelligence, June 29, 1965, SC No. 07353/65, "Developments in South Vietnam During the Past Year," Vietnam Country File, South Vietnam.

19. Memo, George Ball to the President, July 1, 1965, "A Compromise Solution for Viet-Nam" (emphasis added). See his earlier, June 28, 1965, memo to the president, "A Plan for Cutting Our Losses in South Viet-Nam."

20. See memo, McGeorge Bundy to Secretary McNamara, June 30, 1965.

21. See memo, William Bundy to the President, July 1, 1965.

22. Memo, Chester Cooper to McGeorge Bundy, July 20, 1965, *NSC History—Troop Deployment.*

23. *Pentagon Papers,* 4:290–92.

24. Ibid.

25. Memo, first draft, John McNaughton to Secretary McNamara, July 13, 1965, "Analysis and Options for South Vietnam," *Top Secret, NSC History— Troop Deployment.*

26. *Pentagon Papers,* 4:290–92.

27. Memo, Mansfield to the President, July 27, 1965, "Meeting on Vietnam," *NSC History—Troop Deployment.* Mansfield wrote the memo following an afternoon meeting with Senators Russell, Fulbright, Sparkman, Aiken, and Cooper. Mansfield concluded, "there was full agreement that insofar as Vietnam is concerned we are deeply enmeshed in a place where we ought not to be; that the situation is rapidly out of control; and that every effort should be made to extricate ourselves."

28. Memo, McNamara to the President, July 28, 1965, *Confidential Please, NSC History—Troop Deployment* (emphasis added).

29. Taylor, *Swords and Plowshares,* p. 400.

30. Doris Kearns, *Lyndon Johnson and the American Dream* (New York: Harper and Row, 1976), p. 282.

31. Clark Clifford oral history, Johnson Library.

32. Taylor, *Swords and Plowshares,* pp. 401–2.

33. Sharp, *Strategy for Defeat,* pp. 149–50.

34. Taylor, *Swords and Plowshares,* p. 400.

35. Personal letter to the author.

36. BDM Study, vol. 1.

37. Ball ms. For more details, see Ball, *The Past Has Another Pattern.*

38. McGeorge Bundy to Berman, personal letter to the author.

39. Humphrey, *The Education of a Public Man,* p. 323.

40. Johnson, *The Vantage Point,* p. 323. See the entire chapter "Quality of Life," pages 322–46. It is interesting that Johnson placed the discussion of the July 28 decision in that chapter.

41. Ibid., p. 322.

42. Ibid., p. 323.

43. Ibid., p. 326.

44. Memo, McGeorge Bundy to the President, June 30, 1965, "France in Vietnam, 1954, and the U.S. in Vietnam, 1965—A Useful Analogy," *Confidential, NSC History—Troop Deployment.*

45. Ball ms. For more details, see Ball, *The Past Has Another Pattern.*

46. Johnson, *The Vantage Point,* p. 324 (emphasis added).

47. Joseph Alsop, "Mr. Facing Two Ways," *Washington Post,* July 29, 1965 (emphasis added).

48. Letter, John Kenneth Galbraith to the President, June 16, 1965, *Personal and Strictly Confidential* (emphasis added).

49. Letter, Johnson to Galbraith, July 13, 1966.

50. Humphrey, *The Education of a Public Man,* p. 323 (emphasis added).

51. Personal, postpresidential diary of Dwight David Eisenhower, supplied to the author by Prof. Fred Greenstein, Princeton University.

Bibliography

Acheson, Dean. *Present at the Creation*. New York: W. W. Norton, 1969.

Arlen, Michael J. *Living Room War*. New York: Viking Press, 1969.

Austin, Anthony. *The President's War*. Philadelphia: J. B. Lippincott, 1971.

Barnet, Richard J. *The Roots of War*. New York: Atheneum, 1972.

———. *Intervention and Revolution*. New York: New American Library Mentor, 1972.

Bloodworth, Dennis. *An Eye for the Dragon: Southeast Asia Observed: 1954–1970*. New York: Farrar, Straus, and Giroux, 1970.

Boettiger, John R., comp. *Vietnam and American Foreign Policy*. Boston: D.C. Heath, 1968.

Braestrup, Peter. *Big Story: How the American Press and Television Reported and Interpreted the Crisis of Tet 1968 in Viet Nam and Washington*. 2 vols. Boulder, Col.: Westview Press, 1976.

Brandon, Henry. *Anatomy of Error: The Inside Story of the Asian War on the Potomac, 1954–69*. Boston: Gambit, 1969.

Brodie, Bernard. *War and Politics*. New York: Macmillan, 1973.

Bryan, C. D. B. *Friendly Fire*. New York: G. P. Putnam, 1976.

Buttinger, Joseph. *The Smaller Dragon: A Political History of Vietnam*. New York: Praeger, 1958.

———. *Vietnam: A Dragon Embattled*. 2 vols. New York: Praeger, 1967.

———. *A Dragon Defiant: A Short History of Vietnam*. New York: Praeger, 1972.

———. *Vietnam: The Unforgettable Tragedy*. New York: Horizon Press, 1977.

Cairns, James F. *The Eagle and the Lotus: Western Intervention in Vietnam,*

1847–1971. Melbourne, Australia: Lansdowne Press, 1971.

Center for Strategic Studies. *Economic Impact of the Vietnam War.* Washington, D.C.: Georgetown University, 1967.

Chen, John H. M. *Vietnam: A Comprehensive Bibliography.* Metuchen, N.J.: The Scarecrow Press, 1973.

Chomsky, Noam. *American Power and the New Mandarins.* New York: Pantheon Books, 1969.

Christian, George. *The President Steps Down: A Personal Memoir of the Transfer of Power.* New York: Macmillan, 1970.

Clifford, Clark M. "A Viet Nam Reappraisal." *Foreign Affairs* 47 (July 1969): 601–22.

Cohen, Warren. *Dean Rusk.* New York: Cooper Square Publishers, 1980.

Collins, Col. John M. *The Vietnam War in Perspective.* Washington, D.C.: Strategic Research Group, The National War College, 1972.

Cooper, Chester L. *The Lost Crusade.* New York: Dodd, Mead, 1970.

Draper, Theodore. *Abuse of Power.* New York: Viking Press, 1967.

Ellsberg, Daniel. *Papers on the War.* New York: Simon and Schuster, 1972.

Fair, Charles. *From the Jaws of Victory.* New York: W. W. Norton, 1972.

Fairlie, Henry. *The Kennedy Promise.* Garden City, N.Y.: Doubleday, 1973.

Fall, Bernard. *Street Without Joy: Indochina At War, 1946–54.* Harrisburg, Pa.: Stackpole, 1961, 1963.

———. *Vietnam Witness, 1953–66.* London: Pall Mall Press, 1966.

———. *Hell in a Very Small Place: The Siege of Dien Bien Phu.* Philadelphia: J. B. Lippincott, 1966.

———. *Last Reflections on a War.* Garden City, N.Y.: Doubleday, 1967.

———. *The Two Vietnams: A Political and Military Analysis.* New York: Praeger, 1963.

Fall, Bernard, and Raskin, Marcus, eds. *The Vietnam Reader.* New York: Vintage, 1965.

Fifield, Russell H. *Americans in Southeast Asia: The Roots of Commitment.* New York: Thomas Y. Crowell, 1973.

Fishel, Wesley, ed. *Vietnam: Anatomy of a Conflict.* Itasca, Ill.: F. E. Peacock, 1968.

Fitzgerald, Frances. *Fire in the Lake.* Boston: Little, Brown, 1972.

Fulbright, J. William. *The Arrogance of Power.* New York: Random House, Vintage, 1967.

———. *The Crippled Giant: American Foreign Policy and Its Domestic Consequences.* New York: Random House, 1972.

Furgurson, Ernest B. *Westmoreland, the Inevitable General.* Boston: Little, Brown, 1968.

Galloway, John. *The Gulf of Tonkin Resolution.* Rutherford, N.J.: Fairleigh Dickinson University Press, 1970.

Galluci, Robert L. *Neither Peace Nor Honor.* Baltimore: Johns Hopkins University Press, 1975.

Gavin, James. *Crisis Now.* New York: Random House, 1968.

Gelb, Leslie H. "Vietnam: The System Worked." *Foreign Policy* 1 (Summer 1971): 110–73.

————. "The Essential Domino: American Politics and Vietnam." *Foreign Affairs* 50 (April 1972): 459–75.

Gelb, Leslie, and Betts, Richard. *The Irony of Vietnam: The System Worked.* Washington, D.C.: Brookings Institution, 1979.

George, Alexander. *Presidential Decisionmaking in Foreign Policy: The Effective Use of Information and Advice.* Boulder, Colo.: Westview Press, 1979.

Geyelin, Philip L. *Lyndon B. Johnson and the World.* New York: Praeger, 1966.

Giap, Gen. Vo Nguyen. *Big Victory, Great Task.* New York: Praeger, 1967.

Goldman, Eric F. *The Tragedy of Lyndon Johnson.* New York: Dell, 1969.

Goodwin, Richard N. *Triumph or Tragedy: Reflections on Vietnam.* New York: Random House, 1966.

Goulden, Joseph C. *Truth Is the First Casualty.* Chicago: Rand McNally, 1969.

Graff, Henry F. *The Tuesday Cabinet: Deliberation and Decision on Peace and War under Lyndon B. Johnson.* Englewood Cliffs, N.J.: Prentice-Hall, 1970.

Halberstam, David. *The Making of a Quagmire.* New York: Random House, 1965.

————. *The Best and the Brightest.* New York: Random House, 1972.

Harvey, Frank. *Air War—Vietnam.* New York: Bantam Books, 1967.

Herring, George C. *America's Longest War.* New York: John Wiley and Sons, 1979.

Hilsman, Roger. *To Move a Nation: The Politics of Foreign Policy in the Administration of JFK.* Garden City, N.Y.: Doubleday, 1967.

Hoopes, Townsend. *The Limits of Intervention.* New York: David McKay, 1970.

Humphrey, Hubert H. *The Education of a Public Man.* Garden City, N.Y.: Doubleday, 1976.

Janis, Irving L. *Victims of Groupthink.* Boston: Houghton Mifflin, 1972.

Johnson, Haynes B., and Gwertzman, Bernard M. *Fulbright: The Dissenter.* Garden City, N.Y.: Doubleday, 1968.

Johnson, Lady Bird. *A White House Diary.* New York: Holt, Rinehart and Winston, 1970.

Johnson, Lyndon B. *The Vantage Point: Perspectives of the Presidency.* New York: Holt, Rinehart and Winston, 1971.

Kahin, George. "The Pentagon Papers: A Critical Evaluation." *American Political Science Review* 69 (June 1975): 675–84.

Kahin, George, and Lewis, John. *The United States in Vietnam.* New York: Dell, 1969.

Kalb, Marvin, and Abel, Elie. *Roots of Involvement: The United States in Asia, 1784–1971.* New York: W. W. Norton, 1971.

Kattenburg, Paul. *The Vietnam Trauma in American Foreign Policy, 1945–75.* New Brunswick, N.J.: Transaction Books, 1980.

Kaufman, William W. *The McNamara Strategy.* New York: Harper and Row, 1965.

Kearns, Doris. *Lyndon Johnson and the American Dream.* New York: Harper and Row, 1976.

Kendrick, Alexander. *The Wound Within: America in the Vietnam Years, 1945–1974.* Boston: Little, Brown, 1974.

Kinnard, Douglas. *The War Managers.* Hanover, N.H.: University Press of New England, 1977.

Kraft, Joseph. "Washington Insight: The Enigma of Dean Rusk." *Harper's Magazine,* July 1965, pp. 100–3.

Krause, Patricia A., ed. *Anatomy of an Undeclared War: Congressional Conference on the Pentagon Papers.* New York: International Universities Press, 1972.

Lake, Anthony, ed. *The Vietnam Legacy: The War, American Society, and the Future of American Foreign Policy.* New York: New York University Press, 1976.

Lewy, Guenter. *America in Vietnam.* New York: Oxford University Press, 1978.

Littauer, Raphael, and Uphoff, Norman, eds. *The Air War in Indochina.* Boston: Beacon Press, 1972.

Lodge, Henry Cabot. *The Storm Has Many Eyes: A Personal Narrative.* New York: W. W. Norton, 1973.

May, Ernest. *Lessons of the Past: The Use and Misuse of History in American Policy.* New York: Oxford University Press, 1973.

Mecklin, John. *Mission in Torment: An Intimate Account of the U.S. Role in Vietnam.* Garden City, N.Y.: Doubleday, 1965.

Millet, Allan, ed. *A Short History of the Vietnam War.* Bloomington: Indiana University Press, 1978.

Miroff, Bruce. *Pragmatic Illusions.* New York: David McKay, 1976.

Morgenthau, Hans. "We Are Deluding Ourselves in Vietnam." *New York Times Magazine,* April 18, 1965, pp. 25, 85ff.

Mueller, John E. *War, Presidents and Public Opinion.* New York: John Wiley and Sons, 1973.

O'Neill, Robert J. *The Strategy of General Giap Since 1964.* Canberra: Australian National University Press, 1969.

Paolucci, Henry. *War, Peace, and the Presidency.* New York: McGraw-Hill, 1968.

The Pentagon Papers: The Defense Department History of U.S. Decision-Making on Vietnam. Senator Gravel Edition, 4 vols. Boston: Beacon Press, 1971.

Pike, Douglas. *War, Peace, and the Viet Cong.* Cambridge, Mass.: M.I.T. Press, 1969.

Randle, Robert F. *Geneva 1954: The Settlement of the Indochinese War.* Princeton, N.J.: Princeton University Press, 1969.

Raskin, Marcus G. *The Vietnam Reader: Articles and Documents on American Foreign Policy and the Vietnam Crisis.* New York: Vintage Books, 1967.

Roberts, Charles W. *LBJ's Inner Circle.* New York: Delacorte Press, 1965.

Roherty, James. *Decisions of Robert S. McNamara: A Study of the Role of the Secretary of Defense.* Coral Gables, Fla.: University of Miami Press, 1970.

Rostow, Walt W. *The Diffusion of Power: An Essay in Recent History.* New York: Macmillan, 1972.

Schandler, Herbert. *The Unmaking of a President.* Princeton, N.J.: Princeton University Press, 1977.

Schoenbrun, David. *Vietnam: How We Got In, How To Get Out.* New York: Atheneum, 1968.

Schlesinger, Arthur M., Jr. *A Thousand Days.* Boston: Houghton Mifflin, 1965.

———. *The Bitter Heritage: Vietnam and American Democracy.* Boston: Houghton Mifflin, 1967.

———. *Robert Kennedy and His Times.* New York: Ballantine Books, 1981.

Schurmann, Franz; Scott, Peter Dale; and Zelnik, Reginald. *The Politics of Escalation in Vietnam.* Boston: Beacon Press, 1966.

Sharp, Admiral U. S. Grant, USN. *Report on the War in Vietnam: Section I, Report on Air and Naval Campaigns Against North Vietnam and Pacific Command-Wide Support of the War, June 1964–July 1968.* Washington, D.C.: U.S. Government Printing Office, 1969.

———. *Strategy for Defeat: Vietnam in Retrospect.* San Rafael, Calif.: Presidio Press, 1978.

Sheehan, Neil; Smith, Hedrick; Kenworthy, E. W.; and Butterworth, Fox, eds. *The Pentagon Papers as Published by the New York Times.* New York: Quadrangle Books, 1971.

Sherrill, Robert. *The Accidental President.* New York: Pyramid Books, 1968.

Sidey, Hugh. *A Very Personal Presidency: LBJ in the White House.* New York: Atheneum, 1968.

Sorenson, Theodore. *Decision-Making in the White House.* New York: Columbia University Press, 1963.

Stavins, Ralph; Barnet, Richard J.; and Raskin, Marcus G. *Washington Plans an Aggressive War.* New York: Vintage, 1971.

Stoessinger, John. *Crusaders and Pragmatists.* New York: W. W. Norton, 1979.

Sullivan, Cornelius D.; Eliot, George Field; Gayle, Gordon D.; and Corson, William R., eds. *The Vietnam War: Its Conduct and Higher Direction.* Washington, D.C.: Center for Strategic Studies, Georgetown University, 1968.

Taylor, Maxwell D. *The Uncertain Trumpet.* New York: Harper, 1959.

———. *Swords and Plowshares.* New York: W. W. Norton, 1972.

Thompson, James Clay. *Rolling Thunder.* Chapel Hill: University of North Carolina Press, 1980.

Thompson, Sir Robert G. K. *No Exit from Vietnam.* London: Chatto and Windus, 1969.

Thompson, W. Scott, and Frizzel, Donaldson, eds. *The Lessons of Vietnam.* New York: Crane, Russak, 1977.

Thomson, James, Jr., "How Could Vietnam Happen: An Autopsy." *Atlantic Monthly,* April 1968, pp. 47–53.

Trewhitt, Henry L. *McNamara: His Ordeal in the Pentagon.* New York: Harper and Row, 1971.

Tuchman, Barbara. "History by the Ounce." *Harper's,* July 1965, p. 6.

Ungar, Sanford J. *The Papers and the Papers: An Account of the Legal and Political Battle over the Pentagon Papers.* New York: E. P. Dutton, 1972.

U.S., Congress, House, Committee on Armed Services. *United States–Vietnam Relations, 1945–1967: A Study Prepared by the Department of Defense.* 12 vols. Washington, D.C.: U.S. Government Printing Office, 1971.

U.S., Congress, Senate, Committee on Appropriations. *Supplemental Defense Appropriations Bill, 1967.* H.R. 13546, Senate Report no. 1074, 89th Cong., 2d sess., March 17, 1966.

————, Committee on Armed Service. *Air War Against North Vietnam.* Hearings before the Preparedness Investigating Subcommittee, 90th Cong., 1st sess., 1967.

————, Committee on Foreign Relations. *The Vietnam Conflict: The Substance and the Shadow. Report of Senator Mike Mansfield and Others.* 89th Cong., 2d sess., Committee Print, January 6, 1966.

————. *Conflicts Between United States Capabilities and Foreign Commitments.* Hearings, 90th Cong., 1st sess., with Lt.-Gen. James M. Gavin, U.S. Army, Ret., February 21, 1967.

————. *Background Information Relating to Southeast Asia and Vietnam.* 6th rev. ed. Washington, D.C.: U.S. Government Printing Office, June 1970.

————. *U.S. Involvement in the Overthrow of Diem, 1963.* Staff study based on the Pentagon Papers. Washington, D.C.: U.S. Government Printing office, July 20, 1972.

U.S., Commission on the Organization of the Government for the Conduct of Foreign Policy. *Commission on the Organization of the Government for the Conduct of Foreign Policy.* June, 1975. Summary and vols. 1–7. Washington, D.C.: U.S. Government Printing Office, 1975.

U.S., Department of Defense. *United States–GVN Relations.* 12 vols. Washington, D.C.: U.S. Government Printing Office, 1972.

U.S., Department of State. *Aggression from the North: The Record of North Vietnam's Campaign to Conquer South Vietnam.* Publication 7339, February 1965.

U.S., Military Assistance Command, Vietnam. *1967 Wrap-up: A Year of Progress.* Saigon: U.S. Military Assistance Command, Vietnam, 1968.

U.S., President. *Public Papers of the Presidents of the United States: Lyndon B. Johnson, 1965.* 2 vols. Washington, D.C.: U.S. Government Printing Office, 1966.

————. *Public Papers of the Presidents of the United States: Lyndon B. Johnson, 1967.* 2 vols. Washington, D.C.: U.S. Government Printing Office, 1968.

————. *Public Papers of the Presidents of the United States: Lyndon B. Johnson, 1968–69.* 2 vols. Washington, D.C.: U.S. Government Printing Office, 1970.

Valenti, Jack. *A Very Human President.* New York: W. W. Norton, 1975.

Westmoreland, Gen. William C. *Report on the War in Vietnam: Section II, Report on Operations in South Vietnam, January 1964–June 1968.* Washington, D.C.: U.S. Government Printing Office, 1969.

————. *A Soldier Reports.* Garden City, N.Y.: Doubleday, 1976.

White, Ralph K. *Nobody Wanted War: Misperceptions in Vietnam and Other Wars.* Garden City, N.Y.: Doubleday, 1968.

Wicker, Tom. *JFK and LBJ: The Influence of Personality upon Politics.* Baltimore: Penguin, 1972.

Windchy, Eugene C. *Tonkin Gulf.* Garden City, N.Y.: Doubleday, 1971.

Appendix A

SUBJECT: Program of expanded military and political moves with respect
to Vietnam

Introduction. Our objective is to create conditions for a favorable settlement by demonstrating to the VC/DRV that the odds are against their
winning. Under present conditions, however, the chances of achieving this
objective are small—and the VC are winning now—largely because the ratio
of guerrilla to anti-guerrilla forces is unfavorable to the government. With
this in mind, we must choose among three courses of action with respect to
South Vietnam: (1) Cut our losses and withdraw under the best conditions
that can be arranged; (2) continue at about the present level, with US forces
limited to, say, 75,000, holding on and playing for the breaks while recognizing that our position will probably grow weaker; or (3) expand substantially
the US military pressure against the Viet Cong in the South and the North
Vietnamese in the North and at the same time launch a vigorous effort on
the political side to get negotiations started. An outline of the third of these
approaches follows.

I. *Expanded military moves.* The following military moves should be taken
together with the political initiatives in Part II below.

A. *Inside South Vietnam.* Increase US/SVN military strength in SVN
enough to prove to the VC that they cannot win and thus to turn the tide
of the war.

1. *Increase combined US/GVN ground strength to the level required effectively to counter the current and likely VC ground strength.* * On the assumption that GVN strength holds its own, a decision should be made now to bring the US/3d-country deployments to 44 battalions within the next few months. Their mission would include hounding, harassing and hurting the VC should they elect not to stand and fight. General Westmoreland says that infusion of such forces with such missions on the schedule proposed "should re-establish the military balance by the end of December." He continues that "it will not per se cause the enemy to back off."** General Westmoreland's recommendations are shown below:

MACV RECOMMENDED FOR 1965

III MAF	9 bn (2 due 7/5)
173d Abn Bde	2 bn
1st Inf Div	9 bn (3 due 7/15; 6 could arrive 9/1)
101st Abn Div	3 bn (due 7/28)
Air Mob Div	8 bn (due 9/1)
1 MAF	
	<u>3 bn</u> (1 due 7/1; 2 could arrive in 12 days)
Total US	34 bn (175,000)
A/NZ	1 bn
ROK (or US?)	
	<u>9 bn</u> (could arrive approx. 10/15)
TOTAL	44 bn

2. *Deploy 13 additional US helicopter companies and 5 additional Chinook platoons to increase effectiveness of US/GVN forces.*

3. *Deploy additional US artillery batteries and engineers to reinforce ARVN divisions and corps.*

4. *Carry out 800 B-52 sorties a month in strikes against VC havens* (followed promptly by entry of ground-forces into the struck areas).

*Discuss with Ky his view of the military outlook, his plan for improving the situation and his appraisal of the extent to which an increase in US presence along these lines (a) would arrest the deterioration and/or (b) would have a net counter-productive "French colonial" effect. If he suggests the latter, ask how he can offset the VC strength advantage without using additional US forces.

**Westmoreland reports that he "cannot now state what additional forces may be required in 1966 to gain and maintain the military initiative." He says that "instinctively, we believe that there may be substantial US force requirements." He has a study under way, with a fairly solid estimate due soon.

B. *Against North Vietnam.* * While avoiding striking population and industrial targets not closely related to the DRV's supply of war material to the VC, we should announce to Hanoi and carry out actions to destroy such supplies and to interdict their flow into and out of North Vietnam.

1. *Quarantine the movement of war supplies into North Vietnam—by sea, rail and road.*

a. *Mine the DRV harbors.* Seaborne traffic accounts for 80% of the DRV foreign trade, including practically all POL, the single import most vital to the DRV (the DRV armed forces consume 40% of the POL and transportation most of the remainder). Sixty per cent of the bottoms are Free World under charter mainly to China, but almost all POL is carried by Communist tankers. Practically all of the seaborne traffic moves through four ports. Mining of those ports could be launched on 72 hours notice, and delayed fusing (three days) could be employed to permit ships time to exit after the fields were laid. A full mining effort to plant all fields would require 97 sorties; the fields could be sustained with 38 sorties per month.

b. *Destroy rail and highway bridges leading from China to Hanoi.* There are 15 highway, 5 railroad and 8 railroad/highway bridges north and east of Hanoi. The railroads now carry between 1600 and 1900 short tons per day. Roads to Hanoi from China can support considerable truck traffic. It would take approximately 1000 sorties to carry out strikes on the 28 bridges, with 85% probability of dropping one span in each case.

c. *Conduct intensive armed reconnaissance of the LOCs from China.*

2. *Destroy the war-making supplies and facilities of North Vietnam wherever they may be located.* There are 56 unstruck targets in this category —1 explosive plant, 1 airfield, 5 supply and ordnance depots, 7 ammunition depots, 9 POL storage, 12 military barracks/headquarters, 2 communications facilities, 6 naval base/port facilities, and 13 power plants. Approximately 1650 strike sorties would be required to attack all of these targets. About half of them would be suitable for B-52 attack. Only three are likely to lead to more than 100 civilian casualties under daylight alert conditions.

3. *Interdict movement of war supplies within and out of North Vietnam by an expanded strike and armed reconnaissance program against LOCs west and south of Hanoi.*

a. *Expand strike program against bridges, ferries, railroads and roads.* Other than 6 locks-and-dams targets, only 4 bridges and 4 railroad shops and

*Because of the short lead-times involved in all of these actions, no decision with respect to them is needed now. Actions to quarantine the ports or to intensify the strike program against the North can on short notice be made a part of an increasing-pressures program.

yards remain unstruck in this category. These eight targets would require approximately 266 sorties. Two of them—both railroad yards in Hanoi—would probably result in more than 100 civilian casualties. Three of them—the two Hanoi railroad yards and the Yen Vien railroad yard—would be suitable for B-52 strike.

b. *Expand armed reconnaissance against LOCs.* These LOCs south and west of Hanoi, together with the LOCs north and east of Hanoi referred to in para 1c above, should be struck by 1000 sorties a week. This would increase the total strike-plus-armed recce [reconnaisance] sorties against North Vietnam from 1800 to 5000 a month. (Efforts should be continued in Laos to interdict the "trail" there, and at sea preventing infiltration by water.)

4. *Be prepared to destroy airfields and SAM sites as necessary to accomplish the objectives of sub-paras 1–3 above.*

C. *In the United States.* Even if US deployments to Vietnam are no more than 100,000 men, we should:

1. *Call up selected reserve forces* (approximately 100,000 men).
2. *Extend tours of duty in all Services.*

II. *Expanded political moves.* Together with the above military moves, we should take the following political initiatives in order (a) to open a dialogue with Hanoi, Peking, and the VC looking toward a settlement in Vietnam, (b) to keep the Soviet Union from deepening its military involvement and support of North Vietnam until the time when settlement can be achieved, and (c) to cement the support for US policy by the US public, allies and friends, and to keep international opposition at a manageable level. While our approaches may be rebuffed until the tide begins to turn, they nevertheless should be made.

A. *Political Initiatives.*

1. *Moscow.* Place a high level US representative in contact with Moscow to discuss frankly and fully with Soviet leaders our intentions and our desire to find common ground to work with them rather than come into conflict. We would reiterate that US objectives are limited but at the same time we have a firm determination to achieve them. [sentence deleted during declassification] We would press the Soviets to avoid any deeper involvement. We would emphasize that continuation of the military phase can only be harmful to the Communist cause and urge the Soviets to step in (perhaps with British Co-Chairman) to move the situation away from war and toward a peaceful settlement.

2. *United Nations.* As a prelude to expansion of the military effort, we should consider once more putting before the UN the Vietnam question for

discussion with the Chicoms and North Vietnamese present. They will almost surely refuse to attend and will provide us with a better position for expanding military action; but if they accept we will have the prospect of negotiations without having stopped our bombing.

3. *Other international forums.* In all international forums and contacts, public and private, continue to demonstrate to the world who is responsible for the trouble in Vietnam and persuade them that our course of supporting the South, including bombings, must be accepted and if possible supported. Whenever we can provide further demonstrations of Communist intransigence and refusal to treat reasonably on this question, this will strengthen our case.

4. *Geneva Conference.* US should propose a Geneva Conference of all world powers (including France) with the subject, "Peace in Southeast Asia."

5. *NLF and DRV.* GVN—and US after consultation with the GVN—should initiate contacts with the Liberation Front and North Vietnam, making clear a readiness to discuss ways and means of achieving settlement in Vietnam.

6. *Chicoms.* If there is any sign of Chinese willingness to begin discussions, US should contact the Chinese to set forth US position including our limited objective and the dangers to China of continuation of the war, and should press the Chinese to bring the aggression against the South to an end.

7. *UK, Canada, India, France, U Thant.* Consult individually with the British, Canadians, U Thant, Indians, French and possibly other neutrals to enlist them in taking peace initiatives bilaterally, multilaterally or through international organizations however best calculated to bring about the participation of Communist Governments.

8. *Other initiatives.* In connection with paras 1–7 above, US and GVN would make it clear they stand ready to take any reasonable action which does not endanger their military posture which might improve the chances of success of any peace initiatives. This could include a bombing "pause." It could include an explicit restatement of US intention of withdrawing from South Vietnam at the appropriate time, a South Vietnamese announcement of responsible treatment of NLF–VC personnel who remain in the South, emphasis on implementation of President's April 7 offer for economic development in South East Asia, etc.

B. *Initiatives inside South Vietnam.* Take steps to induce VC defections and to increase support for the Ky government—among other steps, these:

1. *Economic program.* Sharply expand program of economic aid in South Vietnam—including a major construction program, junk building, increased rice and pig output, improved distribution and marketing procedures.

2. *Chu Hoi program.* Improve and expand Chu Hoi program—with a good man in charge on the US side, and bounties, amnesties, work and educational opportunities, and other inducements.

III. *Evaluation of the above program.*

A. *Domestic US reaction.* Even though casualties will increase and the war will continue for some time, the United States public will support this course of action because it is a combined military-political program designed and likely to bring about a favorable solution to the Vietnam problem.

B. *Communist reaction to the expanded programs.*

1. *Soviet.* The Soviets can be expected to continue to contribute materiel and advisors to the North Vietnamese. Increased US bombing of Vietnam, including targets in Hanoi and Haiphong, SAM sites and airfields, and mining of North Vietnamese harbors, might oblige the Soviet Union to enter the contest more actively with volunteers and aircraft. This might result in minor encounters between US and Soviet personnel.

2. *China.* So long as no US or GVN troops invade North Vietnam and so long as no US or GVN aircraft attack Chinese territory, the Chinese probably will not send regular ground forces or aircraft into the war. However, the possibility of a more active Soviet involvement in North Vietnam might precipitate a Chinese introduction of land forces, probably dubbed volunteers, to preclude the Soviets' taking a pre-eminent position in North Vietnam.

3. *North Vietnam.* North Vietnam will not move towards the negotiating table until the tide begins to turn in the south. When that happens, they may seek to counter it by sending large numbers of men into South Vietnam.

4. *Viet Cong.* The VC, especially if they continue to take high losses, can be expected to depend increasingly upon the PAVN forces as the war moves into a more conventional phase; but they may find ways of continuing almost indefinitely their present intensive military, guerrilla and terror activities, particularly if reinforced with some regular PAVN units. A key question on the military side is whether POL, ammunition and cadres can be cut off and if they are cut off whether this really renders the Viet Cong impotent. A key question on the political side is whether any arrangement acceptable to us would be acceptable to the VC.

C. *Estimate of success.*

1. *Militarily.* The success of the above program from a military point of view turns on whether the increased effort stems the tide in the South; that in turn depends on two things—on whether the South Vietnamese hold their own in terms of numbers and fighting spirit, and on whether the US forces

can be effective in a quick-reaction reserve role, a role in which they have not been tested. The number of US troops is too small to make a significant difference in the traditional 10–1 government–guerrilla formula, but it is not too small to make a significant difference in the kind of war which seems to be evolving in Vietnam—a "Third Stage" or conventional war in which it is easier to identify, locate and attack the enemy. (South Vietnam has 141 battalions as compared with an estimated equivalent number of VC battalions. The 44 US/3d country battalions mentioned above are the equivalent of 100 South Vietnamese battalions.)

2. *Politically.* It is frequently alleged that such a large expansion of US military personnel, their expanded military role (which would put them in close contact and offer some degree of control over South Vietnamese citizens), and the inevitable expansion of US voice in the operation of the GVN economy and facilities, command and government services will be unpopular; it is said that they could lead to the rejection of the government which supported this American presence, to an irresistible pressure for expulsion of the Americans, and to the greatly increased saleability of Communist propaganda. Whether these allegations are true, we do not know.

The political initiatives are likely to be successful in the early stages only to demonstrate US good faith; they will pay off toward an actual settlement only after the tide begins to turn (unless we lower our sights substantially). The tide almost certainly cannot begin to turn in less than a few months, and may not for a year or more; the war is one of attrition and will be a long one. Since troops once committed as a practical matter cannot be removed, since US casualties will rise, since we should take call-up actions to support the additional forces in Vietnam, the test of endurance may be as much in the United States as in Vietnam.

3. *Generally (CIA estimate).* Over the longer term we doubt if the Communists are likely to change their basic strategy in Vietnam (i.e., aggressive and steadily mounting insurgency) unless and until two conditions prevail: (1) they are forced to accept a situation in the war in the South which offers them no prospect of an early victory and no grounds for hope that they can simply outlast the US and (2) North Vietnam itself is under continuing and increasingly damaging punitive attack. So long as the Communists think they scent the possibility of an early victory (which is probably now the case), we believe that they will persevere and accept extremely severe damage to the North. Conversely, if North Vietnam itself is not hurting, Hanoi's doctrinaire leaders will probably be ready to carry on the Southern struggle almost indefinitely. If, however, both of the conditions outlined above should be brought to pass, we believe Hanoi probably would, at least for a period of time, alter its basic strategy and course of action in South Vietnam.

Hanoi might do so in several ways. Going for a conference as a political way of gaining a respite from attack would be one. Alternatively it might reduce the level of insurgent activity in the hopes that this would force the US to stop its punishment of the North but not prevent the US and GVN from remaining subject to wearying harassment in the South. Or, Hanoi might order the VC to suspend operations in the hopes that in a period of temporary tranquility, domestic and international opinion would force the US to disengage without destroying the VC apparatus or the roots of VC strength. Finally, Hanoi might decide that the US/GVN will to fight could still be broken and the tide of war turned back again in favor of the VC by launching a massive PAVN assault on the South. This is a less likely option in the circumstances we have posited, but still a contingency for which the US must be prepared.

Robert S. McNamara

Appendix B

THE WHITE HOUSE
WASHINGTON

June 30, 1965

MEMORANDUM FOR
THE SECRETARY OF DEFENSE

This memorandum is designed to raise questions and not to answer them, and I am afraid it may sound unhelpful.

The draft memorandum to the President of June 26 seems to me to have grave limitations.

1. It proposes a doubling of our presently planned strength in South Vietnam, a tripling of air effort in the north, and a new and very important program of naval quarantine. It proposes this new land commitment at a time when our troops are entirely untested in the kind of warfare projected. It proposes greatly extended air action when the value of the air action we have taken is sharply disputed. It proposes naval quarantine by mining at a time when nearly everyone agrees the real question is not in Hanoi, but in South Vietnam. My first reaction is that this program is rash to the point of folly.

2. The memorandum itself points out that the test of the success of any program in the near future will be in South Vietnam. I agree with this view. But I think it far from clear that these drastic changes will have commensu-

rate significance in this decisive field. In particular, I see no reason to suppose that the Viet Cong will accommodate us by fighting the kind of war we desire. Fragmentary evidence so far suggests that they intend to avoid direct contact with major US forces and concentrate their efforts against the Vietnamese Army. I think the odds are that if we put in 40–50 battalions with the missions here proposed, we shall find them only lightly engaged and ineffective in hot pursuit.

3. The paper does not discuss the question of agreements with the Vietnamese Government before we move to a 200 thousand-man level. The apparent basis for doing this is simply the increasing weakness of Vietnamese forces. But this is a slippery slope toward total US responsibility and corresponding fecklessness on the Vietnamese side.

4. The paper also omits examination of the upper limit of US liability. If we need 200 thousand men now for these quite limited missions, may we not need 400 thousand later? Is this a rational course of action? Is there any real prospect that US regular forces can conduct the anti-guerrilla operations which would probably remain the central problem in South Vietnam?

5. The suggestion of a naval quarantine is particularly drastic and highly important. I think it should be separated from the rest of the paper. A blockade by mining would have both greater risks and much greater impact. It needs a kind of study it has not had (as far as I know) before it is seriously proposed.

6. This paper omits certain additional possibilities that should be considered before a specific program of pressure is adopted:

(1) It is within our power to give much more drastic warnings to Hanoi than any we have yet given. If General Eisenhower is right in his belief that it was the prospect of nuclear attack which brought an armistice in Korea, we should at least consider what realistic threat of larger action is available to us for communication to Hanoi. A full interdiction of supplies to North Vietnam by air and sea is a possible candidate for such an ultimatum. These are weapons which may be more useful to us if we do not have to use them.

(2) The paper passes by the possibility that stronger interdiction of north-south traffic might be possible by combining land, sea, and air action. I am not persuaded by what I have heard in casual comments of the impossibility of tightening these pressures by combined action. Is there no prospect that special forces could hold critical strong points in Laos along the Ho Chi Minh Trail? Is it impossible to tighten controls along the DMZ? Have we *really* done all we can in naval patrol?

7. The timing of an expanded effort needs examination. It is not at all clear that we should make these kinds of decisions early in July with the very fragmentary evidence available to us now on a number of critical points: the

tactics of the VC, the prospects of the Ky Government, and the effectiveness of US forces in these new roles.

8. Any expanded program needs to have a clear sense of its own internal momentum. The paper does not face this problem. If US casualties go up sharply, what further actions do we propose to take or not to take? More broadly still, what is the real object of the exercise? If it is to get to the conference table, what results do we seek there? Still more brutally, do we want to invest 200 thousand men to cover an eventual retreat? Can we not do that just as well where we are?

McGeorge Bundy

Appendix C

THE WHITE HOUSE
WASHINGTON

Thursday, July 1, 1965
8:20 P.M.

MEMORANDUM FOR THE PRESIDENT

I attach four documents which are for consideration at the 11:00 o'clock meeting tomorrow.

At Tab 1 is Dean Rusk's four-page statement of the basic issues.*

At Tab 2 is George Ball's paper on a compromise solution.*

At Tab 3 is Bob McNamara's recommendation for expanded military action.*

At Tab 4 is my brother Bill's program offering a middle course for the next two months.*

The positions within the government are roughly as follows: McNamara and Ball honestly believe in their own recommendations, though Bob would readily accept advice to tone down those of his recommendations which move rapidly against Hanoi by bombing and blockade.

*Not included in this Appendix.

Dean Rusk leans toward the McNamara program, adjusted downward in this same way.

The second-level men in both State and Defense are not optimistic about the future prospects in Vietnam and are therefore very reluctant to see us move to a 44 battalion force with a call-up of reserves. So they would tend to cluster around the middle course suggested by my brother. They would like to see what happens this summer before getting much deeper in.

The Joint Chiefs are strongly in favor of going in even further than McNamara. Specifically they want now to take out the SAM site, the IL-28s, and the MIGs in the Hanoi area.

My hunch is that you will want to listen hard to George Ball and then reject his proposal. Discussion could then move to the narrower choice between my brother's course and McNamara's. The decision between them should be made in about ten days, which is the point at which McNamara would like a final go-ahead on the air mobile division. I think you may want to have pretty tight and hard analyses of some disputed questions like the following:

1. What are the chances of our getting into a white man's war with all the brown men against us or apathetic?

2. How much of the McNamara planning would be on a contingency basis with no decision until August or September?

3. What would a really full political and public relations campaign look like in both the Bundy option and the McNamara option?

4. What is the upper limit of our liability if we now go to 44 battalions?

5. Can we frame this program in such a way as to keep very clear our own determination to keep the war limited? (This is another way of stating question 4).

6. Can we get a cold, hard look at the question whether the current economic and military situation in Vietnam is so very bad that it may come apart even before this program gets into action? (I don't believe that it is that bad, but no one seems to be really sure of the facts today).

Friday's meeting is not, repeat not, for decisions, but for sharpening of the issues that you want studied.

McG.B.

Appendix D

TOP SECRET

July 1, 1965

MEMORANDUM FOR MR. MC GEORGE BUNDY

THE WHITE HOUSE

Subject: My paper on Viet-Nam

I am attaching my paper on "A Compromise Solution for South Viet-Nam" for inclusion in your book for the President.

George W. Ball

A COMPROMISE SOLUTION FOR SOUTH VIET-NAM

1. *A Losing War:* The South Vietnamese are losing the war to the Viet Cong. No one can assure you that we can beat the Viet Cong or even force them to the conference table on our terms no matter how many hundred thousand *white foreign* (US) troops we deploy.

No one has demonstrated that a white ground force of whatever size can win a guerrilla war—which is at the same time a civil war between Asians—in jungle terrain in the midst of a population that refuses cooperation to the white forces (and the SVN) and thus provides a great intelligence advantage to the other side. Three recent incidents vividly illustrate this point:

(a) The sneak attack on the Danang Air Base which involved penetration of a defense perimeter guarded by 9,000 Marines. *This raid was possible only because of the cooperation of the local inhabitants.*

(b) The B-52 raid that failed to hit the Viet Cong *who had obviously been tipped off.*

(c) The search-and-destroy mission of the 173rd Airborne Brigade which spent three days looking for the Viet Cong, suffered 23 casualties, and never made contact with the enemy *who had obviously gotten advance word of their assignment.*

2. *The Question to Decide:* Should we limit our liabilities in South Viet-Nam and try to find a way out with minimal long-term cost?

The alternative—no matter what we may wish it to be—is almost certainly a protracted war involving an open-ended commitment of US forces, mounting US casualties, no assurance of a satisfactory solution, and a serious danger of escalation at the end of the road.

3. *Need for a Decision Now:* So long as our forces are restricted to advising and assisting the South Vietnamese, the struggle will remain a civil war between Asian peoples. Once we deploy substantial numbers of troops in combat it will become a war between the United States and a large part of the population of South Viet-Nam, organized and directed from North Viet-Nam and backed by the resources of both Moscow and Peiping.

The decision you face now, therefore, is crucial. Once large numbers of US troops are committed to direct combat they will begin to take heavy casualties in a war they are ill-equipped to fight in a non-cooperative if not downright hostile countryside.

Once we suffer large casualties we will have started a well-nigh irreversible process. Our involvement will be so great that we cannot—without national humiliation—stop short of achieving our complete objectives. *Of the two possibilities I think humiliation would be more likely than the achievement of our objectives—even after we had paid terrible costs.*

4. *A Compromise Solution:* Should we commit US manpower and prestige to a terrain so unfavorable as to give a very large advantage to the enemy—or should we seek a compromise settlement which achieves less than our stated objectives and thus cut our losses while we still have the freedom of maneuver to do so?

5. *Costs of Compromise Solution:* The answer involves a judgment as to the costs to the United States of such a compromise settlement in terms of our relations with the countries in the area of South Viet-Nam, the credibility of our commitments, and our prestige around the world. In my judgment,

if we act before we commit substantial US forces to combat in South Viet-Nam we can, by accepting some short-term costs, avoid what may well be a long-term catastrophe. I believe we have tended greatly to exaggerate the costs involved in a compromise settlement. An appreciation of probable costs is contained in the attached memorandum (Tab A).*

6. With these considerations in mind, I strongly urge the following program:

A. *Military Program*

(1) Complete all deployments already announced (15 battalions) but decide not to go beyond the total of 72,000 men represented by this figure.

(2) Restrict the combat role of American forces to the June 9 announcement, making it clear to General Westmoreland that this announcement is to be strictly construed.

(3) Continue bombing in the North but avoid the Hanoi-Haiphong area and any targets nearer to the Chinese border than those already struck.

B. *Political Program*

(1) In any political approaches so far, we have been the prisoners of whatever South Vietnamese Government was momentarily in power. If we are ever to move toward a settlement it will probably be because the South Vietnamese Government pulls the rug out from under us and makes its own deal *or* because we go forward quietly without advance pre-arrangement with Saigon.

(2) So far we have not given the other side a reason to believe that there is *any* flexibility in our negotiating approach. And the other side has been unwilling to accept what *in their terms* is complete capitulation.

(3) Now is the time to start some serious diplomatic feelers, looking towards a solution based on some application of the self-determination principle.

(4) I would recommend approaching Hanoi rather than any of the other probable parties (the National Liberation Front, Moscow or Peiping). Hanoi is the only one that has given any signs of interest in discussion. Peiping has been rigidly opposed. Moscow has recommended that we negotiate with Hanoi. The National Liberation Front has been silent.

(5) There are several channels to the North Vietnamese but I think the best one is through their representative in Paris, Mai Van Bo. Initial feelers with Bo should be directed toward a discussion both of the four points we have put forward and the four points put forward by Hanoi as a basis for

*Not included in this Appendix.

negotiation. We can accept all but one of Hanoi's four points and hopefully we should be able to agree on some ground rules for serious negotiation— including no pre-conditions.

(6) If the initial feelers lead to further secret exploratory talks we can inject the concept of self-determination that would permit the Viet Cong some hope of achieving some of their political objectives through local elections or some other device.

(7) The contact on our side should be handled through a non-governmental cutout (possibly a reliable newspaperman who can be repudiated.)

(8) If progress can be made at this level the basis can be laid for a multi-national conference. At some point obviously the government of South Viet-Nam will have to be brought on board but I would postpone this step until after a substantial feeling out of Hanoi.

(9) Before moving to any formal conference we should be prepared to agree that once the conference is started (a) the United States will stand down its bombing of the North, (b) the South Vietnamese will initiate no offensive operations in the South, and (c) the DRV will stop terrorism and other aggressive acts in the South.

(10) Negotiations at the conference should aim at incorporating our understanding with Hanoi in the form of a multi-national agreement guaranteed by the United States, the Soviet Union and possibly other parties, and providing for an international mechanism to supervise its execution.

George W. Ball

Index